T0301411

THE LABOR OF REINVENTION

The Labor of Reinvention

Entrepreneurship in the New Chinese Digital Economy

Lin Zhang

Columbia University Press   New York

Columbia University Press
Publishers Since 1893
New York   Chichester, West Sussex
cup.columbia.edu
Copyright © 2023 Columbia University Press
All rights reserved

Library of Congress Cataloging-in-Publication Data
Names: Zhang, Lin, 1984– author.
Title: The labor of reinvention : entrepreneurship in the new Chinese digital economy / Lin Zhang.
Description: New York : Columbia University Press, [2023] | Includes bibliographical
    references and index.
Identifiers: LCCN 2022021811 (print) | LCCN 2022021812 (ebook) | ISBN 9780231195300
    (hardback) | ISBN 9780231195317 (trade paperback) | ISBN 9780231551298 (ebook)
Subjects: LCSH: China—Economic conditions—2000– | Entrepreneurship—China. |
    High technology industries—China.
Classification: LCC HC427.95 .Z434248 2023 (print) | LCC HC427.95 (ebook) |
    DDC 330.951–dc23/eng/20220519
LC record available at https://lccn.loc.gov/2022021811
LC ebook record available at https://lccn.loc.gov/2022021812

Columbia University Press books are printed on permanent and durable acid-free paper.
Printed and bound by CPI Group (UK) Ltd, Croydon, CR0 4YY

Cover image: © Getty Images (*top*); © Tony Vingerhoets / Alamy Stock Photo (*bottom*)

Contents

Preface

The Cult of Entrepreneurialism

On a wintry day in 2016, shortly after the Chinese New Year, I walked into one of the countless incubators/coworking spaces lining the streets of Zhongguancun (ZGC) neighborhood for an interview. Known as China's Silicon Valley, ZGC is packed with high-tech companies, research institutes and universities. I had come to "InnoWay" street to meet Min, a middle-aged entrepreneur whose start-up had recently been selected from among hundreds of applicants for a spot in one of the area's new incubators. This meant that Min's team had access to free office space and equipment for at least the next six months and to other free services provided by the incubator. He met me in the lobby and showed me the office his team shared with three dozen other start-ups before we sat down to talk about his journey there.

A fortysomething former billionaire who had spent time in prison and bounced back from bankruptcy, Min was older and more experienced than most entrepreneurs I met in ZGC. During our conversation, I came to realize that his life story encapsulated the themes I wanted to explore in this book: the appeal of entrepreneurialism, the inherent risks and precarity of entrepreneurial labor, the contradictions of entrepreneurial reinvention in post-Mao China, and the experiences of countless individuals—not just in China but also around the globe—who have remade themselves as tech entrepreneurs in the wake of the 2008 financial crisis.

The youngest of eight siblings, Min was born in the early 1970s to poor peasants in southeastern China's Fujian Province. From an early age, Min saw business as a way to escape the life of a peasant and make something of himself. When I asked where he thought his entrepreneurial spirit came from, he said, "entrepreneurship is in my blood," adding:

> Fujian people are very entrepreneurial. In my home village, we didn't have much land to plant food. And we are coastal folks, living far away from the center [of power] in the North. For generations, people [from Fujian] migrated overseas to Southeast Asia, Europe, and America to become laborers and small entrepreneurs. We are everywhere in the world, just trying to make a living. My mom worked hard to raise us. My dad was a migrant worker in the city and was absent most of my life. But he sent money home regularly.

A sensitive, artistic teenager, Min apprenticed himself to a distant relative, an artist who painted for a living in a nearby county. For several years, he worked and lived in his master's home studio, learning how to paint and eventually earning enough to support himself. He left at the age of eighteen to study art at a local teachers' college. It was a sensible career path for a poor rural youth in the 1980s: teachers' colleges charged no tuition and guaranteed a job upon completing the program. After graduating, the local government assigned Min to teach art in a middle school in Fuqing, a small town near the coast.

At that time, the Chinese economy was just taking off following Deng Xiaoping's famous 1992 Southern Tour.[1] Business opportunities were especially abundant along the country's southern coastline. Sections of the coast designated by the government as experimental sites for market reform were opened up to foreign investment earlier than the rest of the country. Riding this early entrepreneurial wave, Min accumulated a small fortune. First, he moonlighted by teaching after school. Then, he expanded his one-man enterprise into a training school with help from a well-off relative who had migrated to Taiwan. "It was a great time for small entrepreneurs," Min explained. "If you were brave, willing to take risks and work hard, you would succeed." However, in the early reform years, untamed markets brought risks as well as opportunities. Min began investing in cafés and dance halls, and this brought him into the orbit of local gangs. He was dragged into a turf war and served six months in prison in 1998.

Eager to start fresh and make a clean break from his old life, Min migrated to Beijing, arriving in the capital with nothing but a single suitcase. It was a new millennium, and China was entering a new era of economic expansion. Foreign investment skyrocketed following the country's admission to the World Trade Organization in late 2001. China was about to transform into the "world's factory"; however, mounting anxiety over foreign monopolies prompted new policies in support of local businesses and brands. Min's entrepreneurial acumen and training as an art teacher served him well in his new environment. Starting as a sales agent for a clothing store, he quickly climbed the ladder in the garment manufacturing and sales industry before launching his own brand. A self-made businessman with an eye for design and fashion, he succeeded by adopting the business models of companies like H&M and Zara, adapting the latest high fashion styles into affordable clothing for young people. In doing so, he took advantage of China's garment manufacturing capacity and market opportunities afforded by its rapidly expanding middle class. At its peak in 2006, Min's business boasted annual sales of more than 1 billion yuan.

When Min's business began to falter after 2008, it was partially due to fallout from the global recession, but also because of China's wholehearted embrace of digitalization and e-commerce. Min told me he learned his lesson the hard way: The era of "traditional industries" was over; it was time for a new model. "The internet is the future," he declared. "IT start-ups are capital's new darlings. Compared to traditional businesses, IT companies develop very fast and have very high valuations." Sounding like a digital utopian, he elaborated:

> It's the promise of sustained development and a different lifestyle in the future: the unlimited potential of technology and financial capital. That's not like, say, the garment industry, which is slow, heavy, and has low margins. How on earth can you compete with the future? After 2008, I realized that I couldn't hire the best

people in Beijing no matter how much I was willing to pay. Young talents today all want to start their own IT company or join an IT business. They all want to go to Zhongguancun!

Min closed his south Beijing-based company in 2008, sold his real estate holdings in the capitol and back home in Fujian, and joined the wave of IT entrepreneurs descending on northwestern Beijing's ZGC neighborhood. "As I drove all my belongings from the south to start afresh in northern Beijing, it felt like history was repeating itself; only this time, I was no longer a young man," Min recalled with emotion. "It's taken me sixteen years to walk across the city," he added. "I admit that I hit a wall. There are hundreds and thousands of people like me who feel left behind and are trying to catch up with what's going on. I made it this far, but even I don't know whether I will survive here in Zhongguancun."

Min was right. He was not alone in his desire to reinvent himself to fit in the new global economy. Since the 1990s, cultivating entrepreneurship has been hailed as the universal path to empowerment: a silver bullet for a whole host of individual and collective ills. The resulting worldwide cult of entrepreneurialism is pushing individuals and nations alike to become more enterprising by reinventing themselves in profitable new ways.

Yet, as Min's story suggests, the fervor underlying the cult of entrepreneurialism and its attendant imperatives to personal and collective reinvention are concealing *actually existing experiences of life* beneath ideological euphoria. The years following the 2008 global financial crisis represent a paradoxical moment in the history of the global neoliberal order: despite the unprecedented proliferation of IT entrepreneurialism around the world, there is a growing awareness of the limits of entrepreneurialism, along with mounting popular demands for stronger social programs and structural changes to the economy.

This book examines the everyday labor of entrepreneurial reinvention. In this process, individuals assume the risks and benefits of identifying themselves not as workers, but as self-reliant entrepreneurs and investors. The labor of entrepreneurial reinvention involves navigating the pain and pleasure of raising one's personal valuation in accordance with the capricious demands of capital and sustaining it at the highest level. Individuals must strategically appropriate and incorporate their traditions, social positionings, and identities to meet new challenges.

Attending to the labor of entrepreneurial reinvention brings into focus the contradictions and frictions generated by the hybrid assemblage of old and new, global and local, self and other, as well as the ingenuity, courage, and persistence of those living with and through those contradictions. By examining digital entrepreneurship as *labor* and situating this labor in the history, unevenness, and cultural specificities of global capitalism, I challenge this uncritical celebration of entrepreneurialism.

Riding on global capitalism's changing currents and taking advantage of his geographic positioning, kinship networks, and the state's developmentalist and pro-social policies, Min transformed himself from a poor peasant into the millionaire owner of a fashion company in two decades. Internalizing the individualizing logic of the neoliberal economy, he willingly accepted the manifold structural risks brought about by China's rapid marketization, draconian policing, capitalist crises, and financialization, viewing them instead as "opportunities" for personal reinvention. Min did not question or criticize the hardships of his bankruptcy and imprisonment or the struggles inherent in starting anew and adapting to rapid technological shifts in middle age. For him and others like him, these trials are not symptoms of a structural crisis but a normal part of life under global financial capitalism.

Min's story of personal entrepreneurial reinvention is one of hundreds that I collected in the course of my research. China has no shortage of such stories. If anything, this capacity to innovate by melding ideas and concepts appropriated from the outside world with local abilities and traditions is what defines modern Chinese history, whether it be its distinct approach to socialism or post-Mao implementation of "capitalism with Chinese characteristics." The creative bricolage of old and new, foreign and local, sits at the heart of the so-called economic miracle of post-Mao China—and gives rise to many of its contradictions.

This book focuses on China's economic and social restructuring following the 2008 global economic crisis, after which the country heavily promoted mass entrepreneurship and innovation, especially in tech. I focus on three groups of entrepreneurs intersectionally positioned with respect to class, gender, locale, and age. This wide-angle approach permits a better view of China's surging entrepreneurialism as the state, the market, and individuals search for alternatives to the unsustainable national development model against the backdrop of a global financial crises, the U.S.-China trade war, and the Covid-19 pandemic. Instead of a radical break with the past, I found that the labor of entrepreneurial reinvention in China involves rearticulating global technological and economic shifts within existing regimes of production and systems of meaning. It blends elements of the global trend toward labor individualization with culturally specific practices of self-making and nation-building. The labor of entrepreneurial reinvention in China is a means of shaping hybrid selves, remaking the nation, and reinventing global capitalism. Specific temporal and spatial articulations open new opportunities for innovation while giving rise to new precarities, contradictions, and inequalities.

From the late 2000s to the late 2010s I traveled back and forth between the United States and China and journeyed extensively throughout China's growing urban centers and countryside. Spending time with start-up entrepreneurs in ZGC's coworking spaces, I saw their faces light up as they talked about the thrills and freedom of starting their own businesses. I also witnessed the inequalities separating elite and grassroots entrepreneurs as they navigated a maze of state policies, strategically riding the coattails of political campaigns while deploying longstanding discourses of developmentalist technonationalism and grassroots politics to mobilize resources. These stories are told in chapters 2 and 3.

Living in an e-commerce village in northern China, I observed how peasant e-commerce entrepreneurs built on the legacies of rural family production to develop a new industrial chain centered around selling handicrafts online. Then, I watched them struggle to upgrade local industry and preserve the traditional bonds of community and solidarity in the face of mounting competition. These stories appear in chapters 4 and 5.

Finally, I spoke with Chinese middle-class female entrepreneurs who use social media to resell Western products, purchased overseas, to consumers in China. These women hoped to reconcile competing desires to live their own lives and maintain more traditional homes by starting home-based internet businesses. Chapter 6 relates how old tensions often manifested in new ways as they struggled to maintain a semblance of balance, even as their businesses erased distinctions between work and home.

The goal of this book is to demystify entrepreneurialism by locating the source of capital's increased profits in the new regime of labor and changing production relations.[2] This puts me in conversation with more than two decades of scholarship about flexible, digital, and cultural labor under neoliberal capitalism since the 1970s.[3] Despite enormous contributions, this scholarship focuses on white middle-class workers in Western metropolitan centers like Silicon Valley and Silicon Alley.[4] More recently, the rise of transnational digital platforms has fueled new studies of platform-based gig workers as networked and "placeless" individuals disembedded from the larger socioeconomic context in which they are situated.[5] Yet, it becomes problematic when experiential knowledge abstracted from Western creative hubs is turned into "a universalizing and essentializing 'view from nowhere,'" and "elevated to a global and universal mechanism of action."[6] It is equally problematic, I would argue, when non-Western lived experiences are essentialized as "cultural" or reduced to the "realm of the static"[7]—that is, when they are deployed as negative examples of Western norms, as neutral case studies to "test" Western theories, or as a positive "alternative" imaginary to solving Western ills.

Until recently, China was often portrayed by scholars of digital and cultural labor as a site of exploitative manufacturing labor, the antithesis of Western free, creative, and affective labor.[8] Emerging literature regarding digital and cultural work in China offers exciting new perspectives and experiences, but there is still a tendency to mechanically apply theories gleaned from Western creative centers to Chinese cases, albeit in more contextualized ways.

To complicate the existing literature on digital and cultural labor, I have theorized the global entrepreneurialization of labor as a dynamic process of "reinvention." This underlines its heterogenous configurations, continuities, and ruptures from earlier regimes of work; its local embeddedness; and its contentious and contradictory nature. In doing so, I have drawn extensively from the abundant scholarship produced on China and other emerging/non-Western economies,[9] These works depart from the neoclassical and Western-centric premises of the neoliberal capitalist market to highlight different, less antithetical state/market relationships and the resilience of the family, both as an economic unit and as a source of cultural identity.[10]

Instead of treating socialist China as a negative case compared to the capitalist free market ideal or attributing China's post-Mao success solely to its adoption of market mechanisms, I have expanded on the work of scholars who recognize the path dependency of China's traditional, socialist, and post-Mao developmental models. Their institutional legacies and constraints have produced a contested and fragmented polity in a state of constant evolution. Thus, my book is situated in the emerging body of research on digital and cultural labor outside the West's traditional confines and on nonwhite and/or working-class communities within Western societies.[11]

China's economic success over the past three decades has led some scholars to search for a "China model," particularly during the years following the 2008 financial crisis. I share their concerns about cultural specificities and historical continuities and agree that China's experiences offer important lessons about how capitalism has been organized historically and at the current conjuncture. However, I reject the notion of Chinese essentialism and exceptionalism and instead explore the syncretism, intersectionality, inequalities, and contradictions involved in the labor of entrepreneurial reinvention.

As this book neared completion, the U.S.-China bilateral relationship went into free fall. China's emerging technological strength became a target for American sanctions and containment amid the unfolding trade war—a topic that is also examined in these pages. Enthusiasm about the China model subsided, and the conversation turned to concerns over the "China threat." Complex, nuanced representations of Chinese society faded from mainstream American media and policy discourse, to be replaced by reductionist caricatures and stereotypes. The latter is perhaps best represented by former U.S. Secretary of State Mike Pompeo's July 2020 speech at the Richard Nixon Presidential Library in California. Reviving Cold War dichotomies and the language of the Red Scare, Pompeo framed China as a "Marxist-Leninist regime" and fanned fears that Chinese students and immigrants in the United States might be spies engaged in intellectual property theft and espionage.[12]

The idealized version of the "China model" once helped observers imagine alternatives to the current unipolar world order. Now, reductionist framing of the "China threat" may well contribute, at least in the short term, to the unification of an otherwise divided American society against a foreign enemy. Either way, I believe it is more productive to overcome the "categorical formalism" of both the "China model" and the "China threat" and, instead, to speak of a "Chinese paradigm," to borrow a phrase from Arif Dirlik.[13] As I elaborate in the epilogue regarding the specific implications of the China paradigm, the Chinese experience is not a finished project to be emulated universally but rather "a work in progress," an ongoing experiment in how global principles articulate to historical circumstances and local reality in the process of nationbuilding. This means focusing not only on successes and potentialities but also on limitations and mistakes, not only on those who have benefited but also on those who have lost out. It is to see and depict China for what it is in all its complexity and contradictions.

My work has been particularly inspired by Kuan-Hsing Chen's concept of "geocolonial historical materialism"[14] and Nancy Fraser's interpretation of the crisis of neoliberal financial capitalism.[15] Following them, I look at "the actually existing" experiences of entrepreneurial reinvention to find both labor and its exploitation via unequal relations of production (constituted by the complex intersectionality of class, gender, race/ethnicity, nationality, locale, etc.) to be important sources of capitalist growth and profits.[16]

In contesting mainstream neoliberal policy discourses and approaches to entrepreneurship, I turn to digital and cultural labor studies, China studies, critiques of neoliberalism, and a substantivist approach to capitalism informed by postcolonial, feminist, and Polanyian perspectives.[17] Following Aihwa Ong and Stephen J. Collier, I consider the labor of entrepreneurial reinvention to involve heterogeneous processes in which participants who are disparately positioned culturally and geographically partake in labor's remaking.[18] As a "global form," China's regime of entrepreneurial labor has been defined by globally dominant neoliberal ideals like individualization, economization, flexibility, and risktaking. Simultaneously, as a "global assemblage," China arose from the temporally and geographically contingent processes of integration into global capitalist production after the late 1970s.[19] My work highlights China's "centralized minimalist" tradition, in which the economy is embedded in the persisting but contradictory logics of the state and the lingering, malleable significance of the family.[20] Locating my analysis in "actual global" space allows me to depict the heterogeneous and contentious formation of China's entrepreneurial labor as a dynamic process where local conditions are reinvented through constant interaction and negotiation with global neoliberal ideals.[21] Particular attention is paid to frictions generated and contradictions experienced when different rationalities compete or negotiate to shape the lived experiences of entrepreneurial workers.

This intersectional approach appears in the book's tripartite structure and in my analytical attention to inequalities and differences within each entrepreneurial scene. Each of the book's three parts tells a different story of the labor of entrepreneurial reinvention in post-2008 China. Urban, rural, and transnational perspectives contribute to an emerging labor regime that reflect the experiences of middle-class and working-class urbanites, peasants and peasant workers, and young, transnationally mobile middle-class women. Together, their perspectives show how the labor of entrepreneurial reinvention has been carried out in tandem with the remaking of the Chinese self, and how this labor connects to China's national project of economic and social restructuring after 2008.

Chapter 1 lays out my theoretical framework in detail, traces entrepreneurial reinvention through the history of post-Mao China, and recounts details of my research journey for this book. My goal here, to quote Larry Grossberg, is "to produce better conjunctural stories: to better understand 'economic' events, practices, relations, etc., by contextualizing them, and to better understand the context by inscribing economies into it."[22] Near the end of our conversation, Min asked me what I planned to do with the stories I collected from him and others. When I told him that I wanted to write a book, his face suddenly brightened, and he offered sage advice about how to pitch my ideas, identify target readers, and come up with a catchy title. "Most important, you have to get the stories right," he stressed. I hope I haven't let him down.

This book is dedicated to my family.

THE LABOR OF REINVENTION

CHAPTER ONE

The Labor of Entrepreneurial Reinvention

Elevation of, investment in, and enthusiasm for the individualized entrepreneur as a heroic driver of economic development and faith in the
frictionless economization of individual differences as a way to energize
capitalism are the chief ingredients of what I call *entrepreneurialism*. Its
proliferation in China at the post-2008 historical conjuncture is not
unique. Individuals and institutions around the world are being called
upon to reinvent themselves as entrepreneurs, that is, to run themselves
as enterprises in a competitive global market by transforming cultures,
social positionings, and histories into resources that can be converted
into profit.

This trend can be seen in the "entrepreneurialization of arts and
culture" in Britain, where the proliferation of freelance work and self-
employment in the cultural industries has coincided with the deepening economization of arts and culture since the late 1990s.[1] It echoes in
the branding discourses of the late-twentieth- and early twenty-first-
century United States, which celebrated individualized cultural entrepreneurs as participants in a "radically 'free' market."[2] After India's liberalization in 1991, entrepreneurialism there took on more collectivist
and developmentalist undertones in the form of "entrepreneurial citizenship," which promised that everyone, "from the least to the most privileged," is "potentially an entrepreneur" and asked middle-class entrepreneurial citizens to "find the opportunities for value amid the diversity

and marginality of India's poor."[3] It could also be heard in the mid-2000s, when the small Caribbean island of Barbados launched a strategic nation-building plan titled "Global Excellence, Barbadian Traditions." The program sought to expand entrepreneurship—and cut back on social welfare and state obligations—by reinventing the local tradition of "reputational flexibility."[4]

Writing in 1732, Richard Cantillon, an Irish economist, defined the entrepreneur as a risk-taker who profits by arbitraging between workers and consumers.[5] In classical economics, entrepreneurship was largely subsumed in other elements of production, either as "skilled labor" or as "providers of capital."[6] However, after neoclassical economic theory elevated the market as a counterweight to the state in the mid- to late twentieth century, the entrepreneur—not labor—came to be seen as the motor of economic development.[7]

Entrepreneurialism, I argue, is the dominant ideology of global financial capitalism. Its emergence and consolidation were the product of two major cultural shifts in the in the mid- to late twentieth century. First, the post-Keynesian rise of neoclassical economics valorized the individual entrepreneur as the ideal economic subject and provided the intellectual basis for the hegemonic ascendance of neoliberal politics around the world.[8] "Stagflation" in the 1970s needed a quick fix. The heroic self-made entrepreneur emerged as a powerful symbol of the free market—the antithesis of stodgy bureaucrats and hapless social welfare beneficiaries.[9] Second was the post–Cold War emergence of what George Yúdice has called "the expediency of culture": a new episteme in which differences (race, sexuality, nation, locale, etc.) were papered over by a discourse of multiculturalism and diversity and capitalized via market competition.[10]

Post-Mao China appropriated the discourse of entrepreneurialism after the country's gradual reintegration into global capitalism began in the late 1970s.[11] Liberal-minded intellectuals joined Western mainstream economists to confirm and reinforce, rather than problematize, neoliberal norms of deregulation, market freedom, and private property rights.[12] In economics, this took the form of neo-institutionalism—a Chinese variant of neoclassicism that emphasizes the role of institutions. Chinese proponents of market liberalism viewed their country as a successful example of laissez-faire capitalism that confirmed their neoliberal worldviews,[13] or, conversely, as a "negative lesson," where "weak property rights, weak contract enforcement and the extensive involvement of government in business affairs" created an "unfavorable" environment for entrepreneurs.[14]

Chinese culturalists, meanwhile, fused nativism with market fundamentalism to celebrate the post–Cold War rise of the "Confucian entrepreneur" in China and other Asian countries benefiting from the new global division of labor. Although helpful in decentering Euro-American-dominated capitalist theory and raising the cultural confidence of people on the periphery of global capitalism, these culturalist celebrations of entrepreneurial reinvention reduced temporally and spatially contingent economic relations and processes and the complex mutual constitution of economy and culture to essentialized cultural differences, often in ways that served the interests of political and economic elites.[15]

What neoclassical, neo-institutional, and culturalist approaches to entrepreneurship share in common is reduction of the culturally specific, often messy, and always dynamic lived experiences of being an entrepreneur at this current historical conjuncture to static theoretical abstractions serving the capitalist status quo. This is true whether they are based on the "pragmatic presentism" of the market-defined economic individual or the "timeless culturalism" of quasi-religious Confucian morality.[16] Better suited to mythologizing neoliberal global capitalism than revealing actual conditions, they encourage the proliferation of entrepreneurialism as a universalist ideology.

Indeed, entrepreneurialism has become an ideology—a system of ideas and ideals that does not always reflect how the world works. As an analytic, the *labor of entrepreneurial reinvention* problematizes universalist promises of inclusivity, empowerment, and freedom by examining actual experiences of individual and collective entrepreneurial reinvention. Within this framework, my book examines lived experiences of entrepreneurialism and labor in post-2008 China as spatiotemporally specific responses to a protracted crisis of global financial capitalism. At the current historical moment, the line between "entrepreneur" and "labor" is blurred, as self-employment becomes increasingly common and workers—like entrepreneurs—are expected to be self-reliant, flexible risk-takers. The actual processes of "reinvention," described herein, highlight the historical continuities, cultural distinctions, and hybrid nature of this new regime of labor, and acknowledge the contradictions and friction generated as heterogeneous factors shape and reshape entrepreneurial workers' lives.

Although unevenly distributed among differently positioned workers, the appeals of entrepreneurial labor are real: freedom, flexibility, self-actualization, creativity and the (remote) possibility of becoming a capitalist. Because of its proven power to disrupt discriminatory forms of social and economic production, entrepreneurial labor can be particularly appealing to people traditionally excluded from such privileges (i.e., women, racial and ethnic minorities, people in capitalist peripheries).

Ultimately, however, entrepreneurialism reduces labor costs via offloading—in the name of freedom and individual choice—the expenses associated with training, reskilling, and reproduction and the risks of participating in global capitalism onto a new entrepreneurial labor force. Over the past two decades, widening wealth disparities, mounting precarity, debt crises, and the decline of social safety nets have combined to render this global, financialized form of capitalism increasingly unsustainable and unlivable.

Entrepreneurialism prevailed in the post–Cold War world, but it became both ubiquitous and highly contested following the 2008 global recession. The financial crisis of 2008 resulted from inherent contradictions in the capitalist economy, but also from social reproductive, political, and ecological crises rooted in the "inter-realm contradictions" of Nancy Fraser's expanded view of capitalism.[17] It is illustrative to compare situations in the United States and China—the countries that benefited the most from financial capitalism's post–Cold War expansion, albeit under different developmental models.

After 2008, the United States witnessed an expansion of entrepreneurialism and deepening crises of debt, social reproduction, and the environment. Simmering discontent erupted along class (the 99 percent versus the 1 percent), racial (#BlackLivesMatter), and gender (#MeToo) lines. Amid the broader economic slump, Silicon Valley reemerged as one of the economy's few bright spots, due in large part to social media, the sharing economy, and digital platforms like Uber, WeWork, and Airbnb. These took off at a time of intensifying entrepreneurialism, appropriating people's struggles for emancipation to reenergize capitalism.[18] Uber, for example, thrived by branding itself as a platform empowering drivers, regardless of background, to "be your own boss."[19] Yet, critiques of neo-liberalism and entrepreneurialism grow louder, as puff pieces about do-it-yourself careers sat awkwardly next to headlines like "Entrepreneurs Are the New Labor" and "How the Uberization of Work Is Rooted in the Cult of 'Shareholder Value.'"[20]

Across the Pacific, China's post-2008 economic rebalancing involved protracted restructuring of its mixed economy. This came not only in response to the global financial crisis, but also to mounting social, political, and ecological crises resulting from China's integration into the global capitalist system. In particular, the 2008 crisis heightened Chinese anxieties about the unsustainability of its export-oriented, investment-led development model. The Hu-Wen administration (2002–2012) distributed a massive fiscal stimulus package as a temporary Band-Aid, but as the new Xi-Li administration took over in late 2012, signs pointing toward an economic slowdown were impossible to ignore. Concerns escalated over whether China, the world's second largest economy, could maintain reasonable growth while transitioning to a more socially, economically, and environmentally sustainable development model.

In this climate of anxiety, IT-related entrepreneurialism emerged to play a pivotal role in China's restructuring and re-imagining. Compared to the United States, however, China's post-2008 entrepreneurial reinvention was shaped by very different relationships between the state, market, individual, and family.

IT entrepreneurialism coincided with the emergence of an investor state as China's government sought to entrepreneurialize problems of development, social equity, and national technological independence. Now, state policy cycles increasingly dictate business opportunities and decisions. New experiments like mixed-ownership reform (MOR, *guoqi-hungai*) and state-guided venture capital funds (*guojia yindao jijin*) have blurred public-private distinctions. Yet, despite trends toward individualization, the family-based organization of labor persists and is gaining new significance, even in e-commerce industries. To a greater extent than in the United States, the Chinese economy remains a mixed economy: its market is embedded in state power and social reproduction.

China's entrepreneurial euphoria peaked in 2015–2016 amid an unprecedented venture capital boom and state policies promoting "mass entrepreneurship and innovation." However, the 2015 equity market crash, mounting government and corporate debt, and the U.S.-China trade war dampened investor enthusiasm. Public dissatisfaction with exploitative labor conditions is also intensifying, as entrepreneurialized workers of all stripes identify themselves more as laborers than as entrepreneurs. Since 2020, the limits of entrepreneurialism as a solution to manifold capitalist crises have become apparent on both sides of the Pacific. Chinese and American entrepreneurs feel squeezed by capital and by each other, and America's imaginary of China has shifted from a competitive/strategic partnership to an existential threat.

To go beyond uncritical celebrations of entrepreneurialism, an analytical framework must be able to tease out contradictions in the actual labor of individual or collective reinvention. It must articulate global forces, local specificities. the historicity of lived experiences and the unevenness of global capitalism. Examining the historical context of China's post-2008 embrace of entrepreneurialism sheds light on the specific ways in which the "universal" of global financial capitalism has been articulated to the "particular" of contemporary China.

TRACING THE TRAJECTORY OF ENTREPRENEURIAL REINVENTION IN CHINA

My informants' experiences of the labor of entrepreneurial reinvention were shaped by global platformization and financialization, and by their varied participation in reinventing China's hybrid economy—which remains more embedded in the social institutions of state power and kinship networks than the idealized American neoliberal model and its market-driven, autonomous, entrepreneurial self.

Instead of essentializing cultural features, placing them in the spatiotemporal context of China's encounter with global capitalism shows how the labor of entrepreneurial reinvention, as undertaken by various individuals in post-2008 China, was a specific cultural and historical response to capitalism's protracted global crisis. Looking beneath the euphoric veneer of entrepreneurialism reveals contradictions inherent in actual experiences of entrepreneurial reinvention. Tracing these contours in China does not homogenize China, nor does it reify the simplified dichotomy of China versus the West. Instead, it illuminates path dependency in the trajectories of China's recent experiments in radical social and economic transformation.

In comparison with the West, where bourgeois-advocated and state-championed economic liberalism led to a supposedly self-regulating market, the Chinese economy before 1900 remained relatively embedded in social institutions like the state and kinship networks.[21] As an agrarian economy defined by interaction between petty capitalist forces and a tributary state, imperial China differed significantly from Western liberal-capitalist countries. Petty capitalism refers to the organization of agricultural and nonagricultural production into kinship-based groups led by agnatic males and reliance on the free or underpaid labor of teenagers, women, and the elderly. The tributary state extracted surplus value via nonmarket means, such as political diktat or military force.[22] These economic and social structures were responsible (at least partially) for the "underdevelopment" of capitalism and the failure of bourgeois revolutionary movements in China.[23] They also made socialism more appealing in China than in the more industrialized West,[24] pushing the country down an alternative path to modernization and industrialization in the latter half of the twentieth century.

Since the People's Republic of China was founded in 1949, the party-state's three goals—national independence, economic development, and social equity—have interacted at different times and under varying internal and external circumstances to inform CCP policy decisions.[25] Eschewing the liberal capitalist model of industrialization, socialist China's path of state-commanded accumulation combined centrally coordinated, decentralized production with a dual urban-rural structure.[26] This system represented both a continuation of, and a break from imperial-era "centralized minimalism."[27]

In Maoist China, the primary unit of labor organization was the state-led collective. In cities, the state tackled tensions between development and social equity by establishing a *danwei*-based "socialist social contract."[28] The primary feature of this social contract was the "iron rice bowl," which guaranteed urban workers lifelong employment and benefits, backed by a soft government guarantee for underperforming enterprises.[29] Ostensibly egalitarian, the urban work regime continued to be characterized by intra-class and gender inequalities: permanent male workers in state-owned danwei were treated as superior socialist subjects, to the disadvantage of female and temporary workers. In the country-side, the state abolished private property rights, established communes, and set up a residence registration system to extract agricultural sur-pluses in support of urban industrialization. This dichotomy led to con-temporary China's rural-urban divide. Yet, although the rural economy stagnated, the commune system provided peasants with basic social wel-fare benefits.[30]

In pursuing its alternative path to modernization, the socialist state disembedded individuals from the longstanding Confucian family-individual axis and reembedded them in a new state/individual axis mediated by work units and communes. The resulting tug-of-war between developmentalism and egalitarianism became a source of constant ten-sion that culminated in the decade-long Cultural Revolution.

China's state-dominated, urban industrialization drive reached its limits by the late 1970s. Weakened by years of political turmoil, its econ-omy sank into a prolonged slowdown.[31] Still, normalization of U.S.-China relations earlier in the decade set the stage for what political scientist and historian Evan Feigenbaum called "one of the most dramatic stories of policy reversal in the twentieth century."[32] The "reform and opening-up" policy initiated by China's party-state in the late 1970s coincided with the financialization and deindustrialization of developed Western econo-mies. As the power and influence of manufacturing labor faded in the West, jobs were outsourced abroad or shifted to immigrant workers.[33] After more than a decade of isolation from both the U.S.- and Soviet-led systems, post-Mao China was reintegrated into the global neoliberal order in the 1980s. Soon, other late-industrializing economies across Asia and Latin America became major destinations for labor outsourcing.

In a bid to renew economic growth and maintain power, the Chi-nese Communist Party (CCP) forged an alliance with global capital and free market forces. Beginning in the 1980s, China refashioned its Maoist legacy. Its strong grassroots mobilization capacity, extensive network of state-owned enterprises and skilled workers, and vast pool of healthy and relatively well-educated peasant labor became the centralized socialist state's "comparative advantage" in the global capitalist marketplace.

Reintegration into the global capitalist system required reinventing local traditions so as to parallel global trends toward entrepreneurializing labor. The moderately paced state-managed marketization of the 1980s is generally considered a "reform without losers."[34] The countryside benefited from the dissolution of communes, the restoration of household-based production quotas, and the establishment of new township and village enterprises (TVEs). For example, the village of W, the protagonist of chapters 3 and 4, witnessed a revival of its traditional handicraft businesses and home-based, gendered weaving labor in the 1980s and early 1990s, largely due to the emergence of handicraft-exporting TVEs. Urban reform lagged behind until the mid-1980s when many workers struck out on their own. Some were in the first generation of ZGC IT entrepreneurs.

Under the surface, however, China's post-Mao transformation was riven with internal tensions. In addition to runaway inflation, contradictions between an increasingly liberal political environment and the rampant corruption of post-Mao China's first generation of "bureaucratic capitalists"[35] came to a head during the 1989 Tiananmen protests. After a short period of retrenchment, Deng Xiaoping "Southern Tour" in the spring of 1992 sought to resolve the party-state's legitimacy crisis and renew enthusiasm for economic reform, while tightening political control and stoking nationalist sentiment.[36] Deprived of access to capital by international sanctions post-Tiananmen and worried by the Soviet Union's collapse, the party-state embarked on a campaign of state-led self-capitalization without political liberalization to begin the second phase of expedited marketization.[37] This model of export-oriented, investment-led development in the 1990s facilitated rapid GDP growth, but it came at the cost of rampant labor exploitation, environmental degradation, and geographically uneven development.

By the turn of the millennium, two decades of state-led entrepreneurialization had unleashed economic growth, but also exacerbated divisions within Chinese society. The power of the bureaucratic capitalists, including ZGC IT entrepreneurs who had secured their first fortunes in the 1980s and early 1990s, grew more entrenched through financial and real estate investments. They were soon joined by a new generation of IT entrepreneurs who returned from overseas or had connections with foreign investors. A symbolic moment in the rise of this new class came at the CCP's Sixteenth National Congress in 2002, when Chinese President Jiang Zeming invited private entrepreneurs to join the party as "advanced elements of a new social strata."[38]

Meanwhile, the costs of these reforms were borne by an estimated 30 million urban workers who were laid off by mid-2001[39] and by peasants and migrant workers in the country. In the early 1990s, the state had abandoned its pro-rural stance and reverted to urban developmentalism. Soon after, a large number of TVEs had gone bankrupt or been privatized, including handicraft enterprises in the W Village. The countryside's declining capacity to absorb excess labor, coupled with surging foreign direct investment (FDI) in urban areas, generated a massive wave of labor migration to the cities.[40]

Some of these migrants joined what Chinese journalist Ling Zhijun called the "ant army" (*mayi xiongbing*, 蚂蚁雄兵) of grassroots entrepreneurs. They resembled the vendors who filled up ZGC's electronics malls looking for opportunities in export-driven electronics production and the urban real estate boom. In W Village, bankrupt handicraft TVEs were replaced by private, family-run businesses. Most young men in the village sought opportunities in the city, while women remained at home weaving for private handicraft export companies instead of the TVEs. All of this laid foundations in the village for expanding handicraft e-commerce in the late 2000s.

China's reintegration into global capitalism in the 2000s was a period of transition. China continued to walk the tightrope of GDP-driven, export-oriented, and investment-led development while making adjustments around the edges trying to restructure what had become an increasingly imbalanced economy. The 1999 U.S.-China trade agreement and China's entry in the WTO two years later turbocharged its national export in the first decade of the new millennium.

The inflow of foreign capital and businesses opportunities benefited some in China more than others. Icons of IT entrepreneurialism, like Jack Ma of Alibaba and Charles Zhang of Sohu, became celebrities. Their life stories were widely publicized in Chinese media as the country's answer to Steve Jobs, Bill Gates, and Mark Zuckerberg. These cultural narratives of heroic IT entrepreneurship foreshadowed the post-2008 entrepreneurial proliferation.

China's state-enforced rural-urban divide prevented the formation of urban ghettos and a pauperized class, like those found in many other emerging economies, but it created a huge "floating population" of rural-to-urban migrants, disadvantaged groups who came to constitute

China's "neglected" army of informal labor.[41] By 2009, 120 million peasant migrant workers were without an urban *hukou*, the household-registration system enacted since the Maoist years that bars the free rural-urban or urban-rural migration of Chinese citizens. "Second-class citizens," they were excluded from labor protections and unions and bore "the added burden of no health benefits and special school fees for their children."[42] That number doesn't include the 50 million urban residents, many recently laid off by state-owned or collective enterprises, who found informal employment or self-employment in the expanding services sector.[43]

To mitigate the growing social deficit and problems of uneven development, the Hu-Wen administration introduced an urban minimum income guarantee program in 2002, and in 2006 established public housing for the urban poor and basic universal health insurance for urban residents. As part of the campaign to "build a new socialist countryside," a number of policies to facilitate rural reconstruction were also enacted between 2003 and 2007.[44]

By the late 2000s, the People's Republic of China had come far from its Maoist roots. At double-digit annual growth rate, it was overtaking Japan as the world's second largest economy. However, in many ways it remained a mixed economy on the semi-periphery of global capitalism. The relative embeddedness of China's economy in state power and familial networks, the persistent state control over "pillar industries" like telecommunications and finance, the deep involvement of local government in economic activity, and the semi-proletarian peasant workers under the institutionalized rural-urban divide set China apart from most Western developed economies. Yet, China's pursuit of GDP-driven developmentalism had come to overshadow goals of national independence and social equity. This imbalance threatened not only the legitimacy of the CCP but also the sustainability of the so-called China model. It lies at the heart of contradictions that plague the labor of entrepreneurial reinvention in post-2008 China.

The 2008 global financial crisis shook China's economy to its core.[45] The sudden contraction in overseas demand and trenchant debt woes of many Western developed economies convinced China's ruling elites and general public alike of the unsustainability of the export-oriented economic model and the vulnerability of the American model of financial capitalism.[46] Subsequently, the "adjustments" of the 2000s morphed into a national project of economic and social restructuring. Instead of a radical departure from neoliberal global financial capitalism, however, the search for alternatives ushered in a new era of entrepreneurial reinvention where, in a continuation of China's centralized minimalism, entrepreneurialism proliferated even as state power and family institutions strengthened. New opportunities for empowerment opened up, but new forms of precarity and regimes of inequality were also created.

By late 2008, weakening global demand exerted strong downward pressure on the Chinese economy, causing an economic slowdown, a wave of bankruptcies among export-oriented factories, and rising unemployment.[47] The government reacted with a Keynesian stimulus, and pumping 4 trillion yuan into the economy in the form of investment in public projects led to a temporary recovery. The protracted nature of the global recession made this recovery short-lived, however. In response, Chinese policymakers embraced the concept of the "investor state." Continuing trends already visible in the mid-2000s, the investor state model combined a financialized approach to governance with socialist technonationalism and campaign-style mobilization.

In a gesture reminiscent of Mao's Great Leap Forward (*dayuejin*), Premier Li Keqiang kicked off a nationwide campaign in late 2014 to advance "mass entrepreneurship and innovation." He called on individuals from all socioeconomic backgrounds to become entrepreneurs and on businesses and government to encourage bottom-up innovation and entrepreneurialism. A year later, Li promoted the Internet Plus initiative (*hulianwangjia*, 互联网+), a new policy that blended technological innovation with China's existing strengths in manufacturing, agriculture, and infrastructure.

When I was conducting fieldwork in China in 2015 and 2016, I witnessed a massive nationwide surge in platform-based, VC-backed entrepreneurship. Chinese from a wide variety of backgrounds and at different career stages were rushing into the brave new world of venture start-ups, microentrepreneurship, and self-employment. In this new era of entrepreneurial reinvention, digital entrepreneurialism emerged as China's engine of economic restructuring. Home- and family-based digital entrepreneurship and self-employment were reimagined as new sites of economic growth, and as flexible and fulfilling alternatives to existing working-class and middle-class jobs.

But the celebratory rhetoric surrounding entrepreneurialism concealed inequalities that separated out "digital entrepreneurs." Different backgrounds produced different propensities for managing the twists and turns of personal and collective reinvention, and the tensions generated by a confluence of seemingly contradictory forces like state control, patriarchal familial structures, and individualization. Tensions arising from the state's need to balance GDP-driven developmentalism, technonationalism, and social equity and between central and local authorities were products of China's ever-evolving centralized minimalist regime of governance.

THE JOURNEY TAKEN

My initial decision to write a book about Chinese IT entrepreneurs was informed not just by the growing international visibility of the country's IT firms after 2008, but also by something more personal: a desire to use my understanding of social theory to make sense of my family's and friends' experiences in a period of rapid economic and social change. It all started in the summer of 2010 on an excursion to the Chinese countryside to visit my extended family. Our reunion soon became fieldwork of sorts as I learned about the e-commerce village of W. Located in northern Shandong Province, the village hardly fit the typical profile of an IT entrepreneurship hub, yet my experiences there soon had me rethinking everything I thought I knew about internet entrepreneurship. The week I spent with my cousin and his family awakened me to the ways peasants were investing in the new economy and transforming themselves to fit its demands. For the first time I came to see entrepreneurship as a new regime of autonomous and flexible labor. Later, this idea became the focus of my field research.

After 2008, weak overseas demand depressed export-oriented manufacturing, forcing export businesses and their workers to seek alternative opportunities. The state's increased investment in rural infrastructure and social welfare for peasants and peasant workers prepared the way for digital platforms to make inroads in rural China. In 2010, Shandong's rural e-commerce industry was just taking off, and my cousin introduced me to a few trailblazing peasant e-commerce entrepreneurs in W and other villages in B County. I returned to W Village for ten days in the summer of 2013 and for a week in the winter of 2014 to conduct exploratory research. During that time I spent every day getting to know local e-commerce entrepreneurs, women weavers, and village and county officials. Over the ensuing years, I followed the growth of the e-commerce industry in B County, a trend that mirrored the rise of Taobao village nationwide, reflecting strategic rural expansion to sidestep the rapidly saturating urban market.

In order to better understand what was driving the Taobao village phenomenon—a concept coined by Alibaba's corporate research division AliResearch in late 2010 to describe the rapid rise of rural sellers on the company's consumer-to-consumer e-commerce website, Taobao.com—I attended the inaugural "Taobao Village Summit" in January 2014. This weeklong conference was organized by the Alibaba Group in collaboration with the Lishui municipal government not far from the company's headquarters in Zhejiang Province. At the conference, I got to know peasant entrepreneurs and village officials from across the country. I also met with AliResearch staff, university researchers, and journalists who were invited to the event. Together, these people represented the diverse array of interests involved in constructing China's emerging regime of peasant entrepreneurial labor, although the event itself inadvertently highlighted some of the discrepancies between the "entrepreneurial optimism" promoted by the corporate-state nexus and the lived experiences of peasant entrepreneurs.

Importantly, the conference helped me fit developments in W Village in the context of China's ongoing socioeconomic restructuring. I returned to W Village in March 2015 and spent five months living with a local family of digital entrepreneurs. Most of my data about W Village's e-commerce industry was collected during this time. I interviewed thirty-nine villagers with family-run e-commerce ventures, five urban-to-rural migrant entrepreneurs, nineteen women weavers, and eight village or county cadres.

The continued predominance of family in local e-commerce businesses and the county's outsourcing model of handicraft making focused my attention upon the persistence of traditional models of family-based production. Each family business was managed by at least two people, usually a young husband and wife or, in some cases, two city-born entrepreneur partners. Often, the whole extended family was involved in some form or another. To better understand the origins of this production model, I visited county libraries and archives to collect information about the history of handicraft making in the area.

I conducted another nine interviews with retired managers and workers at the county's two defunct handicraft TVEs and spoke with owners of the previous generation of export-oriented handicraft businesses. This gave me a better sense of the historical evolution of handicraft production in the area before the introduction of e-commerce and the emergence of new entrepreneurial labor regimes in the late 2000s. In July 2018 and again in July 2019, I returned to W Village for about three weeks to conduct follow-up interviews with village entrepreneurs and cadres whom I had previously gotten to know. This kept me abreast of transformations in the local e-commerce industry and in the personal lives of villagers struggling to stay afloat amid growing competition, shifting rural policies, and the mounting toll of the U.S.-China trade war.

My experiences in W Village and the Taobao village phenomenon taught me how rural entrepreneurs, together with tech platforms and different levels of state apparatus, reinvented centuries-old practices of family-based petty capitalist production to construct a new regime of "platformized family production." Valorization of the individualized digital entrepreneur as an ideal subject, fetishization of innovation and creativity under the global intellectual property regime, and privileging of digital and intellectual labor disguised as IT entrepreneurship have brought to the fore tensions inherent in the hybrid regime of platformized family production. Integrating the Chinese countryside into global digital capitalism via e-commerce created new opportunities for peasants and marginalized urban youth to achieve social mobility, but it also shaped a new regime of value that rewards some and marginalizes others, depending on their capacity to transform according to the volatile demands of the new economy.

In 2011, less than a year after my reunion with my cousin, I moved to Los Angeles for graduate school. One day, at a gathering of students from China, I met a fellow graduate student who told me about her social media–based e-commerce business reselling luxury products to consumers in China. Although I knew about this nascent informal economy, I was surprised to learn how large and influential it had become, how bounded it was along gendered and ethnic lines, and how much labor went into managing an online micro-enterprise.

She introduced me to six women *daigou*, informal entrepreneurs who resell overseas purchased products to consumers in China, living in Los Angeles. Three were Chinese international students like us, two were housewives, and one was a small business owner who got involved in the daigou trade to make extra money. I followed them on shopping trips, observing their interactions with sales associates and helping them take product photos; I hung out at their homes and offices to learn how they packaged merchandise, and I got to know some of their families. On a few occasions, they generously allowed me to observe their online interactions with customers. These early encounters with women daigou alerted me to the class-, culture-, locale-, and gender-specific nature of daigou entrepreneurial labor, especially compared to the experiences of rural e-commerce entrepreneurs.

Between 2012 and 2016, my circle of informants expanded. I interviewed forty-two female and four male daigou entrepreneurs across North America, Western Europe, the Middle East, and East Asia whom I got to know through friends or existing informants. I also recruited interviewees who were total strangers, especially focusing on those with more established businesses. I followed their e-commerce shops online, then reached out to them directly as a customer inquiring about the commodities they sold, even purchasing products on occasion. After we had established a sense of trust, I invited them for interviews. I conducted ten face-to-face interviews with U.S.- and China-based entrepreneurs and thirty-six via Skype, WeChat, or phone.

Since then, I have maintained regular online contact with a dozen of them, chatting with them about their businesses and lives. I joined their online customer groups and observed their interactions with clients. In 2015, one entrepreneur invited me to a party in Shanghai that she had organized for her customers. Closely following their social media profiles and online shops—whether on Sina Weibo, Instagram, WeChat, Taobao, Ymatou, or Xiaohongshu—gives me access to regularly archived social media photos they post about their businesses and personal lives. I took screenshots of important messages. Between 2014 and 2015, a friend and I ran our own daigou business on Taobao. This was my first personal experience of the gendered, class-based labor that keeps a daigou business afloat; it was also when I realized all the work that goes into the photos women daigou take of themselves carrying luxury bags or wearing designer jeans. Our e-shop lasted for about a year, and we earned little in the way of profit.

Reading government and corporate policy statements and media coverage of the daigou industry in both Chinese and English complimented my online and offline ethnographic work. Between 2019 and 2020, I conducted fifteen follow-up online interviews with the women resellers I got to know in order to learn how new state policies regarding daigou and the new cross-border e-commerce platforms were transforming their businesses and lives.

The stories I collected following these women daigou agents as they move back and forth between China and abroad, between the virtual realm of social media and e-commerce sites and the physical space of homes and shopping centers, crystallized in discussions of how gendered and classed labor practices utilized by platform-based daigou developed to solve the specific contradictions facing globally mobile middle-class young Chinese women caught between the demands of competing gender regimes in post-2008 China.

At a time of rising individualization and retraditionalization, these female entrepreneurs are reinventing gendered subjectivities and establishing a feminized, community-based transnational commodities circuit. Their efforts illustrate the appeal and limitations of daigou as an emerging labor practice. Undertaking the labor of entrepreneurial reinvention via the strategic performance of gendered identities and networks has allowed some women more choice, autonomy, flexibility, and mobility. But such freedoms are constrained by the biopolitical governmentality of digital capitalism and the patriarchal Chinese state, which encourages consumer citizenship and divides women based on class, race, and nationality, thus rendering employment precarious and atomized.

In August 2015, I returned from my five-month stay in W Village and stopped by my in-laws in Beijing's Zhongguancun area. I wanted to put the small village's entrepreneurial boom in the broader context of China's ongoing socioeconomic restructuring, including the "Mass

Entrepreneurship and Innovation" campaign and "Internet Plus" initiative. As with all mass campaigns in China, national media threw its full weight behind the plans. Morning newspapers were plastered with slogans calling on young people to "create their own jobs instead of seeking jobs," while evening TV news programs featured motivational stories about model entrepreneurs from all walks of life. ZGC was at the center of this entrepreneurial storm. Many of my friends were thinking about leaving or had already left their old jobs to start businesses or join start-ups. I was eager to understand their entrepreneurship experiences as young middle-class working professionals and learn how they differed from those of rural peasants and transnational women.

Between August 2015 and March 2016, I spent six months conducting intensive participant observation in ZGC. My field sites included ZGC's first coworking space, the Garage Café, a chain youth hostel for start-up entrepreneurs called You+, and ZGC InnoWay (figure 1.1), the new street of incubators and government agencies providing services for start-up companies. During regular visits to the electronics malls, I met and talked to small business vendors selling electronic products there.

FIGURE 1.1 Zhongguancun InnoWay in 2016, when I did the bulk of my fieldwork in the district. Credit: Hongzhe Wang.

The golden age of malls was over by the early 2010s. In 2017, they were restructured, and many of the electronics sellers I had met were leaving Beijing. A municipal government campaign to "upgrade" the city evicted migrant workers and other members of what officials termed the city's "low-end population" (*diduan renkou*, 低端人口). By 2018, most small vendors had been driven out of existence, and the malls had become incubator spaces.

During my fieldwork in ZGC, I usually spent my days interviewing entrepreneurs at the Garage Café and You+, observing their daily activities and sponsored events. Some events were "road shows" where entrepreneurs pitched projects to investors. Others were public lectures and workshops featuring successful IT entrepreneurs, or promotions for companies providing start-up company services. An internationally known, government-sanctioned "model" coworking space, the Garage Café enjoyed excellent foot traffic: entrepreneurs, government officials, media personalities, researchers, and tourists from around the world came through its doors every day. The informal conversations I struck up with these visitors were often quite informative, especially when it came to how ZGC's entrepreneurial ethos was influencing start-up culture across China.

During this time, I also visited and interviewed entrepreneurs based at TusStar, an established incubator affiliated with Tsinghua University. These entrepreneurs were better positioned and connected than most of those I met at the Garage Café or You+. Their teams usually consisted of overseas returnees with graduate degrees from famous American universities or from Tsinghua University, combined with technological expertise or extensive industry and government connections.

Juxtaposing sites and types of interviewees gave me a sense of the hybrid, hierarchical nature of ZGC's entrepreneurial scene. This undermined the universal promises of the mass entrepreneurial campaign. I conducted and transcribed fifty-one formal interviews with ZGC entrepreneurs and industry figures and recorded many more informal conversations in my field notes. Reading print media coverage of ZGC since the 1950s and books about the history of ZGC and ZGC-based IT companies contextualized my fieldwork. Historical research helped me grasp the continuities and ruptures defining the latest generation of IT entrepreneurs in ZGC.

In August 2019, I returned to ZGC, staying for a month to revisit coworking spaces and incubators while conducting follow-up interviews with twelve entrepreneurs and incubator administrators whom I had met before. I also interviewed five new entrepreneurs who started businesses after 2016, in part to gain a comparative perspective. Many ZGC entrepreneurs had been impacted by the U.S.-China trade war, so information collected after 2016 was crucial to understanding how geopolitical tensions and national policies altered tech entrepreneurship and the experiences of entrepreneurs. Thus, my research shows how the lives and potentialities of different generations of elite and grassroots entrepreneurs were shaped by uncertainties inherent in local-central state relations under a centralized minimalist political system.

The evolution of variously situated entrepreneurial spaces reflects the tensions between the state's technonationalist drive to enhance national security by fostering technological independence and its desire to boost domestic consumption, residential income, and employment. Contrasting the various experiences of entrepreneurs and entrepreneurial spaces, I argue that China's state-led entrepreneurialization succeeded in the economic restructuring of strategic industries, benefited some well-positioned entrepreneurs, and temporarily eased unemployment. But so far, this financialized approach has failed to generate a sustainable long-term strategy to redress social inequalities and associated problems of underconsumption. Even worse, it subjects disadvantaged individuals to new risks and boom-and-bust cycles. In ZGC, the mass entrepreneurship and innovation campaign was a winner-take-all affair. Despite the state's desire to promote innovation and social equity, its developmentalist logic continues to frustrate the former and marginalize the latter.

These stories of the personal and collective labor of entrepreneurial reinvention highlight the creativity underlying the articulation of global capitalism, Chinese tradition, and contingent realities, as well as the contradictions this process has generated. Hopefully, they faithfully recount the challenges of the contemporary moment, address the potentials and limits of entrepreneurialized solutions to global crises, and suggest potential alternatives to the current paradigm.

As storytellers, scholars, too, are entrepreneurial laborers. Despite relative intellectual agency, we share many of the same challenges Chinese entrepreneurial workers experience under neoliberal capitalism.

Lawrence Grossberg cautions, "telling better stories of the conjuncture will take serious time and even more serious labor" and require us "to reinvent ourselves as intellectuals and scholars, to change our intellectual practices and to produce new kinds of collective and collaborative scholar-subjects."[48] Writing this book has taken me to unexpected places, exposed me to new ideas, both academic and otherwise, and produced new friendships and alliances. I think of it less as a monograph and more as a collection of cocreated stories formed through intersubjective relationships with my interviewees and, of course, plenty of hard entrepreneurial labor.

PART ONE

City in Transition

CHAPTER TWO

Navigating the Investor State

Elite and Grassroots Entrepreneurs
in Zhongguancun

Dan is CEO of the start-up Serica Crypto-Chip Technologies. I first met him at an incubator affiliated with Tsinghua University in 2016, at the height of China's "mass entrepreneurship and innovation" campaign. One of several industrial policies adopted after the 2008 financial crisis, the ambitious campaign was designed to rebalance China's export manufacturing and investment-driven economic model, enhance indigenous technological innovation, and expand domestic consumption. Explosive growth in China's venture capital market accompanied a host of recent technological and economic transformations, including the proliferation of 3G and 4G wireless data, the burgeoning platform economy, and research and investment in artificial intelligence. These initiatives lay the groundwork for the boom in IT entrepreneurship that I wanted to study.

Just thirty-four years old, Dan was one of many entrepreneurs from relatively elite backgrounds whom I met in Zhongguancun (ZGC). "China's Silicon Valley" is the birthplace of many top tech companies, including Lenovo, TikTok and Douyin (subsidiaries of ByteDance), the e-commerce platform JD.com, and the ridesharing platform DiDi Chuxing. It is also home to some of China's top academic institutions, including Tsinghua University and Peking University (figure 2.1).

In 2010, Dan quit his doctoral program in the United States and returned to China to launch his own start-up, specializing in the design and production of "crypto chips." A self-proclaimed technonationalist,

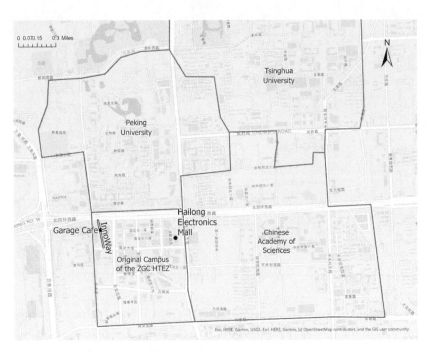

FIGURE 2.1 A map of Zhongguancun proper, showing the principal sites mentioned in the text. Credit: Tu Lan.

Dan strongly supported China's state efforts to enhance local innovation. He named his company Serica (Latin for "silk") because he wanted his chips to emulate the unrivaled superiority and sophistication of ancient Chinese silkmaking. Dan brought more than chip-design expertise back with him: his experiences in the United States shaped his management style. After a summer internship at Google, he wanted to incorporate its "people-centric" management culture into his Beijing start-up. His small team enjoyed plenty of autonomy and Google-style perks—including a free snack bar.

When I first interviewed Dan in 2016, however, he expressed frustration at the continued dominance of state-owned IT monopolies and scorned the cronyism, shortsightedness, and inefficiency of China's start-up scene. Nevertheless, he still had faith in China's system of state-led, market-driven high-tech innovation.

By 2019, Dan's market instincts and technonationalist commitment were paying off. A year into the U.S.-China trade war over access to technology as much as markets, his company received series A funding from a consortium led by a state-owned venture capital firm to develop cutting-edge semiconductor technologies. This sector was singled out for additional investment in President Xi Jinping's "Made in China 2025" industrial strategy. Subsequent American sanctions only strengthened China's determination to become technologically self-reliant.

Dan's elite background and success set him apart from other IT entrepreneurs I met in ZGC's famous coworking space, the Garage Café. These self-identified "grassroots" entrepreneurs lacked Dan's technological expertise, educational credentials, and institutional networks. Many had been drawn to ZGC by sensationalized media coverage of a mass entrepreneurship campaign featuring grassroots entrepreneurs who had leveraged brilliant ideas into big business investments.

Fu, for example, worked at the Zhengzhou campus of the Taiwanese electronics manufacturer Foxconn before joining the digital entrepreneurial gold rush in 2014. Early on, he spent most of his time in the Garage Café socializing with aspiring entrepreneurs and meeting with angel investors searching for fundable projects. To save money, he slept on a Café sofa and ate at a university canteen. Like many grassroots entrepreneurs in ZGC, Fu worked on several projects, wrote business proposals, and pitched ideas to investors, but in vain. The last time I talked to him, in the summer of 2019, he was working as a waiter at the Garage Café, now part of InnoWay's avenue of government-backed café incubators, coworking spaces, and exhibition sites showcasing state progress in promoting entrepreneurship and innovation. Although he had yet to hit it big, he told me he couldn't go back to factory work now that he saw himself as an entrepreneur.

Dan and Fu are among those whose lives have been transformed by China's post-2008 entrepreneurial reinvention. Although the Western market-fundamentalist model of entrepreneurship is more familiar, state-led entrepreneurialization sits at the heart of China's ongoing project of national reinvention. ZGC's outsized role in science and technology (S&T) development and its strategic location in Beijing made it an ideal vantage point for observing the Chinese process of entrepreneurialization, along with its strengths and weaknesses.

The contrasting experiences of these two entrepreneurs reflect larger tensions embedded in the state's embrace of IT entrepreneurship after

2008. The increasingly financialized approach to governance; persistent technonationalist interests in fostering independent development and strengthening national security; and desire to boost domestic consumption, income, and employment converged in what Hao Chen and Meg Rithmire term the Chinese "investor state."[1]

Since at least the Mao era, China has struggled to balance a nationalist preference for independent development with its socialist mission to promote social equity. The investor state is its latest attempt to manage this tension.[2] Its origins can be traced to the mid-2000s, when Hu-Wen leadership advanced a suite of technonationalist industrial and pro-social policies to redress problems that arose during China's reintegration into global capitalism. This shift toward a financialized approach to governance was reinforced by the state's response to the 2008 global economic crisis. Seeking to invest the nation out of the financial crisis, the state haphazardly pumped 4 trillion yuan into preexisting policy initiatives.

Envisioning the state as an investor—guiding and facilitating, rather than directly managing a market-driven, entrepreneurial economy—became official policy under the Xi-Li leadership at the Third Plenum of the Eighteenth Party Congress in 2013.[3] Eager to restructure the imbalanced economy without unduly sacrificing GDP growth, the new leadership leaned heavily on China's socialist toolkit and learned from the experiences of countries like the United States, Japan, Germany, Singapore, and Israel.[4] Over the ensuing decade, Chinese policymakers appropriated foreign concepts like Industry 4.0 and maker culture,[5] blending reinvented Maoist campaign-style mass mobilizations and technonationalism in the service of a financialized regime of governance.

One of the earliest IT entrepreneurship centers in China, ZGC pioneered state-led entrepreneurial reinvention. The post-Mao entrepreneurialization of labor was shaped by tensions between dependent and independent development paths, and between development and social equity—all products of China's efforts to reenter the global capitalist order while building a socialist market economy at home. Thus, the "high-tech innovation," developmentalist, and nationalist motives driving China's S&T policies must be considered together with its residual socialist redistributive rationalities and desires—factors that are often neglected. IT entrepreneurship studies that adopt a liberal free market framework and innovation scholarship that conceives of the Chinese state as merely nationalist and developmentalist miss its redistributive aims.[6]

In China's centralized minimalist governance, multipronged state influence engages with decentralized power at local levels. Thus, local institutional resilience and central/local government relations impact regional IT entrepreneurship and shape local innovation models.[7] This dichotomy has shaped generations of IT workers and entrepreneurs and caused the actual entrepreneurial labor of reinvention in ZGC to be riddled with contradiction. Stories of setbacks, frustrations, and failure coexist with celebrations of individual accomplishment and policy success. Despite the state's triumphant narrative, people and places in ZGC have experienced the contradictions inherent in Beijing's S&T policies, and the disjuncture between the central state's agenda and local government interests and modes of implementation.

The following pages situate the post-2008 proliferation of IT entrepreneurialism in ZGC within the history of Mao-era and post-Mao development. State power did not retreat in the reform era. Rather, the state's relation with entrepreneurialism evolved as it sought to advance China's position in the global capitalist system. These efforts both nurtured and constrained ZGC entrepreneurs at different points in time.

After the 2008 global financial crisis, the Chinese investor state emerged to facilitate the major economic and social restructuring required to create a more sustainable developmental model based on indigenous innovation and domestic consumption. State-led financialization created conditions that fostered the entrepreneurialization of labor on an unprecedented scale, particularly in ZGC. The three stories in this chapter of elite and grassroots entrepreneurs highlight the varied, profoundly contradictory experiences of entrepreneurial reinvention in ZGC. By "rendering entrepreneurial" development and social equity, the state offloaded the risks of financialized economic and social restructuring onto individuals who had to reinvent themselves according to the logic of the new hybrid economy.[8] Economic restructuring of strategic sectors benefited a few well-positioned entrepreneurs and temporarily eased unemployment. But the state's financialized approach has yet to generate a sustainable strategy for redressing social inequalities and the problem of underconsumption, even as disadvantaged individuals are subjected to new financialized risks and boom-bust cycles.

THE EVOLUTION OF STATE-ENTREPRENEUR RELATIONS IN ZGC

Red Scientists and Engineers in the Socialist Danwei (1950s to Late 1970s)

Contemporary tensions between development, national security, and redistribution can be traced to the 1950s when ZGC emerged as socialist China's nascent S&T research and development center.[9] During the Maoist years, the state's competing desires to promote rapid industrialization and simultaneously achieve socialist egalitarianism resulted in a tug-of-war between the technocratic, centrally planned economy and Mao-style mass mobilizations carrying out class struggle and ensuring grassroots participation in politics and the economy.

The "red" scientists and engineers who first worked in ZGC became increasingly entangled in struggles between these two visions of socialist development. Many of that first generation had been educated overseas and returned to China after the founding of the PRC. Soon they were joined by a younger generation trained in the new socialist education system. The scientists and engineers at ZGC's elite research and educational institutions—especially overseas returnees—received salaries and welfare benefits that were higher than those of the urban working class and much higher than those of peasants living outside ZGC's walled compounds.[10]

For Mao Zedong and his followers, the rising power of the technocratic elite threatened the legitimacy of the CCP as the representative of workers and peasants—the "vanguard of the proletariat"—and left China overly reliant on the Soviet Union's technocratic model of socialist modernization. Conflict between the Maoist and technocratic visions oscillated between periods of relative political and economic stability and frenzied mass political campaigns—notably the Great Leap Forward (1958–1962) and the Cultural Revolution (1966–1977).[11]

After Mao's death in 1976, Deng Xiaoping became China's paramount leader. Part of the "conservative," technocratic faction within the

CCP, Deng abandoned class politics in favor of prioritizing economic development. China switched gears and reentered the global capitalist market, albeit gradually and cautiously. Yet, tensions inherent in the social-national-developmental model, wide swings between periods of political control (*shou*, 收) and liberalization (*fang*, 放), and Maoist anti-bureaucratic decentralization persisted well into the post-Mao era as legacies of China's socialist experiment.

The Scientists Turned IT Entrepreneurs of Electronics Street

Compared to Mao-era scientists and engineers, whose careers and life trajectories were largely shaped by Cold War politics and the socialist state agenda, the scientists and IT entrepreneurs of the early reform era faced a complex of state and market logics. A welter of global market forces, technological shifts, and state policies pushed "red" scientists and engineers to "jump into the sea of commerce" (*xiahai jingshang*, 下海经商) in the storm of "reform and opening-up" (*gaige kaifang*, 改革开放).[12] Building "socialism with Chinese characteristics" was a contested process. Eventually, a hybrid model emerged in which state and market forces were thoroughly entangled.

A decline in central state funding in the 1980s accentuated the disconnect between research and market demands and deepened the frustration of ZGC scientists. Many of them joined existing nongovernmental IT businesses or became entrepreneurs and launched their own ventures. Many embraced Silicon Valley–style entrepreneurialism as a counterweight to the socialist command economy and the monopolies of state-owned enterprises (SOEs) in key sectors.[13] In reform-era ZGC, socialist ideals like the "iron rice bowl" (*tie fanwan*, 铁饭碗), denoting the security and welfare provided by the state, became associated with laziness, inefficiency, and lack of ambition.[14] Unlike socialist danwei, which subjected scientists and engineers to the state's political agenda, ZGC's new IT companies emphasized human agency and autonomy.[15]

Yet disembedding individuals from socialist institutions was gradual and incomplete, as the state continued to control significant aspects of entrepreneurs' lives and opportunities. The piecemeal, fragmented manner of the reforms deepened decentralization. Local governments and danwei officials were incentivized to encourage and even participate in privatizing socialist assets and entrepreneurializing labor.[16] The ZGC IT firms founded in the 1980s were spinoffs of state-owned research institutes and universities. Prior to privatizations in the mid-1990s, IT companies could be registered only as "state- or collectively owned, non-governmental enterprises."[17] In the early stages of these companies, many entrepreneurs relied heavily on their mother danwei for start-up funds, technology transfers, office space and facilities, human resources, and access to political networks.[18]

Beijing's municipal authorities and Haidian District's government also encouraged nongovernmental IT companies. In the 1980s, ZGC companies were driving local economic growth, generating tax revenues and employment opportunities, and boosting real estate value. Local officials who increasingly embraced entrepreneurial ways allied with the IT entrepreneurs, and the rapid expansion of ZGC's Electronics Street benefited from their noninterventionist stance.[19]

Soon, however, the emergence of this new technocratic-commercial elite revived class tensions and ideological disputes. The "capitalist versus socialist" (xingzi xingshe, 姓资姓社) debate—a manifestation of earlier debates between Maoist development and social equity—epitomized the struggle taking place over reform in ZGC. After its establishment in 1985, Electronics Street attracted particular criticisms from ZGC researchers and professors, officials and journalists, and the public (figure 2.2).

Critiques ran the gamut from disrupting China's research establishment for personal enrichment, to acting as a hotbed for capitalism, embezzlement, scamming, corruption, and smuggling. In response to mounting pressure, central government investigations during the 1980s led to the downfall of several ZGC entrepreneurs and companies.[20] Discontent over corruption and the growing wealth gap, exacerbated by rampant inflation, reached a breaking point during the 1989 Tiananmen protests, sparking a national crisis. Yet, Electronics Street weathered this storm. Reform-minded officials in the central government and local government and danwei officials valued it as a test site for the commercialization of China's S&T sector.[21] Most of the entrepreneurs who survived in those years were not only business-smart but also politically shrewd and well connected.

FIGURE 2.2 Zhongguancun Electronics Street in the early 1980s. Source: Zhong-guancun Yearbook, https://www.zgcyqz.cn/zjtp/index_2.jhtml#.

After Deng Xiaoping reaffirmed China's commitment to reform and opening up in 1992, ZGC entered a new phase. However, old tensions between dependent and independent development resurfaced once more as economic growth, framed as the "rejuvenation" of Chinese civilization, came to underscore the CCP's political legitimacy. Tensions were acute in ZGC as fear of technological and economic dependence on the outside world stirred up deep-rooted technonationalist sentiments.

Sharp reductions on electronics tariffs in 1993, and a business environment increasingly friendly to foreign companies and investors, attracted an influx of foreign IT firms to ZGC.[22] Fierce competition from multinationals looking to expand their market share in China quickly reduced Chinese IT companies to little more than sales agents for brands like Dell, IBM, and Apple.[23] By the mid-1990s, once-dominant Chinese hardware and software manufacturers accounted for less than one-fifth of the domestic market.[24] In a flare-up of technonationalist sentiments in ZGC, Chinese IT entrepreneurs lobbied the state to implement protectionist policies against a "foreign takeover" of the IT industry.[25]

Many domestic companies went bankrupt around this time. Those that survived did so by deploying a mix of commercial and political tactics. In the turbulent early reform years, ZGC entrepreneurs carefully positioned themselves in relation to their political patrons, whether reform-minded or conservative, while simultaneously learning from and guarding against multinational corporate (MNC) "foreign wolves."[26] During a 1998 meeting with China's new premier Zhu Rongji, Lenovo's founder and CEO Liu Chuanzhi pointedly remarked that ZGC's nongovernmental IT entrepreneurs, unlike their Silicon Valley counterparts, were at the mercy of both markets and state policy.[27] Straddling the state-run danwei system and burgeoning IT markets, first generation ZGC entrepreneurs found success atop a mixture of socialist legacies and aspirational Silicon Valley–style market liberalism.

Dot-Com Entrepreneurs and Electronics Vendors

The turn of the millennium coincided with the peak of Silicon Valley's dot-com bubble. Global venture capital endorsed and supported a new generation of internet entrepreneurs in ZGC who largely benefited from China's opening up and embrace of foreign investment. Prominent figures included Charles Zhang, CEO of Soho.com and an MIT-educated physicist, and Zhidong Wang, founder of Sina.com and an accomplished computer programmer out of Peking University. The majority of ZGC's dot-com entrepreneurs had never worked in state-owned business but enjoyed extensive overseas connections or had recently returned from overseas. If Silicon Valley existed only as a vague cultural imaginary for first-generation ZGC entrepreneurs, the generation emerging in the late 1990s was unfettered by socialist ideology and living the Silicon Valley dream.[28]

ZGC was experiencing a Silicon Valley makeover. Having been "rediscovered as a poster child of indigenous technological innovation" by the central state, ZGC was designated a "national-level science park" (*guojiaji kejiyuanqu*, 国家级科技园区)in 1999.[29] In comparison to its laissez-faire approach in the 1990s, the central government proactively promoted S&T development after 2000. Boosting ZGC's innovation capacity became a key policy goal. Hence, the government invested in new infrastructure, offered tax breaks to ZGC-based IT companies, loosened household registration controls to allow private firms to hire college students from elsewhere in the country, and attempted to attract overseas returnees by setting up high-tech start-up incubators affiliated with local governments, research institutes, and universities.[30] These institutes and universities also benefited from state largesse during this period, with increased funding for strategic and basic research.[31]

If greater state involvement in nongovernmental IT businesses offered protection from foreign competition, it also constrained their autonomy and fostered a clientelist relationship between the entrepreneurs and the state.[32] Along with overdependence on foreign venture capital, which preferred low-risk "copy-to-China" business models, clientelism compromised the innovation capacity of ZGC companies.[33] Exacerbating inherent tensions within central state S&T policies, the local governments responsible for implementing them and distributing investment often had stakes and interests distinct from those of the central authorities.

Nevertheless, between 1994 and 2005, ZGC doubled in size, expanding beyond historical Zhongguancun to include ten additional "high-tech parks" scattered around Beijing.[34] The main rationale for this expansion was to enhance ZGC's ability to compete with other regions for foreign direct investment and central government support. It was also a ploy to raise local government revenues by commercializing state-owned land, sometimes in ways that clashed with central state desires for domestic innovation. Many new IT start-ups struggled with ZGC's rising office rents and could not compete for talent with well-funded MNCs and state-owned enterprises.[35] By the mid-2000s, ZGC was no longer the undisputed mecca of China's IT industry: compared to the rising star of Shenzhen in the south, its fortunes were fading.

As China became the world's largest electronics manufacturer in the 2000s, ZGC emerged as a base for growing numbers of "grassroots" IT entrepreneurs. Many entrepreneurs with humble backgrounds came from the ranks of small vendors operating out of electronics malls that sprouted in the area after the late 1990s. Their rapid expansion in the 2000s, another product of local government pursuit of GDP-driven growth, helped generate new employment and entrepreneurial opportunities, and facilitated social mobility for non-elite entrepreneurs during a period otherwise defined by developmentalism and declining social egalitarianism.[36]

The majority of small businesses in ZGC's electronics malls (figure 2.3) employed fewer than three people, and the boundaries between employer and employee were fluid.[37] Some store owners were young college graduates interested in tech who preferred being their own boss to working at a larger firm. Others were migrants from small towns or the countryside who came to Beijing for business opportunities. Those with start-up capital had often borrowed it from family and friends. Others worked in the shops to acquire skills, accrue resources, and build networks before striking out on their own. Most ZGC businesses offered little employment security and few benefits. Companies popped up and disappeared on a regular basis. Overtime was the norm. Many grassroots entrepreneurs lived in shacks, in rental apartments in inner city ghettos (*chengzhongcun*, 城中村), or on the fringes of the city.[38]

Unlike elite entrepreneurs, grassroots IT entrepreneurs operating out of ZGC's electronics malls between the late 1990s and the late 2000s were

FIGURE 2.3 Zhongguancun Electronics Malls in 2005. Source: Zhongguancun Yearbook, https://www.zgcyqz.cn/zjtp/index_2.jhtml#.

culturally marginalized and largely invisible. They were often stigmatized as underhanded dealers who cheated their customers.[39] In contrast to the fawning media profiles of titans like Charles Zhang, positive depictions of ZGC electronics vendors were rare, except for those few who had joined the ranks of the elite IT entrepreneurs.[40]

ZGC's retail electronics industry did little to foster domestic innovation, but it offered tens of thousands of opportunities with low entry thresholds to ranks of aspirants and generated enormous tax and real estate revenues for the local government. In ZGC in 2006, the number of registered small vendors exceeded five thousand, with an estimated thirty thousand sellers offering ten thousand types of electronic products to consumers.[41] The sales volume of ZGC's electronic malls reached over 100 million yuan per day—9 percent of China's retail electronics market.[42]

In the absence of substantive redistributive measures from the state, the entrepreneurialization of labor by grassroots electronics vendors provided a channel for upward social mobility in ZGC. Thus, China's growing investment in technological innovation, IT entrepreneurship, and social equity in the 2000s hinted at major economic and social restructuring on the horizon and foreshadowed its broad entrepreneurial reinvention after 2008.

THE ZIGZAG PATH TO
ENTREPRENEURIAL REINVENTION

In September 2011, fresh off a visit to ZGC, the American tech entrepreneur and academic Vivek Wadhwa published an article in the *Washington Post*, "What We Really Need to Fear About China." While he questioned the value of Chinese-published academic papers and patents filed by Chinese inventors as metrics for innovation capacity, he praised the entrepreneurial spirit of China's younger generation and the country's vibrant IT start-up scene. He spoke highly of the Tsinghua University students he met and singled out the Garage Café as an exemplar of China's new entrepreneurial spirit. These were the "real threat" to America's continued tech dominance.

Wadhwa was on to something. By the early 2010s, IT entrepreneurship was gaining popularity and legitimacy as a desirable alternative to more conventional employment options, including, in his description, "working for a stodgy state enterprise, an autocratic government, [or] an opportunistic foreign multinational."[43] He was prescient in recognizing the importance of new infrastructure, like the Garage Café and Tsinghua University's Berkeley-backed entrepreneurship program, which trained China's new entrepreneurial labor force. Still, Wadhwa's Silicon Valley perspective and optimism, expressed at a time when U.S.-China bilateral relations were more collaborative, prevented him from seeing the state's complex role in China's entrepreneurial reinvention and the convoluted path it traveled in the 2010s. For an alternative ZGC-centered perspective, let us look back to the immediate aftermath of the 2008 global financial crisis.

In December 2008, Premier Wen Jiabao paid an official visit to ZGC. The impact of the recent global financial crisis had been acutely felt in the area, since 40 percent of ZGC's GDP came from the export-oriented electronics industry.[44] Wen toured two state-owned high-tech companies specializing in biotech and nano materials before stopping at a privately owned software development firm. Declaring that ZGC should serve as a national example for the coming economic restructuring, he stressed that its core mission was to promote indigenous technological innovation and help the country move up the value-added chain from "made in China" to "created in China." According to Wen, this could only be achieved via a "combination of market mechanisms, government intervention, and science and technology innovation."[45]

To reverse China's overdependence on the production of low-value-added goods for foreign markets, the central government embarked on a major economic and social restructuring campaign aimed at transitioning to a more sustainable development model based on indigenous innovation and domestic consumption. This is the context of the post-2008 state-led collective and individual reinvention of entrepreneurship and IT innovation. Faced with maintaining a socially and politically acceptable GDP growth rate while spearheading domestic innovation, curbing unemployment, and boosting domestic consumption, the state turned once more to its socialist toolkit, incorporating technonationalism and mass mobilization in its financialized push for entrepreneurship and innovation. Encouraged and guided by the investor state, IT entrepreneurship would alleviate long-standing contradictions between development, technological autonomy, and social justice. Still, this optimistic new development model followed a winding path to realization. Whether or not they liked it, ZGC's new generation of elite and grassroots entrepreneurs found themselves on a bumpy ride.

Testing Ground for the Investor State

In March 2009, three months after Wen Jiabao's visit, the State Council officially designated ZGC as China's first "National Indigenous Innovation Demonstration Zone" (*zizhu chuangxin shifan qu*, 自主创新示范区). The idea was to use ZGC as a testing ground for China's financialized approach to governance—an experimental site where state-led initiatives to commercialize science and technology development would be tested first, then rolled out nationally. These initiatives included establishing a new incentive mechanism for university researchers to commercialize their work, providing better access to venture capital for start-ups, expanding government procurement of high-tech products, and strengthening intellectual property protection. There was precedent for this: in 2002, ZGC pioneered the use of "government-guided funds" (*zhengfu yindao jijin*, 政府引导基金), which funneled public money into private enterprises in strategic sectors, comparable to DARPA in the United States. These policies were backed by initiatives like the "Thousand Talents Program" (*qianren jihua*, 千人计划) unveiled in 2008. An attempt to reverse China's brain drain, the program funded universities to recruit international experts in academic research, innovation, and entrepreneurship.

A key driver of the state's financialized approach to S&T development was the Zhongguancun Development Group (ZGC Group). Founded in 2010 as a state-owned, market-driven company with eighteen shareholders—all state-owned companies or asset-management groups—ZGC Group was tasked with managing all affiliated high-tech parks and innovation spaces, as well as investing in young IT companies on behalf of the Beijing government. Relying on ZGC's rich legacy of S&T development and the Beijing municipal government's political clout, ZGC Group operated simultaneously as an angel investor, a start-up incubator, a local government financing vehicle, and a real estate development and management company.

In a 2012 interview, ZGC Group's General Manager, Xu Qiang, described the company as representative of an ongoing "shift in government function and institutional innovations." It aimed to utilize market mechanisms to better allocate resources for the new ZGC Indigenous Innovation Demonstration Zone.[46] Xu summarized the ZGC Group's founding principles with the formula "2+3." The "2" referred to its two missions: first, serving the state's development goals while fulfilling its social responsibilities (its political-social mission), and second, generating profits for its shareholders and employees (its commercial mission). The "3" referred to the company's three primary business responsibilities: industrial investment, high-tech park management, and high-tech venture capital investment.[47] To illustrate the kinds of projects ZGC was interested in, Xu highlighted two successful investments: a memory chip company founded by an overseas returnee and Tsinghua graduate, and a civil/military project developing applications for the Beidou Navigation Satellite System, China's Global Positioning System (GPS). These investments were so successful that the Trump administration put ZGC Group on the entity list.[48]

While state agents like ZGC Group were facilitating entrepreneurship in strategic high-tech sectors like semiconductors and navigation, parallel state-led promotion of the telecommunications industry, and liberalization of financial markets opened a floodgate of opportunities for start-ups and private capital in mobile computing.[49] The years following 2008 witnessed the birth of many of today's top tech firms, such as the food delivery platform Meituan (2010), the ride-hailing app DiDi Chuxing (2012), the fintech platform Yiren Digital (2012), the e-commerce platform Pinduoduo (2014), and TikTok's parent company, ByteDance (2012). The most popular investment targets were either online-to-offline (O2O) platforms that connected digital users to physical businesses via their smartphones or peer-to-peer (P2P) lending platforms that directly linked people in need of loans with potential lenders.

These two IT entrepreneurship tracks—strategic technologies and the consumer internet—set the stage for an entrepreneurial boom. Sudi, cofounder and former investment manager of the Garage Café, was among the first to see it coming. In a 2016 interview, he told me he had been inspired to found the café in 2011 as one of ZGC's earliest privately owned incubators after witnessing the hustle and bustle of ZGC's post-2008 entrepreneurial scene. "Every time I walked into a café near those big internet companies, I would run into groups of young start-up team members," he recalled. "Some were brainstorming their business proposals, others were working on their demos. And private investors, eager to find new projects to invest in, were banging down my door for advice and recommendations. So, I knew things were heating up."

The Booms and Busts of Campaign-Style Entrepreneurialization

By the time the Xi-Li administration took over in late 2012, financialization of China's economy had grown to such a degree that they faced a conundrum: how could the market and financial capital be further utilized to drive economic growth without fully losing state control?[50]

Their response to these challenges came in late 2013 during the Third Plenum of the Eighteenth Party Congress. The "Decision on Major Issues Concerning Comprehensively Deepening Reform" mapped out plans for a mixed economy in which the market would play a "decisive" role, but the state would remain "dominant."[51] In essence, the idea was to enhance the state's financialized approach to governance while simultaneously expanding the reach of the market. In theory, this would boost the economy, strengthen the CCP's dominance and governing capacity and foster stronger bonds with Chinese citizens via new entrepreneurship opportunities.[52]

Xi and Li ramped up the Hu-Wen administration's appropriation of Maoist technonationalism to justify expanding the role of state industrial policy in China's economy. The best-known example of this was Xi's "Made in China 2025" initiative: industrial policies rolled out in May 2015 that sought to strengthen technological independence and innovation in ten strategic sectors. Unlike the Hu-Wen goal of transforming "made in China" into "created in China," Xi's initiative put more emphasis on maintaining and advancing China's manufacturing edge. The plan's technonationalist framing attracted heavy criticism in Washington and became a *casus belli* for the Trump administration's trade war in 2018.[53]

The expansion of industrial policy paralleled a qualitative transformation of the investor state begun under Hu and Wen and consolidated under Xi and Li. Over a decade, the state's economic role transformed from managing the assets of state-owned enterprises to "the expansion of state investment beyond the state sector." It was increasingly willing to work with and empower "firms and managers that the CCP does not control through its own organization department and personnel systems."[54]

In ZGC, expanding state investment took form in the "ZGC Billions Science and Technology Financial Services Platform," established in 2013 and affiliated with ZGC Group. It aimed to use 10 billion yuan in government funds to attract hundreds of billions more from private investors that would be channeled into strategic sectors such as semiconductors.[55] State-owned high-tech firms, like Tsinghua University's network of affiliates, underwent mixed-ownership reforms. At the same time, private entrepreneurs were welcomed into state-owned enterprises as CEOs or board members in a bid to further separate business management from university management. Distinctions between public and private became increasingly blurred as China combined state-led financialization with the socialist strategy of "concentrating power to do big things" in order to reinvent the socialist "whole state system" to produce a "new-style whole state system" (*xinxing juguotizhi*, 新型举国体制).[56]

The financialized approach to fostering innovation also derived momentum from Maoist mass mobilization methods. Through campaign-style promotion of the stock market, China's government turned a "arbitrary opportunity," offered by new links between the Shanghai and Hong Kong stock exchanges, into a "speculative frenzy" that culminated in the burst of the equity bubble in the summer of 2015.[57] As economist Thomas Orlik documented, China's top leaders, beginning in 2012, "cheered the market higher, with their words echoed and reechoed in the state press." Their enthusiasm for the "reform dividend" drew "novice investors with more enthusiasm than experience" into the stock market.[58]

Campaign-style entrepreneurship promotion culminated in Premier Li Keqiang's initiative to promote "mass entrepreneurship and innovation," announced at the 2014 World Economic Forum in Davos. The initiative appeared in the government's annual work report in March 2015, alongside another new initiative, "Internet Plus," intended to restructure and upgrade China's service, manufacturing, and agricultural industries through computing technologies and information networks.[59] Whereas Xi's "Made in China 2025" technonationalist policy aimed to resolve tensions between innovation-driven and foreign-based development, Li's mass entrepreneurship and innovation campaign carried the additional mission of easing unemployment and restoring social equity. As Li put it: "Promoting entrepreneurship and innovation helps restructure the system of wealth redistribution and enhances social justice. This also opens up space for young people, especially those from poor families, to seek social mobility. We promote mass entrepreneurship and innovation because we want more people to get rich and realize their life's meaning" (*shixian rensheng jiazhi*, 实现人生价值).[60]

Two months after announcing these new policies, Li visited ZGC's InnoWay Street—newly constructed and managed by the government as a model of state-led mass entrepreneurship and innovation initiatives across the nation. Following Li's widely covered visit in May, InnoWay welcomed an influx of aspirational entrepreneurs, visitors, and journalists from across the country and abroad. State-subsidized "mass makerspaces" (*zhongchuang kongjian*, 众创空间) popped up across China as state media churned out motivational stories of entrepreneurs from widely different backgrounds, including overseas returnees, students, and workers migrating between the countryside and urban areas. With mass entrepreneurship and innovation established as the new political yardstick, local governments competed to implement the policy.

At the peak of the 2015 boom, the number of ZGC-based entrepreneurs exploded as overseas returnees and white-collar professionals left their jobs at established companies or government institutions. However, many of these latecomers had less experience or technical training than those who arrived before 2013. A large proportion of the InnoWay entrepreneurs I met in 2016 bore a striking resemblance to the grassroots entrepreneurs of ZGC's electronic malls in the 2000s. They were migrant workers, peasant entrepreneurs, and ordinary college graduates from humble family backgrounds. They came to ZGC with dreams of becoming their own boss, motivated by media stories of grassroots entrepreneurs just like them whose lives were transformed by the opportunities opened up by recent reforms. In 2015, around 32 percent of the nation's venture capital (VC) investment was concentrated in ZGC, accounting for 24.8 percent of all funds invested nationwide. The following year, 24,607 start-ups were founded in ZGC.[61]

One of my informants likened this mass entrepreneurship mobilization campaign to the "Up to the Mountains and Down to the Countryside Movement" (*shangshan xiaxiang yundong*, 上山下乡运动), which attempted to ease urban unemployment and poverty after the Great Famine of 1959 to 1961 and again during the Cultural Revolution by sending urban youths to the countryside to learn from the peasant masses. Li's initiative shared a concern over urban unemployment with its Mao-era antecedent, but this time, my informant explained, the message communicated by the state was that "you're responsible for creating your own job." Just as the "Down to the Countryside" movement burned out after the Cultural Revolution, nationwide entrepreneurial fervor peaked in the summer of 2015, right before the equity bubble burst in July, which cooled capital investment considerably.

By August 2015, the long list of bankrupted online-to-offline (O2O) start-ups circulating in the Chinese IT community was sending chills down the spines of entrepreneurs nationwide. Many were already worried about an impending "venture capital winter" (*ziben handong*, 资本寒冬) as excess liquidity dried up. Riding the coattails of Silicon Valley ventures like Uber and Airbnb as well as Chinese success stories like Didi Chuxing and Meituan, the O2O bubble had benefited from the Internet Plus policy, which promoted digital platforms as a way to reinvent traditional industries, create new consumer demand, and generate entrepreneurialized jobs.

Another overheated sector, peer-to-peer (P2P) finance, also showed signs of contraction by mid-2015. Boosted by state promises to liberalize the financial market and populist rhetoric like "inclusive finance," the sector witnessed explosive growth between 2013 and 2015.[62] Emboldened by laudatory media profiles, lay investors embraced fintech despite its risks.[63] Several P2P lending platforms started to wobble in late 2015, most prominently Ezubao, an industry dynamo that was later discovered to be a Ponzi scheme.[64]

The real turning point of the mass entrepreneurship and innovation campaign came in January 2016, when the party mouthpiece, *People's Daily*, published an interview with an individual identified only as an "authoritative person" (*quanwei renshi*, 权威人士).[65] Widely believed to represent the viewpoints of President Xi Jinping, the anonymous interviewee called for "supply-side reform" and laid out five goals for the future:

reducing overcapacity in industry, reducing inventory in real estate, deleveraging the economy, reducing costs for administrative approvals, and patching up weak points.

In ZGC, this interview slammed the brakes on the overheated VC market even as the state was directing resources away from "speculative," frothy O2O and P2P industries and toward the strategic semiconductor, electronic vehicle, and artificial intelligence sectors. This adjustment benefited some ZGC entrepreneurs but left many companies and their employees in the lurch. To some extent, the state succeeded in redirecting investment away from speculative start-ups and toward investment-starved tech companies in strategic sectors. However, it was less successful in deflating the real estate bubble and reversing China's debt-financed infrastructure construction boom, traditional safe havens that benefited from the outflow of O2O and P2P investments.

ZGC's electronics malls, shopping centers, and restaurants were a poor fit for the state's new goals. Plans to "upgrade" the area had been floating around since 2009 but took on new significance after 2016. That year, ZGC Group, together with the Haidian District state-owned Assets Supervision and Administration Commission (SASAC) and the Tsinghua-affiliated firm TusHoldings, pooled 8 billion yuan to transform a 7.2-kilometer stretch of real estate into an enlarged version of InnoWay.[66]

Suddenly, businesses and vendors that for years had generated enormous tax and land sales revenue for Beijing's government, and employment and entrepreneurship opportunities for migrants and others, were pushed out of ZGC to make room for businesses and institutions specializing in "R&D, innovation and creativity, and technology-related finance."[67] Already weakened by competition from e-commerce platforms, electronics malls were particularly hard-hit. Small vendors shut down or transitioned into "start-up incubators" or "customer experience centers" for high-tech companies. During my fieldwork, I met quite a few former electronics vendors who, after being forced out of business, tried their luck on the brand-new InnoWay. Yet, "upgrading" ZGC produced a glut of vacant office space. Many of the tenants that moved in were government subsidy–sucking incubators and mass makerspaces.

The state's financialized solution for promoting indigenous innovation and social equity, while maintaining GDP growth, proved the least successful. While it channeled resources and talent into strategic sectors and generated new industries and entrepreneurial and employment opportunities, it also precipitated economic speculation, engendered financial risks, and made work more precarious. Many have correctly identified the post-2008 moment in China as ushering in the "advance of the state" (*guojin*, 国进),[68] but few acknowledge the macro global and domestic economic contexts—particularly the failure of free market economics—that made a more active state role an imperative. Even in liberal capitalist democracies like the United States, the state has an important role in financialization. In China's party-state, greater control over its economy and society allowed for more effective financial, human, and cultural resource mobilization—in service of its vision of economic development.[69] But as the boom-and-bust cycle between 2009 and 2015 proved, such power can spiral out of control with each new decision and policy direction.

The growing state role in supporting high-tech and strategic industries was reinforced by the outbreak of the U.S.-China trade war in 2018 and ensuing geopolitical tensions between the two nations during the Covid-19 pandemic. Yet, however much the party-state's latest transformation owes to socialist technonationalism and mass mobilization techniques, its financialized approach to innovation and social equity hardly represents a return to the military S&T developmental model or the radical redistributive class politics of the Mao era. For ZGC entrepreneurs along the elite-grassroots continuum, China's shifting economic policies have had mixed implications as benefits and risks remain unevenly distributed. In the wake of the 2015 equity crisis, it is clear that the negative consequences of state-led financialization continue to fall disproportionally on the most vulnerable.

ELITE VS. GRASSROOTS ENTREPRENEURS

In her study of maker culture in Shenzhen, Silvia Lindtner aptly notes how the state's support for indigenous innovation and mass entrepreneurship was interpreted by Chinese entrepreneurs as a "commitment to supporting people's own desires to achieve parity with the West—the CCP was seen as serving citizens' interests to achieve happiness."[70] In reinforcing the ahistorical dichotomy between the CCP and Chinese citizens, however, she missed historical continuities between the Maoist and post-Mao states, as well as the multiplicities and contradictions within state structure. The rise of an investor state combining financialized governance with socialist technonationalism and mass line politics simultaneously enabled and constrained entrepreneurial reinvention in ZGC. While the individualization of risk and digital elitism characteristic of Silicon Valley and Silicon Alley are prominent features of life in ZGC, the key role played by the investor state in determining macroeconomic cycles and the life choices of variously positioned entrepreneurs presents us with a unique case.

Despite the universalist claims of the entrepreneurship and innovation campaign, the capacity to mobilize resources in the name of self-reinvention differs significantly among entrepreneurs. Within a few months of beginning my fieldwork in ZGC, I had a sense of the social hierarchy among entrepreneurs, what my informants liked to call the "chain of contempt" (*bishilian*, 鄙视链). "At the very top of the hierarchy sit the overseas returnees, who are well-trained and technically proficient," one of my informants, a former private investment firm employee who had left to found his own O2O business, explained. "Many came with their own patent technologies. Equally well-positioned are former employees of established Chinese internet companies like BAT [Baidu-Alibaba-Tencent], big SOEs, or foreign MNCs. . . . It is the entrepreneurs, more than their businesses or products, which the investors are betting on."

Heng, the SOE Engineer Turned Start-Up Entrepreneur

Heng is indisputably one of the most elite entrepreneurs I met in ZGC. A former engineer at a national-level SOE (*yangqi*, 央企) and an alumnus of Peking University (PKU), Heng and his weather technology start-up have benefited from the rise of the investor state, especially efforts like mixed-ownership reform that blur boundaries between the private and public sectors.

I got to know Heng in the mid-2000s, when he was still a college student majoring in atmospheric sciences at PKU. Hailing from coastal Zhejiang Province, a region famous in China for its entrepreneurial spirit, Heng's father rode the wave of reform that swept China in the early 1990s, leaving his danwei to found his own company. This entrepreneurial spirit passed from father to son: At a time when many of his classmates in the physics department were stressing over their GPAs or cramming for the GRE so they could go abroad for graduate school, Heng had already founded an e-commerce business with a friend. Eventually, he opted to stay in China and pursue graduate studies at PKU.

There, Heng's life took an unexpected turn. Influenced by his two roommates—one of whom had started PKU's Taoism Studies Society and the other its Sinology Studies Society—he started to read avidly about Taoism and neo-Confucianism. "Traditional Chinese philosophy encourages you to seek satisfaction in the status quo by curbing your own desires and maintaining inner peace," Heng told me. His newfound desire to go with the flow led him to take a low-stress job as an engineer at a national SOE specializing in wind energy. During his four years at the SOE, however, he grew frustrated by its bureaucracy, workplace hierarchy, and lack of incentives. "I tried to just accept the rules of the system and focus on climbing up the bureaucratic ladder, but while I found some solace in the teachings of traditional Chinese philosophy, deep down I knew I was not happy."

China's promotion of entrepreneurship and innovation transformed his life. Beginning in the 2013, an increasing number of his colleagues started leaving the company to start their own firms or to work for start-ups. "The messages from the top suggest that the state indeed wants SOE employees to quit and strike out on their own," Heng explained to me in 2016. "As a former SOE employee, I wholeheartedly support this. There are so many young talents in SOEs who feel underappreciated and trapped." Yet Heng's experiences working in the state-owned sector also gave him valuable insights into the operations of China's political system. For example, he knew that despite state encouragement of entrepreneurship, state capital would continue in its dominate role in China's economy. "The state will never give up its command over the economy, but the higher-ups know the state-owned sector is not working efficiently, and the best way to restructure the bureaucratic SOEs is to mobilize bottom-up entrepreneurial energy."

In 2013, one of Heng's colleagues at the SOE approached him about quitting and starting their own weather technology business. As the two strategized about where to begin, they were thrilled to learn about two new state initiatives: one encouraging mixed-ownership reform at SOEs, the other gradually increased public access to government-collected big data, including weather data. These initiatives were part of the new Xi-Li regime's plan to speed up economic restructuring. As described earlier in this chapter, MORs were an attempt to revitalize the state sector with infusions of private management and capital; open data rules sought to enhance the capacity, efficiency, and transparency of governance.[71] Both initiatives generated abundant entrepreneurial opportunities for public-private partnership.

These new opportunities encouraged Heng and his colleague to quit their jobs in late 2014 and set up their own weather tech company. Thanks to the experiences they accumulated and connections they developed at the SOE, they closed a deal with a state-owned media and data firm affiliated with the China Meteorological Administration. Responding to the state's call to embrace public-private partnerships while maintaining independent management and ownership, Heng and his partner established a separate joint venture with the media and data firm in 2015. In collaboration with Alibaba's cloud platform, Aliyun, their new joint-owned company's main business is a digital platform that processes and analyzes weather data collected by state-owned satellites, radar facilities, and weather stations across the country. Using this dataset, Heng's firm generates reports tailored to the needs of its clients—mostly energy, aviation, and environmental companies, many of them SOEs. Within two years, the start-up's niche market positioning, coupled with political backing from their SOE co-owner, helped Heng attract considerable investment, mostly from private VC firms. This private and public fusion illustrates a larger trend under the Xi-Li leadership, in which the boundaries between state and private businesses are increasingly blurred amid tightening CCP control.[72]

When I interviewed Heng in early 2016, his company was headquartered in a building owned by the Beijing Meteorological Bureau. I registered with a security guard at the front desk, showing my ID card before I was given a temporary pass to swipe myself in. On the ninth floor, where Heng's company was located, I entered an office indistinguishable from those of all the other start-ups I visited during my fieldwork. The space was packed with cubicles occupied by busy, overworked young employees. Reflecting on abandoning the "iron rice bowl" offered by his SOE employer and becoming his own boss, Heng told me it was the "best decision." As he put it: "The feeling of being needed and appreciated makes me feel alive. I was dying in my old job. . . . Now I feel like every day is a roller-coaster ride. The excitement is addictive."

Heng told me that he had been giving regular talks at events organized by PKU's alumni association to encourage more young people to strike out on their own. His sense of excitement was shared by many elite ZGC entrepreneurs who spoke with me at the peak of the mass entrepreneurship and innovation campaign in 2015 and 2016.

When we met again in 2019, ZGC's entrepreneurial boom was threatening to bust. Venture capital deals had plummeted amid the escalating U.S.-China trade war.[73] Of the couple dozen start-ups I had been tracking, Heng's company was one of the few that had beaten the odds. The company had expanded over the previous three years and moved part of its operations into a new office building. Heng's business had weathered the trade war well. "Exports are down, but government investment is up," he explained. "Most of our clients are in the state sector, so we are shielded from the trade war as we rely mostly on government procurement."

With a steady stream of revenue and a rich capital reserve, Heng's company was expanding into "weather derivatives"—a new market that had emerged from the liberalization of the China's financial sector. However, after seeing so many start-ups fail over the past few years, Heng had become more cautious when giving advice to would-be entrepreneurs: "The start-up world is full of risks and while I am one of the lucky few, there's still a long way to go."

In 2011, Vivek Wadhwa noted how Chinese students who wanted to become entrepreneurs had altogether different motivations from their American peers: "American students usually talk about building wealth or changing the world. The Chinese said they saw entrepreneurship as a way to rise above 'the system,' to be their own bosses and to create their own paths to success."[74] Heng's story of entrepreneurial reinvention was certainly about rising above the system. If he had stayed at his SOE, he told me, he would have remained a cog in the bureaucratic machine. "Now I am a business partner to my former bosses, and I socialize with them like a peer. I also hired two of my former supervisors as consultants. I couldn't even dream about this when I was just a mid-level engineer at the SOE."

Yet, instead of striving for autonomy from the system, Heng reintegrated himself into it. Along the way, he benefited from state policies aimed at reform. For Heng and many of his fellow entrepreneurs in ZGC, entrepreneurial reinvention is about reimagining and transforming the system and the self by hybridizing the old (experiences, skills, and connections) with the new (technologies, markets, and management regimes). The pro-entrepreneurship investor state is a pragmatic ally of this group, not only providing access to government-controlled data, but crucial political backing that can buffer start-ups against the mounting financial risks stemming from campaign-style entrepreneurialism. Sometimes the appeal of this relationship is about more than business: for a number of ZGC entrepreneurs I spoke with, including Dan, who was introduced at the start of this chapter, the nation-state also serves as a site of cultural identification.

Dan, the Oversees Returnee

When I first met Dan in early 2016, and his four-year-old company was about to take off, he criticized government handling of the stock market crash the year before and scorned the proliferating O2O start-ups as "a waste of resources." He explained, "I understand that the top leaders have to balance many different priorities. Keeping the economic engine going and generating employment are important, but all that investment in these food delivery and P2P lending companies doesn't help much when it comes to real high-tech innovation. . . . [Meanwhile,] we struggled to stay alive. Fortunately, things are turning around."

Dan is another member of ZGC's IT elite. Born to a doctor and an engineer in southeastern China, he became fascinated with mathematics and computers after his parents bought him a Lenovo in the late 1990s. In middle school, Dan's mathematical talent won him a medal at the International Olympiad in Informatics. But math wasn't his only interest. Recalling his middle school years, Dan told me that he was equally passionate about culture, history, and philosophy. Perhaps because of these formative experiences, Dan was more outspoken and articulate than many ZGC entrepreneurs I had met who came from purely scientific and engineering backgrounds. Nevertheless, his experiences and thinking are representative of the new generation of IT elites in ZGC.

Dan's master's degree came from the Chinese Academy of Sciences Institute of Computing, the institute that had designed China's first CPU chip and nurtured generations of IT entrepreneurs, including Lenovo's founders. After graduating in 2007, Dan took the well-worn path to America: "We used to joke about how the best and brightest Chinese went abroad to build the USA," he recalled with a laugh.

Working toward a PhD in California, Dan got involved in an applied research project that gave him hands-on experience in chip design. Outside of the lab, Dan was eager to learn about American culture and society. "I took several courses outside of my discipline, in the humanities and social sciences, and I received an 'A' in an elective course about the history of Western philosophy," he recounted with pride. During the summer of his second year he interned at Google and enjoyed its famously relaxed corporate culture. "I gained quite a few pounds at Google because I really liked the free food they offered," he recalled, smiling. His experiences at Google helped him set up his own start-up. "Chinese society does not respect individuals," he explained. "American tech firms like Google know better how to unleash individual creativity and agency."

Yet, Dan's thinking took a technonationalist turn during his sojourn in the United States. A series of events eventually prompted him to quit his PhD and return to China. The first trigger, Dan told me, was during the 2008 Beijing Olympics torch relay in San Francisco. He went to the event with a group of pro-China university students, and they got into a fierce debate with pro-Tibetan independence protestors on the street. "I was so disillusioned with American democracy after I saw the biased national and local media reporting on the event," he told me. "The pro-China voices were completely muffled by media because they just assumed we had been brainwashed by the CCP." The 2008 financial crisis further dampened his enthusiasm for "American-style capitalism" as many of his Chinese engineer friends were laid off by Silicon Valley companies. "They lost their jobs overnight. Because of their visa status, they were the first to go."

Struggling with culture shock and loneliness and alienation as an international student, the growing signs of China's robust economic recovery made Dan increasingly restless. One day a news story about a famous Chinese cryptology professor caught his attention. The professor, who later became Dan's advisor at Tsinghua, stunned the global cryptography community when her team exposed a weakness in a key U.S. government encryption code previously thought to be virtually unbreakable. "They called her 'the magician from the Orient,'" Dan recalled. The story sparked his interest: "I immediately realized that I could combine cryptography with my training in chip design. That could be my niche." The next day, Dan wrote a letter to the professor expressing his desire to study cryptography with her at Tsinghua. He was admitted the same year.

After three years in the United States, Dan returned to ZGC with a master's degree in electronic engineering and enrolled at Tsinghua as a PhD student. Two years later, while finishing his dissertation, he launched a start-up firm specializing in the design of crypto-chips. The early going was rough. Most private investors were reluctant to invest in capital-intensive technologies that would take years to become profitable. At one point, Dan sold off his family's old apartment to make payroll.

But his market instincts, persistence, and technonationalist commitment eventually began to pay off. In 2014, Dan's company received seed funds from the Tsinghua-affiliated TusStar incubator. That same year, the central government set up the "Big Fund"—a state-backed "fund of funds" aimed at promoting national self-reliance in semiconductors. In 2015, Dan was recruited into China's highly selective "Thousand Talents Program" and Beijing municipal government's "Overseas Talent Aggregation Project" (*juhai jihua*, 聚海计划). With that came not just individual financial reward and preferential policy treatment, but the all-important stamp of political approval for his company.

In a system where state policy mobilizes resources and dictates economic cycles, a political endorsement of this sort opens many doors. Between 2015 and 2017, Dan's company received two rounds of angel investment from incubators affiliated with Tsinghua University and Beijing's Haidian District. A few months before our first interview, Dan leveraged a recommendation from ZGC officials to secure a deal with the Ministry of Transportation to participate in the design and manufacture of China's next-generation public transportation card.

Still, he resented the monopolistic SOEs that had tried to take over his young company for its patents and the unprofessional financial agents and investors who wanted to make quick money off his work. His luck turned only with the U.S. trade and technology war against China.

Threatened by American restrictions on chip exports, the Chinese state ramped up efforts to strengthen domestic chip design and manufacturing capacity. Earlier that year, Dan had been named one of China's forty most influential businesspeople under forty by *Fortune* magazine. By the end of 2018, Dan's company had received a major investment from two top state-owned enterprises and two private VC firms known for backing cutting-edge technologies.

In the summer of 2019, I met Dan for a follow-up interview. He had moved his company into one of the most luxurious office complexes in downtown ZGC. As I exited my taxi and walked into the building, I was dazzled by the postmodern artwork on display, abstract sculptures and paintings coexisting seamlessly with traditional Chinese elements like bamboo trees, an arch bridge, and an artificial lake dotted with goldfish. Glancing through the list of tenant companies, I saw the names of successful Chinese SOEs like China International Capital Corporation, private firms like Huawei, and foreign multinationals like Google, Intel, and Apple. At the bottom of the list was Serica. This office was quite an upgrade from the state-owned incubator where we first met three years earlier. Owned and operated by Lenovo and designed by a team of world-famous architects, the building seemed to be the material embodiment of China's future—at least the future envisioned by the Chinese political and business elite—the private and public, Chinese and foreign, high-tech and pastoral, all blended together in perfect harmony (figure 2.4).

Dan's assistant greeted me at the entrance and led me past a line of meeting rooms named after Western philosophers like Schopenhauer and Heidegger to reach his office. During our conversation, we talked about what had changed over the past three years and the impact of the U.S.-China trade war on his business. Compared with our last meeting, Dan was more confident about China's state-led innovation system and also more reluctant to criticize it, although he deplored how preferential policies and proliferating state and private investment allowed "dishonest" entrepreneurs to take advantage of state support. "I have to thank Trump," he joked. "If not for his sanctions on Huawei and ZTE, Chinese tech companies would never have made up their minds to become more self-reliant in chips. Now they have no choice." He told me that the government would publish an "unreliable entity list" to push Chinese tech

FIGURE 2.4 The lobby of Dan's new office building, a testimonial to his accomplishments as an entrepreneur. Photo by author.

companies to replace imported chips with domestic versions whenever possible. "The state had been promoting semiconductor independence for years, but the market didn't really take it seriously; they thought the government was just crying wolf," Dan told me. "Now the wolf has finally come."

I asked why he named his company's meeting rooms after Western philosophers. He laughed. "I hope it doesn't seem pretentious," he replied. "I think China has a lot to learn from Western philosophy—rationality and being reflexive about rationality, respect for science, just to name a few things. That said, in my opinion, it's the people who identify with Chinese culture and the Chinese way of doing things, but who have been trained in the West in science and engineering, who will lead the Chinese IT industry."

Toward the end of our conversation, Dan asked me if I was going to write another China-bashing book, adding that he knew "pro-China books do not sell well in the United States." I responded by asking how he wanted to see his generation of Chinese IT entrepreneurs represented in English media outlets. He paused for a few seconds and said: "I'd like to see us represented like the socialist scientists and engineers, those who sacrificed the personal interests of their 'small selves' (*xiaowo*, 小我) to serve the collective interests of the nation."

Dan's words played in my mind as I made my way home. They reminded me of work by anthropologist Yunxiang Yan on how individual subjectivities in contemporary China, even after decades of marketization and globalization, are still determined by the power of the party-state.[75] Yan argued that, "The key to understand the Chinese self . . . lies in the Chinese understanding of the individual as the duality of a small self and great self."[76] The rise of the investor state in recent years, in tandem with the state's appropriation of socialist technonationalism, has only strengthened the affective bond between the party-state and elite IT entrepreneurs enjoying state patronage. This is true even as the latter remain clearheaded about the problems that have emerged in this process and about China's own weaknesses. For elite entrepreneurs like Dan, who consider themselves agents of China's technonationalist development and inheritors of its socialist tradition of self-sacrifice, their personal entrepreneurial reinvention is inextricable from the collective nationalist struggle to reclaim China's rightful place, not just in the global division of labor, but as a great civilization equal to the West.

However, as Silvia Lindtner found in her study of makerspaces in Shenzhen, identification with state-championed technonationalism occludes not only exploitation and self-exploitation—as seen in the prevalence of overtime culture and rising mental anxieties tied to overwork and cutthroat competition in China's tech industries—but mounting inequality, even within the tech sector. Most entrepreneurs I spoke to in ZGC had none of the government connections, endorsements, elite education credentials, or alumni networks enjoyed by Heng and Dan, much less the latter's technical expertise. While state championing of entrepreneurship encouraged individual risk-taking, adverse consequences were disproportionately shouldered by grassroots entrepreneurs already disadvantaged by the system. Chinese state efforts to entrepreneurialize social equity by appropriating socialist mass line politics have struggled to redistribute economic opportunities and the alleviate the increased precarity of IT entrepreneurial labor.

Meng, the Grassroots Success Story

I first learned about Meng from a documentary on ZGC entrepreneurs produced by China Central Television (CCTV). The director of the documentary, whom I had met during my fieldwork, invited me to a special screening of the film for a group of administrators at the ZGC branch of the state-run Industrial and Commercial Bank of China (ICBC). The documentary focused on non-elite "grassroots" entrepreneurs in ZGC as they braved the storms of the entrepreneurial campaign. It won numerous awards in 2015. After the screening was over, one bank administrator praised the film as "motivational" (*lizhi*, 励志) and thanked the director for "telling the stories of the grassroots" (*jiceng*, 基层).

"Motivational" was exactly the tone the government was going for as it spun narratives of grassroots entrepreneurs who had created their own jobs. A couple of weeks later, I ran into Meng at one of the coworking cafés on InnoWay. A mutual friend and fellow entrepreneur introduced us and told me that Meng's excavator sharing platform had just received a new round of investment from a private equity firm. Taking advantage of this introduction, I struck up a conversation. After casual small talk, our mutual friend turned to me and said: "[Meng] is quite a celebrity now. Ever since he met the vice premier [Liu Yandong] and became a movie star on CCTV, he's had investors chasing after him." Meng blushed at the compliment and looked embarrassed. "I am just a grassroots entrepreneur who got lucky," he demurred.

A few days later, I sat down with Meng in the same café for a formal interview. I was eager to hear his tale. Despite the many rumors of grassroots success stories I had heard during my fieldwork, Meng was the first self-proclaimed "grassroots entrepreneur" I had met whose start-up had actually been funded. I was curious to learn what set him apart and what he had to say about China's financialized approach to entrepreneurializing social equity. In the documentary, I was struck by a scene in which Meng returns to his home village in East China to visit his father—a garbage collector and trader who disapproved of Meng's entrepreneurial ambitions—so I decided to start our conversation by asking about his family.

Meng grew up in a poor village along the banks of the Yangtze River. His father worked as a sailor for the township's transportation company before being laid off in the late 1990s. As Meng put it: "His state-owned company was squeezed out of the market by its privately owned rivals and their fancy imported cargo vessels." To support his family, Meng's father left for a nearby city, where he found work as a migrant laborer, only to return a few years later to take care of Meng's mother after she fell ill. To get by, he started a small garbage collecting and trading business. Although Meng had been a top student in elementary and middle school, when he took the college entrance exam, he had to face the harsh reality that his family could not afford his tuition and living expenses. So, Meng enrolled in a local teachers' college that didn't charge tuition and returned to his hometown after graduation to teach math. Frustrated by the low pay, he quit teaching after a few years to dabble in small ventures before becoming a sales agent for a construction machinery company in 2008. Riding the coattails of the post-2008 real estate and infrastructure construction boom, Meng quickly accumulated a small fortune. It wasn't enough. Enticed by the seemingly limitless potential of China's nascent digital economy, Meng left his hometown and started a business designing and manufacturing copycat, or *shanzhai*, phones in Shenzhen.

"I think of it as paying my dues" (*jiaoxuefei*, 交学费), said Meng, explaining his failed venture. "I was a rookie with no background who got into an overcompetitive industry," he added. "I learned my lesson."

Still unsure of next steps in late 2013, Meng stumbled across a post on the Chinese microblogging app Sina Weibo touting a coworking café in ZGC. "I actually still have a screenshot of the post," Meng told me, scrolling through a photo album on his phone until he found the post that had changed his life. "Buy a cup of coffee, and you could stay here all day," the ad read. "We organize all types of entrepreneurial events, and there are no entry requirements (*lingmenkan*, 零门槛). Come here and meet with your future investors and business partners!" Eager to know more, Meng looked up the Garage Café online. The news reports only made him more excited. According to one article, the Beijing government was planning on building an entire street of incubators to serve the emerging mass entrepreneurship campaign. "I thought this could be my opportunity," Meng told me. His first encounter with the Garage Café and InnoWay mirrored the experiences of many other grassroots entrepreneurs I interviewed in ZGC. Like them, positive news coverage inspired him to try his luck in the capital.

Meng arrived in ZGC in early 2014, just as the latest round of entrepreneurial fervor was heating up. Like Fu, the former Foxconn worker whose story appears at the beginning of this chapter, Meng hung out at the Garage Café picking up the basics of applying for VC funding. He spent his days socializing with entrepreneurs and investors and working on his business proposals. In the evenings, he crashed at a public bathhouse where, thanks to an annual membership purchased during a sales event, he could wash up and enjoy free breakfasts and cheap evening snacks. "I went to the bathhouse so regularly that the waiters at the front lobby thought I was the manager. At one point, they started to greet me as 'Boss Meng,'" he said, laughing. "In truth, I did start to feel like my own boss." During his first year at the Garage Cafe, Meng pitched a number of business proposals, including a poster-making app and a device attached to landline phones that would record and display caller information. None got funded.

After almost a year of trial and error, it suddenly dawned on him that, instead of creating a brand-new self, he should "reinvent" who he already was—a grassroots entrepreneur—by bringing his old construction machinery sales business online. In late 2014, before the mass entrepreneurship and innovation campaign reached its zenith, Meng's proposal for an excavator and machinery Uber secured seed funding from a domestic VC firm. The idea behind the company was to build a digital platform on which construction teams could rent equipment to reduce cost. Soon after, Meng became a poster child for grassroots entrepreneurial success. Not only was his story featured in the CCTV documentary, but he was also invited to a high-profile event organized by a supervising body, the ZGC Administrative Committee (*Zhongguancun guanweihui*, 中关村管委会). As a representative of ZGC's grassroots entrepreneurs, Meng met face-to-face with Chinese Vice Premier Liu Yandong and talked to her about his start-up.

All this state-sponsored publicity amounted to an implicit political endorsement for his business. This helped him secure another round of investment in early 2016, even as enthusiasm for O2O businesses began to cool. But when I asked Meng if he thought the mass entrepreneurship campaign had been effective in promoting social equity (*shehui gongping*, 社会公平), his response surprised me. "I don't think there will ever be real equity," he told me. "Securing some investment might bring me temporary success, but honestly, I don't feel optimistic about the future of my company." When I asked him why not, he painted a bleak picture of the start-up scene. "Do you know how competitive the start-up world is?" Meng asked, before listing some of his worries and anxieties:

> I know of at least a handful of businesses that are in direct competition with me. From what I know, one company's founder was a former product manager at Alibaba. Another founder worked for a state-owned construction company for many years. If you look at DiDi and Uber, you will see that the game is winner-take-all. I might have won the VC lottery, but I don't have the institutional and personal networks or access to resources needed to win the larger competition. People doubt you because of your background, and you doubt yourself. We were born unequal, and there's only so much I can do. Don't let the media propaganda fool you!

Meng's experiences as a model grassroots entrepreneur and media icon for state-championed mass entrepreneurship speak to the extra-economic and social redistributive logic behind the rise of China's investor state. The same logic drove the state to invest in O2O platforms and encourage private investment to do the same because of their potential to increase domestic consumption and create jobs. State-championed investment fueled the rapid expansion of an O2O bubble between 2013 and 2016. However, the added labor and extraordinary hardship non-elite entrepreneurs go through to get funded, together with lack of sustained institutional support for grassroots entrepreneurs like Meng, reveal the limitations of the financialized reinvention of socialist mobilization politics in redressing structural inequalities.

In the years following my interview with Meng, the Chinese state, fearful of a "hard landing," launched another campaign of supply-side reform to cool down the overheated economy. Grassroots entrepreneurs in ZGC, with no political buffer and few career options, were hit harder than their elite counterparts. The majority were "wantrepreneurs" like Fu whose start-ups had never been funded. A decade ago, they might have hawked electronics products or assembled DIY computers at one of ZGC's electronics malls. In the mid-2010s, after these malls had become incubators and coworking spaces, they embraced the government call for mass entrepreneurship and innovation by reinventing themselves as start-up entrepreneurs, even though most of them lacked the practical ability to achieve their ambitions.

When I returned to ZGC in the summer of 2019, some of these entrepreneurs were still hanging around. Quite a few had become waiters or low-level administrative workers in the area's many new incubators and coworking spaces. Others were driving for DiDi or selling products online to get by while waiting for their next entrepreneurial opportunity. Some had sold their apartments or lost their life's savings. Others had borrowed money from families or friends and were now in debt. Meng's company disbanded in late 2018 after the team exhausted its funding in fierce competition with a rival firm backed by the Chinese tech giant Tencent. In a desperate attempt to stabilize his company's finances, Meng invested some of the company's VC funds in a P2P lending platform. That platform, like almost all the others, went bankrupt in early 2019, leaving him deeply in debt. When we met in August 2019, Meng told me he was involved in a new cryptocurrency start-up, hoping to make quick money and repay his debts. "I can't go back to the small town I came from," he told me. "[But] not many companies in Beijing are interested in hiring a guy like me in his late thirties with few credentials. Crypto is my best bet."

THE RISKS AND REWARDS OF ENTREPRENEURSHIP

The investor state emerged in post-2008 China as a solution to the crisis faced by its export-oriented developmental model: particularly, its lack of technological independence and mounting social inequalities. It was an attempt to promote indigenous innovation, ease unemployment, and drive domestic consumption. Instead of a retreat of the state and a linear path to the individualization of labor, we see the continued power of the state in shaping the lived experiences of different generations of ZGC's IT entrepreneurs, even as it grapples with tensions between developmentalism, nationalism, and socialism and with internal divisions between different levels of state institutions.

The hybrid model of a state-led but increasingly market-driven system of innovation has been effective in incentivizing a new generation of Chinese knowledge elites, such as Heng and Dan, to reinvent themselves as entrepreneurs and unleash their creative potential. Yet, it is too early to evaluate whether and to what extent the financialized approach has actually helped boost China's innovation capacity. The rise of the investor state, Chen and Rithmire argue, "enabled the state to move beyond 'state sector' firms in steering industrial policy and has perhaps made finance available to firms indeed, but it has also generated waste, corruption, excessive risk-taking, and counterproductive international suspicion of Chinese firms of all kinds."[77]

The investor state's record in redressing social inequalities and promoting equity is more mixed. Residual socialist logic and rhetoric helped animate IT entrepreneurship. They created the institutional and cultural conduits to make grassroots entrepreneurship legitimate and endowed state-led entrepreneurialization with an extra-economic valence. But in valorizing individual success, the state confuses tokenism for group success, while obscuring the persistent structural barriers faced by non-elite entrepreneurs like Meng and Fu in their personal entrepreneurial reinventions. The campaign approach to entrepreneurial mobilization intersected with the boom-and-bust cycle of the venture capital industry to render life and work especially precarious for grassroots entrepreneurs. Their struggles point to the limits of the investor state in redressing social equity and the unevenness of China's ongoing entrepreneurial reinvention. I explore this further in the next chapter on the new entrepreneurial spaces that emerged in post-2008 ZGC.

CHAPTER THREE

From Science Park to Coworking

ZGC's Contested Spaces of Innovation

One day in late 2016, Wei, the managing director of TusStar, the Tsinghua University-affiliated incubator, showed me around its newly renovated facilities. Located in Tsinghua Science Park (TusPark), the 190-acre complex of glass and steel sits just outside the university's southeast gate on some of the most expensive, sought-after real estate in all of ZGC. Its neighbors include Procter & Gamble, Google, and NEC, a Japanese corporation.

Initially founded as the "Tsinghua Science Park Business Incubator" in 1999, TusStar was rebranded in 2013 to keep up with changes in China's IT start-up market and culture. That year, TusStar also began disassembling some of its old office cubicles to create an "entrepreneur café" with an open floorplan. This was in response to political calls for innovation, and to competition from popular entrepreneurial spaces like the Garage Café and WeWork China. "We are now a nationally certified Mass Entrepreneurship and Innovation Space (MEIS; *zhongchuang kongjian*, 众创空间)," Wei proudly informed me. Like the TusStar rebrand, the MEIS label was coined by the State Council in 2015 as part of the national campaign to promote mass entrepreneurship and innovation introduced in the previous chapter. MEIS became an umbrella term applied to diverse kinds of entrepreneurial infrastructure, including incubators, accelerators, makerspaces and coworking offices.[1] Within five years, such distinctions had collapsed as China developed more incubators and makerspaces than any other country in the world: numbers rose from 1,464 in 2013 to 4,624 in 2018, according to the Ministry of Science and Technology.[2]

The rapid expansion of the MEIS system in China paralleled the proliferation of for-profit incubators, coworking spaces, and makerspaces around the world. Before the late 2000s, the global industry appeared to shift toward ownership diversification, but most Chinese business incubators remained state-owned. After 2008, however, China's emergence as an investor state and expansion of domestic venture capital pushed state- and university-owned entrepreneurial infrastructures like TusStar to act as market entities and supported privately owned, VC-backed coworking spaces and makerspaces, like the famous Garage Café.

Despite its hip new rebrand and several rounds of "marketization reforms" to "separate enterprises from universities" (*xiaoqi fenkai*, 校企分开), TusStar still operates like a university-affiliated SOE. It remains intimately connected to Tsinghua University and its network of elite alumni, many of whom hold key leadership positions in Chinese government and industry—including China's President Xi Jinping and his predecessor, Hu Jintao. Most of the shares in TusHoldings, TusStar's parent company, are controlled by Tsinghua Holdings, a wholly owned subsidiary of Tsinghua University. And a significant amount of TusStar's venture capital comes from state-owned banks and VC funds or from Tsinghua's alumni network. Tsinghua alumni dominate the TusHoldings board, and the boards of other corporations under the Tsinghua Holdings umbrella. Many TusStar employees and incubatees are Tsinghua alumni or students. Wei, for example, studied nuclear physics at Tsinghua and worked at the University's Education Foundation before joining TusStar in 2014.

University-affiliated enterprises, especially those connected to elite universities, are the vanguard of China's post-2008 drive for technological independence and global leadership. Paradoxically, TusStar's recent market-driven reforms and embrace of financial capital have strengthened its historical connections to the Chinese state and the Chinese Communist Party (CCP). In this sense, TusStar's entrepreneurial labor of reinvention has been both productive and problematic. While it expedited state capacity to develop strategic technologies, it also encouraged risk-taking and rent-seeking behavior and tightened links between political, cultural, and economic capital.[3]

The rise and fall of the Garage Café, on the other hand, shows the contentious convergence and uneasy coexistence of the new and old social logics shaping China's social infrastructure for mass entrepreneurship and innovation. One of China's first privately owned MEIS projects, the Garage Café was founded by angel investors who made fortunes in China's rapidly expanding IT and venture capital industries after 2000. From the beginning, the space felt more like a social enterprise than a business, largely thanks to the idealistic vision of Sudi, its cofounder and manager. Sudi positioned the Garage Café as a zero-threshold platform for early-stage entrepreneurs and prioritized generating social value for entrepreneurs of all backgrounds over profits.[4] Although Sudi met resistance from the Garage Café's more profit-oriented cofounders, local officials supported and later appropriated his "new social" ideals. Ultimately, however, Sudi's ideals were complicated by conflicting redistributive and developmentalist goals at different levels of the party-state.

Three years after the Garage Café opened in 2011, Beijing's municipal government converted Haidian Book City—the two-hundred-meter-long street where the Garage Café was located—into "InnoWay," a complex of café-style coworking spaces and incubators, financial and media institutions, and government exhibition and service centers. Ironically, InnoWay initiated a downturn in the Garage Café's fortunes. Outcompeted by more profit-driven, better-connected new spaces, the café struggled under the weight of its social mission. After Sudi's ouster in 2014, new management began pursuing the same financialized, expansionist tactics as its competitors, while trying to preserve the Garage Café as a socially conscious enterprise. Still, ZGC's grassroots entrepreneurs who identified with the Garage Café's pro-social ideals were alienated and marginalized by this transformation. As mass entrepreneurial fervor cooled after 2015, many of the Garage Café's old customers left ZGC in search of employment and entrepreneurial opportunities elsewhere. Some who stayed struggled to make a living. Although increasingly cynical about the state-led entrepreneurial movement, they saw no viable alternative to it.

Residents like Tu, a grassroots entrepreneur who was fighting a state-owned real estate developer over the rights to his publishing house in Haidian Book City, strike a jarring chord in the government's harmonious melody of innovation and entrepreneurship-driven restructuring. Tu's "nail house" on InnoWay—nail house (*dingzihu*, 钉子户) is a Chinese neologism for a holdout property that refuses to make way for real estate development—his personal struggles, and his ultimate refusal to achieve entrepreneurial reinvention demonstrate the continued hegemony of developmentalism and technonationalism over socialist goals of equality and redistribution. Like the rise and fall of the Garage Café, Tu's story reveals the limits of entrepreneurialism as a governing ideology for empowering the less privileged.

FROM BUSINESS INCUBATORS TO "MASS ENTREPRENEURSHIP AND INNOVATION SPACES"

The explosive growth of MEISs in China should be understood as part of a larger transnational movement unfolding globally after the 2008 financial crisis, as people and institutions attempted to revitalize state and community power and reinvent forms of social, economic, and political participation. A brief genealogy puts the different historical and technological trajectories of Chinese and American innovation spaces in context. Historicizing recent global shifts in technological imagination, including the transnational maker and coworking movements, will clarify the crucial roles of governmental and nonprofit institutions in promoting economic and technological development on both sides of the Pacific after 2008. Yet, as we have seen, China had been appropriating foreign concepts and experiences in the process of developmental and institutional change in the 1980s. Tensions within and between various governmental institutions and the uneasy coexistence of multiple rationalities and conflicting relationships made the path of entrepreneurialization twisted and uncertain.

State-Owned Incubators and High-Tech Zones

China's first business incubator, the Wuhan Donghu Pioneers Center, founded in 1987, grew out of a research project of the Chinese Academy of Science and Technology for Development, which was sponsored by the United Nations Commission on Science and Technology for Development.[5] Much like ZGC, Wuhan City's Donghu District houses a number of state-owned research institutes and universities. In the late 1980s, deep cuts in government funding placed intense pressure on these institutions to become financially self-sustainable. Initially structured as a "public institution" (*shiye danwei*, 事业单位) eligible for subsidies from the municipal Science and Technology Commission, the Pioneers Center incubator became financially independent in 1990.[6]

Prior to this milestone, Wuhan's experiment had become the basis for the "Torch Plan," one of China's earliest post-reform industrial policies. Introduced in 1988, and inspired by Silicon Valley, Boston's Route 128, and other tech clusters in developed countries, the Torch Plan sought to promote high-tech development and innovation in a market-driven way. It intended to establish the social and physical infrastructure that IT entrepreneurship needed to flourish in the post-Mao era, using a suite of policies addressing everything from business incubators and high-tech development zones (HTDZs) to new rules regarding taxation, finance, trade, product pricing, and personnel management. As China transitioned from a command economy to a more market-driven model, these policies encouraged scientists and engineers at state institutions to commercialize their research output.[7] Incubators—often attached to HTDZs—soon began appearing across China.

In drafting the Torch Plan, Chinese policymakers drew inspiration from the "American experience": the government-cultivated system of university/industry technology transfer that emerged after World War II. Ironically, the state's role in this process is often left out of contemporary media and academic accounts of Silicon Valley, which tend to focus on its market-based and hobbyist roots.[8] As Fred Block points out, the American public "has been mostly kept in the dark" about the workings of American innovation system, especially "the role that government plays in this system."[9]

Beginning in the 1970s, most early business incubators in the United States were actually nonprofit institutions supported by universities, local governments, business communities, and occasionally by national government agencies like the National Science Foundation or the U.S. Economic Development Administration.[10] Nor should "corporate venturing" by companies such as the Fairchild Corporation or Kodak be discounted.[11] Between 1985 and 1995, U.S. Small Business Administration initiatives, including the National Business Incubation Association (NBIA), increased the number of incubators in the United States fifteen-fold, from forty to nearly six hundred. Most of them were public or nonprofit.[12] In parallel with this state-backed public innovation system, early hacker-spaces emerged, like the Homebrew Computer Club in the Bay Area, typically within communities of technolibertarians or DIY culture enthusiasts.

By the mid-1990s, the dot-com frenzy had turbocharged the incubator industry. Venture capital-backed, profit-driven incubators and online communities became training camps and networking sites for a new generation of entrepreneurial labor. These institutions and communities helped normalize flexibility and risk as justifiable trade-offs for the sense of self-actualization, freedom, and creativity offered by new styles of working.[13] As the bubble reached its height in the late 1990s, the burgeoning entrepreneurialization trend eclipsed the nonprofit model's reliance on governments, universities, or hobbyist communities. The number of for-profit internet incubators like Idealab soared from thirty-seven in January 1998 to more than four hundred by July 2000.[14] Their blend of cultural bohemianism, free-market entrepreneurial zeal, and techno-determinism —alternatively termed the "Californian Ideology" or "the industrialization of bohemia"—challenged the existence of nonprofit incubators and hobbyspaces and heightened tensions between social and commercial values.[15]

Back in China, the Torch Plan embodied the internal tensions within the country's science and technology development program. Although it was touted as a way to promote innovative high-tech ventures, the plan's investment criteria "focused on proven technologies as a way to jump-start local production and supply a large number of manufacturing jobs."[16] This dilemma between technological advancement and economic development stemmed from China's position in the international division of labor as a manufacturer of low value-added goods. It was exacerbated by growing reliance on fixed asset construction to boost GDP.

State-owned incubators established in the 1990s, like the HTDZs that often hosted them, were caught between their stated mission, championing technological innovation, and their real business, boosting economic growth as measured by GDP. Far from promoting technological innovation, the strongest incentive many local governments and institutions had for setting up HTDZs was to earn revenue from leases, state subsidies and investment and to grow the tax base, along with the usual motives like job creation.[17] This investment-driven and real estate–driven logic of development flourished after China's 1994 fiscal reform put local governments under greater fiscal pressure and incentivized local cadres to prioritize GDP growth at all costs.[18]

ZGC's High-Tech Experimental Zone (HTEZ) had been established in 1988. Built around Electronics Street, it tapped into the dense concentration of educated labor in Beijing's Haidian District. However, "zone fever" soon swept through ZGC. In 1994 its HTEZ expanded to include two additional "experimental zones," satellite campuses of ZGC's High-Tech Experimental Zone on the northern and southern fringes of the city. The HTEZ expanded again in 1999, when ZGC became a national-level science park under the Jiang Zemin–Zhu Rongji regime. China's leaders were rolling out a new "invigorate China through science and education strategy" (*kejiao xingguo zhanlüe*, 科教兴国战略), and two new campuses were added to the newly rebranded ZGC Science Park.[19] In early 2006, after five additional campuses had been built on the city's outskirts, ZGC Science Park was rebranded yet again, this time as a high-tech "platform" consisting of "one district and ten campuses" not confined to a geographic area (figure 3.1). The incentive for this expansion, in addition to increasing land leasing revenue, was local officials' desire to boost ZGC's GDP to better compete with other HTDZs, thereby maximizing access to preferential programs that would attract more business and talent to Beijing.[20]

In parallel with its geographic expansion, ZGC's original campus in Haidian underwent a grand makeover in the late 1990s. The new highrises lining its streets were owned by local government agencies or SOEs, and often managed by commercial real estate contractors. Political and commercial interests united to maximize the value of ZGC real estate. Deep-pocketed MNCs, established Chinese corporations and SOEs, and profitable electronics malls began squeezing out the small and medium high-tech start-ups that once powered Beijing's innovation engine.[21]

At that time, ZGC's trajectory was typical of other HTDZs across the country. Prior to the late 1990s, government institutions and SOEs sponsored the major national incubators. In most cases, incubators were

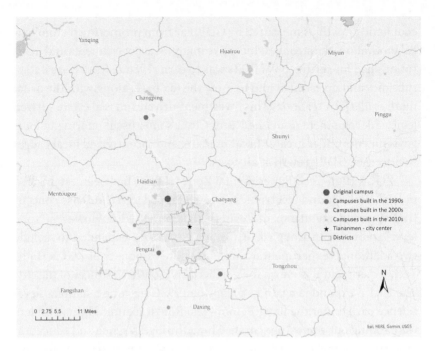

FIGURE 3.1 The expansion of Zhongguancun since the early 1990s, showing its rapid growth into several Beijing districts. Credit: Tu Lan.

conduits for distributing subsidies and implementing China's industrial policies. Services were often limited to providing clients with cheap office space.

This changed abruptly with the expansion of global venture capital, which coincided with China's entry into the WTO, and with the 2001 dot-com bubble.[22] The first privately owned Chinese incubator opened in 2003 on one of ZGC's ten satellite campuses. But while more private agents soon joined the fray—including universities, research institutes, and private and foreign companies—ownership diversification did not create substantial changes in China's incubator industry. Private efforts to promote domestic innovation were still overshadowed by an export and investment development model that relied on imported technologies and second-generation innovation.[23] Qiang, a long-time participant in China's incubator industry, gave me an idea of the dominant role of the state at that time:

I started interning at the incubator in 2007, when I was still in college. It was a state-owned public institution. Unlike most state-owned companies, the employees were all pretty young. Most of them were fresh college graduates like me. . . . Our role was more like that of an intermediary between entrepreneurs and governments or all kinds of state-owned institutions and companies. Many of the entrepreneurs I met were researchers at state-owned institutes and universities who wanted to commercialize their research outputs. In addition to office rentals, we made money based on a commission system whereby we would earn a small percentage of the deals we helped to close. There was no To-C (customer) business and very few To-B (business) deals. The majority were To-G (government).

The Post-2008 Proliferation of MEISs

Much changed between 2007 and 2016. Qiang left the state-owned incubator in 2010 to start his own online education company but went bankrupt in 2013 after exhausting his seed investment. The next year, he became a manager at the ZGC branch of the coliving start-up, You+. At the time, You+ was one of the hottest spots in ZGC: Its valuation soared after it secured series-A funding from Lei Jun, cofounder of the Chinese tech company, Xiaomi. One of the first multipurpose spaces of its kind in China, You+ is an incubator, coworking space, hostel, and social community for young entrepreneurs. Soon, however, the coliving market began to get crowded, like the coworking market from which it evolved, as WeWork unveiled WeLive in April 2016.

Coworking was another product of global entrepreneurial reinvention after 2008, the outcome of an unlikely partnership between entrepreneurs, venture capitalists, politicians, community workers, and educators across the Pacific region. Along with renewed interest in incubators, the proliferation and popularity of coworking and makerspaces was driven by venture capital. At the same time, other agents, including government and nonprofit or civic-minded entities, were crucial participants in the collective experiment with new practices of citizenship and labor organization.

If the entrepreneurial boom in post-2008 America reflected negotiations and collaborations among different agents seeking a new vision for U.S.-led development (i.e., revitalizing American manufacturing, building infrastructure for flexible entrepreneurial workers, and strengthening STEM education), the proliferation of mass entrepreneurship and innovation spaces in China in the 2010s addressed similar desires to reinvent the country's economy and society. It, too, witnessed the coming-together of different agents—albeit not without conflict and friction—seeking to reimagine China as an innovator with a more equal and sustainable economy.

The post-2008 investor state's amalgam of financialized governance, socialist technonationalism, and mass line politics shaped the experiences of a new generation of elite and grassroots entrepreneurs in ZGC. MEISs initially expanded on the periphery of state capitalism after 2008, as China became one of the few bright spots in a bleak global economy.[24] State-led financial liberalization attracted an unprecedented surge in domestic and foreign venture capital. New entrepreneurial opportunities followed technological breakthroughs like 3G, AI, and blockchain. In this climate, a few VC-backed, socially minded entrepreneurial spaces in cities like Beijing, Shanghai, and Shenzhen were set up by cosmopolitan, tech-savvy entrepreneurs who appropriated liberal Western concepts like coworking and makerspaces to reenergize China's economy.

First on the scene was Sinovation Ventures, a capital-rich incubator founded by the Taiwanese-American computer scientist and businessman Kai-Fu Lee. After heading Google China for four years, Lee left the company in 2009 and set up shop across the street from Google's Tus-Park headquarters. Lee founded Sinovation with VC funds from investors like Steve Chan, cofounder of YouTube, Taiwanese electronics manufacturer Foxconn, and Legend Holdings, Lenovo's parent company.

In 2010, David Li, Minlin Hsie, and Ricky Ng-Adam—Silicon Valley alums and influential players in Chinese tech—started a new makerspace in Shanghai: XinCheJian. A year later, the Garage Café opened on the second floor of a rundown hotel in ZGC and quickly distinguished itself from traditional state-owned incubators. Chaihuo Makerspace, one of Shenzhen's first coworking spaces, grew out of former Intel engineer Eric Pan's Seeed Studio.

Local governments moved quickly to channel this capital-driven, bottom-up creative dynamism and reenergize an economy desperate for new opportunities. Previously, government subsidies were reserved for state-owned incubators. After 2011, however, ZGC's Administrative Committee—a government supervisory body—began integrating private entrepreneurial spaces like Sinovation and the Garage Café into its subsidized system of "innovative incubators" (*chuangxinxing fuhuaqi*, 创新型孵化器). Encouraged by the success of privately owned entrepreneurial spaces, Beijing's municipal government opened the reconfigured "InnoWay" in 2013 as complex of incubators and other entrepreneurial infrastructure.

Even as the state turned to private incubators to reenergize SOE innovation, that system was transforming on its own. In 2013, the Tsinghua Science Park Business Incubator became TusStar. Like other university-affiliates across China, the Business Incubator underwent shareholding reform (*gufenzhi gaige*, 股份制改革) in the early 2000s to stimulate more market-oriented behavior.[25] After the 2008 crisis, a new round of "mixed-ownership reform" (MOR) had brought more private capital and management professionals to its parent company, TusHoldings. A key Xi-Li initiative, MOR intended to "separate [university-affiliated] business from the operations of the university."[26] The result would be a more market-driven incubator free of some of the constraints on state-owned businesses—something like TusStar.

In consequence of this economic and social restructuring, boundaries between state-owned and private businesses became increasingly blurred. At its climax in 2015, this reform campaign announced the series of industrial policies described in the previous chapter: the entrepreneurship and innovation campaign, Made in China 2025, and Internet Plus. Made in China 2025 revived the Torch Plan's focus on incubators in order to "upgrade" China's innovation and entrepreneurship service industries.[27] Almost overnight, entrepreneurial spaces of almost every type appeared across the country under the MEIS label.

Tasked with implementing these national policy initiatives, local governments and governmental institutions competed for subsidies and other support by boosting their numbers of incubators and start-ups. In 2016, for example, the Henan provincial government provided a start-up fund of three million yuan to any national-level incubator recognized by the Ministry of Science and Technology. Local governments in other regions offered tax breaks, low rent and utility rates, and start-up insurance to attract local incubators.[28]

Concurrent state efforts to promote a domestic venture capital industry, especially in the public-private partnerships known as "government-guided funds," also benefited the incubator industry. Real estate businesses, which had thrived on China's investment-led development logic, embraced the new innovation-driven model and joined the high-tech entrepreneurial gold rush. Many MEISs during the boom were little more than office rentals passed off as entrepreneurship and innovation spaces. By early 2017, the VC surge had subsided and bankruptcies were sweeping through the start-up scene. Leading industry observers lamented that "there are too many entrepreneurial spaces and too few entrepreneurs to occupy them."[29]

Unanswered are questions of whether, and to what extent, the MEISs helped China build a more innovative, equal, and inclusive society. What new institutional and subjective formations emerged out of collective entrepreneurial reinvention as distinctions between public and private firms grew less substantial? The following three case studies of institutional entrepreneurial reinvention in ZGC offer answers to these questions.

TUSSTAR AND THE FORTUNES OF
ENTREPRENEURIAL STATE CAPITALISM

Since the early 1980s, China's leaders—many of whom were trained as scientists and engineers—dreamed of building a university-industry technology transfer ecosystem like Silicon Valley. Enterprises affiliated with Tsinghua have long played key roles in China's state-led innovation system, borrowing from foreign models while maintaining distinctly "Chinese characteristics." With the financialized approach to promoting indigenous innovation appearing in the late 2000s, Tsinghua's university affiliates again advanced the state's vision—and again found themselves targeted for reform. To understand how these reforms reflect ongoing reinventions of corporate entrepreneurialism, we must quickly look at developments in the past.

University-Affiliated Enterprises as Public-Private Hybrids

Soon after its founding in 1911, the last year of the Qing dynasty, Tsinghua began to operate businesses even as it prepared students to study in the United States.[30] With the PRC's founding in 1949, Tsinghua became the "cradle of red engineers."[31] During the Great Leap Forward (1958–1960), the school responded to Mao's call for universities to train "laborers with socialist consciousness and culture" by expanding its production facilities to better integrate education, research, and production. During the Cultural Revolution's radical egalitarianism, students and professors were required to work in factories and agricultural communes.

In the late 1970s, researcher-founded firms emerged from Tsinghua in parallel with the repudiation of class struggle and the consolidation of technocratic power (figure 3.2).[32] Despite pushback from "conservative" forces, these spinoffs were encouraged by local cadres and university administrators as important revenue sources at a time of budget cuts.[33]

FIGURE 3.2 Photo of Tsinghua students from the Department of Computer Science and Technology in the early 1970s. Source: Department of Computer Science and Technology, Tsinghua University, https://www.cs.tsinghua.edu.cn/yxjj/lsyg.htm.

Tsinghua's spinoffs mushroomed to more than a hundred companies in less than twenty years' time. In 1995, these firms were consolidated via merger and reorganization to form Tsinghua University Enterprise Group.[34] From that point on, Tsinghua's affiliated enterprises followed the path of entrepreneurial state capitalism, combining profit-driven marketization with heavy reliance on the Tsinghua brand and its strong alumni network among China's technocratic elite. Yet, despite successful technology transfers, they generated secondary innovations based on mature technologies.[35] Limited capacity for indigenous innovation left them playing catch-up.

One of these companies, TusHoldings, embodies the contradictions inherent in its ostensible mission of spearheading technological innovation, its residual social function as a university-affiliated enterprise, and its profit imperative. The company was established in 1994, primarily to develop and manage real estate.[36] Five years later, Tsinghua's Science Park Development Center set up the Tsinghua Science Park Business Incubator within TusPark to invest in promising start-up companies, almost all of which were founded by Tsinghua students, professors, or alumni. But R&D investment lagged. Lack of domestic and foreign VC funding,[37] lack of intellectual property protections, abundant government and university red tape, and the onerous hukou population registration system that made recruiting talent from around the country difficult—all these factors constrained innovation capacity.

Tsinghua's affiliated companies trained the university's students in hands-on research and entrepreneurship. However, a portion of company revenue kicked back to the university, and they were often tasked with employing the family members of university administrators, faculty, and staff.[38] This was disadvantageous in competition with MNCs and private domestic IT firms that were free from the economic constraints imposed on university affiliates.

Yet, the Tsinghua brand and its elite alumni network helped secure government procurement contracts and preferential policy support.[39] Financialization provided opportunities in the 2000s. Some firms opted to go public by acquisition and merger with existing publicly traded firms.[40] Some looked to profit from real estate speculation.[41] TusHoldings and other Tsinghua companies invested heavily in real estate, which was more profitable and secure.

After the state boosted Tsinghua's funding in the late 1990s, public anger made profit-making less legitimate. University enterprises became easy targets for critics worried about corruption and the privatization of public assets. The goal of state reform in the early 2000s was to create a "firewall" between the university and its affiliates. Ideally, university firms would become "separate entit[ies] independent from the university administration," either in the form of limited liability or joint-stock companies.[42] TusHoldings, for example, is a joint-stock company founded in 2000 to replace the Tsinghua Science Park Development Center.[43] Yet, corporate reform failed to sever universities from their for-profit subsidiaries because their ties were not simply financial or administrative. The university-affiliated enterprise system facilitates the mutually beneficial transfer of political, cultural, academic, and commercial capital between elites—a relationship at the heart of contemporary Chinese state capitalism.

Pursuit of development at all cost again came under fire after the 2008 global financial crisis, even though growth was needed to end the economic slump. China faced the daunting challenge of deepening market reforms by unleashing financial capital, while at the same time controlling inevitable threats to technological autonomy, national security, social stability, and sustainability. The entrepreneurial reinvention of Tsinghua affiliates encapsulates this challenge.

Mixed-Ownership Reform and Post-2008 Reinvention

China initiated MOR after 2008 to reduce direct state involvement in the operations of university-affiliated SOEs. Mixing state and private capital introduced private sector management practices, making firms better at serving state goals like enhancing indigenous innovation capacity and achieving technological independence. But how could the state ensure that private managers and capital prioritize state agendas, especially those running counter to their own? The answer was to increase CCP presence in corporate governance as a safeguard against corruption and a source of ideological guidance.[44]

China has long treated tech companies affiliated to elite Chinese universities as a special category of state-owned enterprise. If the state wanted them to be market-driven businesses to serve its extra-economic goals, it didn't want to compromise their social functions and academic reputations. It should be no surprise, then, that state-led entrepreneurial reinvention in SOEs was replete with conflict and compromise.

One strategy Tsinghua Holdings used to carry out mixed-ownership reforms in its subsidiaries was to identify successful business owners who were loyal alumni and appoint them as CEOs of Tsinghua-affiliated companies. Wang Jiwu, the new CEO of TusHoldings, was one such figure. In 2012, TusHoldings welcomed Wang as its CEO. A Tsinghua alumnus and real estate magnate, Wang joined TusHoldings during the implementation of Tsinghua Holdings' MOR plan.[45] He owed much of his success in business to his ability to constantly reinvent himself. A 2014 article in *Shuimu Tsinghua* called Wang a "Confucian businessman."[46] In addition to majoring in economic management at Tsinghua, Wang led several student-run interest groups and showed particular interest in Marxist and Leninist theories. His graduation in 1993 coincided with post-Tiananmen China's renewed embrace of the market economy. This motivated his choice to become a real estate developer at a state-owned enterprise. Wang immediately assumed one of its most challenging jobs: relocating residents of buildings marked for demolition during Beijing's rapid 1990s urbanization.

Step by step, Wang ascended the SOE hierarchy and eventually headed its investment branch in Hong Kong. There, he gained experience in financial capital investment and management. In 2003, Wang left the SOE to found his own real estate company and became a billionaire in less than a decade.[47] Throughout, he remained active in Tsinghua's alumni association and regularly donated to the university.[48] According to another *Shuimu Tsinghua* article, Wang's "loyalty" to Tsinghua convinced its president that he was the right candidate to assume the reins of TusHoldings. When the journalist asked Wang why he agreed to take the job, he replied: "All I was thinking at that time was whether there was anything else I could do for the nation and for Tsinghua." The article concluded, "Of all the various ways Wang could have repaid the university, he decided to help Tsinghua earn money."[49] In 2012, Wang and his real estate management team joined TusHoldings to preside over its MOR. At the same time, Wang's private firm became the second largest TusHoldings shareholder.

Under Wang's leadership, TusHoldings became a market-driven agent of state capital focused on technology services and financial investment. Relative to the private incubators and investment firms I studied, TusHoldings was more focused on incubating and investing in designated strategic sectors that might take years to show a return on investment. State priorities included semiconductors, AI, new energy, nanomaterials, and biotechnology, often collectively called "deep tech" or "hardcore" technologies. My interviews with the manager and employees of TusStar hint at how they rationalized gaps between the company's immediate financial interests and the state aims dictating its investment decisions. Almost everyone I spoke with used the Chinese phrase *"you qinghuai"* (有情怀), or "having ideals," to describe TusStar's commitment to cultivating start-ups in strategic deep-tech sectors that most private incubators and investment firms considered too risky. Wei, TusStar's managing director, whose story led off this chapter, attributed these ideals to the company's connections with Tsinghua. "Tsinghua's cultural genes were built into our company. We are very committed to incubating and investing in deep technology companies. Seldom do we get distracted by the comings and goings of market fads. And because we share the Tsinghua spirit of 'actions speak louder than words' (行胜于言), we are not keen on media publicity. Instead, we focus on getting things done."

Wei made a point of distinguishing TusStar from the hype-chasing investors and incubators responsible for the O2O bubble. In particular, he applauded TusPark's (see figure 3.3) decision to kick out a street food start-up despite its high market valuation: "We don't buy into media-generated hype. The start-up did not reflect our core value of advancing 'hardcore' technologies." Lei, a TusStar incubatee who cofounded an e-bike start-up as a PhD student at Tsinghua, shared Wei's criticisms of "low-tech" enterprises. As Lei explained it:

In the end, it's all about the hardcore technology products you can make. Those are the products that change the structure of an industry or break a monopoly. It's those IT start-ups that are worthy of investment. The majority of Chinese IT entrepreneurs are only making business model innovations (*yingxiao moshi chuangxin*, 营销模式创新). It's not so different from constantly coming up with

FIGURE 3.3   TusPark in 2019. Photo by author.

new schemes to trick people into spending more money. That's why we have had very few real technological innovations, despite the booming IT start-up industry in China.

TusStar can focus on risky, hard-to-monetize sectors largely because of its generous government backing. As a national-level MEIS, TusStar enjoys substantial financial and policy support from the state, including reduced rent and tax breaks. TusHoldings' venture capital firms, in their role as state investment agents, also regularly obtain funding and loans from state-owned banks.[50] Government funding and support give Tus-Holdings the resources and incentives to transcend quick profits and align its business vision with the state's long-term extra-economic agenda.

Sometimes the collaboration is direct, as when TusHoldings worked with Zhejiang's provincial government and several private companies to found the Zhejiang Robot Industry Development Corporation as part of China's "manufacturing upgrade" initiative.[51] TusHoldings' investment in blockchain technologies also went against the prevailing speculative trend. Instead of jumping on the cryptocurrency bandwagon, TusHoldings focused on incubating and investing in start-ups that build the basic technological infrastructure for blockchain. With support from a state-owned bank, it established connections with developing countries in Southeast Asia and Africa to help them build a low-cost blockchain payment system: a merger of the state's indigenous innovation drive and its geopolitical aims under the "Belt and Road Initiative."[52]

Yet, despite the success of the Tsinghua Holdings MOR in empowering affiliated companies to better pursue state goals, it was less effective in curbing internal clientelism or stemming excessive dependence on real estate revenue. Both problems are outcomes of China's state-led development model. The country's financialized approach to technological development focuses limited resources on a few successful businesses—often owned by Tsinghua alumni. By "picking winners," incubators and investment funds affiliated with Tsinghua marginalize other less well-connected entrepreneurs. One TusStar incubatee told me he felt threatened by deep-pocketed competitors trying to buy his patents, many of whom were affiliated in some way with Tsinghua Holdings. Other ZGC entrepreneurs I talked with expressed frustration with perceived clientelism at TusStar, where elite Tsinghua alumni often seemed to receive more care and support.

More problematic was the persistence of, or even the amplification of real estate development models within the university-affiliated SOE sector. As of late 2020, TusPark had more than thirty branch campuses across China; TusStar counted more than one hundred branch incubators nationwide and was expanding overseas. The purpose of TusHoldings' national and global expansion is to platformize and deterritorialize its incubation resources to "overcome the geospatial constraints on the development of incubators" and "set up a global support network and a more comprehensive entrepreneurship and innovation ecosystem to more effectively allocate and mobilize resources."[53]

A *China Real Estate Business* investigative report published back in 2012 tells a different story. University-affiliated real estate development companies like TusHoldings used the state economic restructuring campaign to expand their business nationwide. Local officials enthusiastically embraced the chance to restructure local economics, attract political and financial endorsements from the central government, and polish their own political résumés by linking themselves with prestigious universities. In reality, these projects had difficulty transferring geographically specific academic resources to far flung satellite branches. Many new innovation parks and incubators struggled to turn a profit after their government subsidies ran out. Because land costs in parks designated for research and industry were relatively low, local developers snapped up plots, converted them into apartments or office buildings, and pocketed the profits.[54] The post-2008 real estate boom, despite ostensible ties to innovation and economic restructuring, contributed to government and corporate debt burdens over the next decade.[55]

In 2017, the state stepped in to bring these problems under control. As part of "supply-side reforms," the Ministry of Education set up a discipline inspection team (*xunshizu*, 巡视组) within Tsinghua Holdings.[56] The arrival of this anticorruption team—reporting directly to the CCP— was prelude to a new policy issued by the State Council calling for restructuring university-affiliated enterprises.[57] It emphasized the ownership role of state capital. University SOEs were urged to observe "the principles of the market economy" but to remain separate from schools so that schools could concentrate on education.[58]

At Tsinghua Holdings, the practical effect of supply side reforms was to weaken the power of the professional managers and private capital brought in during the previous MOR, while giving more weight to the party-state and its imbedded agents. In 2018, Wang and another Tsinghua company CEO transferred their seats on Tsinghua Holdings' board of directors to two colleagues with experience as party secretaries.[59] In a November 2019 interview with the *Beijing News*, Wang revealed that TusHoldings planned to realign its business more closely with the state's strategic agenda.[60] Central to this new plan was Xiong'an New Area. Located about a hundred kilometers southwest of Beijing, Xiong'an is the crown jewel of China's efforts to pioneer an eco-friendlier, more innovation-driven developmental model. President Xi is personally interested in this project. Wang told the *Beijing News* that TusHoldings had just welcomed the state-owned Administrative Committee of Xiong'an New Area as a new shareholder and strategic investor. During the previous year it had worked closely with the Xiong'an municipal government to build basic infrastructure, including a new TusPark branch to accompany several Xiong'an-oriented VC funds dedicated to incubating businesses in state-designated strategic sectors.

Wang also stressed the importance of management autonomy, albeit under CCP control. Too much intervention could hurt long-term state goals of promoting technological innovation. "TusHoldings is a high-tech company committed to innovation. Technological innovation demands a more dynamic, flexible, and tolerant institutional culture and management regime. In our experiences of incubating and investing in strategic technologies, we have realized that the existing SOE management regime is too rigid and constricting for high-tech companies."[61]

The stories of TusStar and TusHoldings show how China's export-oriented, investment-led, and GDP-centric development model compromised its pursuit of technological independence and indigenous innovation, while fostering the transfer of economic, political, and academic capital among elites. The ongoing challenge is how to effectively utilize market mechanisms and state resources (financial capital, policy support, and so on) in service of the state's strategic agenda without falling into clientelism and corruption. The new private entrepreneurial spaces that emerged on the periphery of state capitalism would follow a very different trajectory of entrepreneurial reinvention.

THE GARAGE CAFÉ AND THE DASHED DREAMS OF SOCIAL ENTREPRENEURSHIP

"Perfect timing, the right location, and cooperation and support from the right people (*tianshi dili renhe*, 天时地利人和)." Sudi answered my question about the roots of the Garage Café's success with a proverb attributed to Mencius, an ancient Chinese philosopher. The proverb encapsulates its almost overnight rise to fame as ZGC's first entrepreneur-oriented café-style incubator and coworking space. As cofounder and former CEO, Sudi played a major role in the incubator from 2011 until he left in 2014, after disagreements with other shareholders over its future direction.

I last interviewed Sudi in 2019, at his new Entrepreneurship Museum, a nonprofit he founded a year earlier as the latest chapter in his battle to promote and document the development of what he called "entrepreneurial spirit" (*chuangye jingshen*, 创业精神) in China. Like TusStar, the story of Sudi's Garage Café is the story of China's post-2008 search for alternative development models. But this tale starts and ends on the margins of state capitalism. New social spaces arose as part of the entrepreneurial labor of reinvention, but state involvement and co-optation eventually complicated the scene.

A VC-Backed Space for Social Entrepreneurship

The story of the Garage Café begins in April 2011, when Sudi—with his own capital and funding from a group of ten angel investors—opened the first café-style coworking space/incubator in ZGC. The thirty-one-year-old Sudi had just quit his high-paying job as director of investment at the Chinese IT service provider ChinaCache. As a poor Beijing student, he had been a nonconformist entrepreneur in college, skipping class to work part-time in computer sales. Before joining ChinaCache in 2006, Sudi had worked in sales and marketing at several IT companies, including Foxconn and 8848.com, one of China's earliest e-commerce companies. His work in broadband internet service sales gained the trust of many of China's current tech giants when they were still start-ups. When he left the business in 2010, he alone accounted for one-seventh of ChinaCache's total sales volume.[62]

Sudi was a self-made IT entrepreneur and professional with little in the way of academic credentials, technological expertise, or connections. His experiences instilled in him a strong affinity for non-elite or, to use his term, "grassroots" entrepreneurs. His own success as a salesman and start-up investor in the WTO-era Chinese tech industry convinced him of the power of free market competition to level the playing field for young grassroots entrepreneurs. His close working relationships with a number of IT start-ups that became successful on the margins of China's state capitalist system also shaped his thinking.

Sudi thought of setting up a social platform for early-stage IT entrepreneurs to work together, exchange ideas, support each other, and meet potential investors while still director of investment at ChinaCache. "At the time," he told me, "most VC people were based in East Beijing, whereas many of the IT entrepreneurs worked in the northwestern part of the city; not only did it take a lot of connections for early-stage entrepreneurs to get the attention of a potential investor, but they also wasted a lot of time stuck in traffic. I noticed that to save money and stay flexible, many early-stage entrepreneurs worked in cafés. So why not start a café for entrepreneurs?"

In 2011, Sudi went to the United States to visit Silicon Valley landmarks in the history of entrepreneurship, like the HP Garage, and investigate emerging coworking and makerspaces. He told me he picked the "Garage Café" name because "the garage is a cultural symbol that represents values like tolerating failure, encouraging tinkering, and granting individuals the freedom to explore their own passions—precisely what's missing in Chinese society today." In a 2011 interview, Sudi told a journalist from the *People's Daily* that

> capital, resources, and networking are all key to the success of early entrepreneurs. It's not that Chinese people are not creative, but they lack the social platforms needed to obtain support and unleash their creativity. The Garage Café is a coworking space for early-stage entrepreneurs, a place where they can tinker with their ideas and products. Spending a day there is only as expensive as a 15 yuan cup of coffee. This kind of low-threshold platform lowers risks for entrepreneurs and allows them to stay flexible.

To lower costs, Sudi rented an eight-hundred-square-meter space on the second floor of an inconspicuous hotel in what was then known as "Haidian Book City"—a block of bookstores and small businesses primarily catering to nearby university students. He had a secondary motivation for choosing a low-profile location: keeping the space open to the public while screening out random customers like tourists or people on dates. Unlike the upscale coworking spaces that followed, the Garage Café was simple and down-to-earth (figure 3.4). Upon entering, the first thing visitors saw was a board where anyone could post calls for start-up team members and contractors. Beyond the coffee bar, the floor was covered with desks and chairs to accommodate as many people as possible. An elevated stage for events stood in front of the room facing the desks.

FIGURE 3.4 The Garage Café's coworking space. Photo by author.

Shelves against the back wall held books on business, technology, and entrepreneurship. As a social platform for early-stage entrepreneurs, it was low-cost, tolerant, participatory, and collaborative.

In its early years, Garage Café ethos was realized in the communitarian entrepreneurial labor of its coworkers, who offered each other both tangible and intangible support. In addition to leveraging coworking labor, Sudi and other shareholders capitalized on their own personal networks to channel investors, media, commercial resources, and political support to the Café in a virtuous cycle that attracted more coworkers, sustaining the community and its ideals. Riding the venture capital wave, the entrepreneurial labor of the Garage Café and its patrons reinvented existing resources and networks to construct a new model of innovation and entrepreneurship in China.

One example of the Garage Café's tangible, community-based support was its "open-source technology team." Founded and led by Zhaodong, a programmer turned serial entrepreneur who sold his first startup in 2011, the team consisted of programmers and Garage Café regulars who freely volunteered their consulting services to fellow coworkers. Leveraging the coworkers' entrepreneurial labor and its shareholders' personal connections, the Café partnered with tech companies to provide exclusive perks to entrepreneurs who paid a small membership fee. These included free cloud services from Alibaba, free Microsoft Windows and Office software, and free testing platforms for Android apps. But the most attractive perk was meeting face-to-face with angel investors and investment managers who visited the Garage Café regularly looking for promising start-ups.[63] These benefits, Sudi stressed, were the result of the aforementioned virtuous cycle, created by the whole community. Big IT corporations provided services because they saw Garage Café members as potential long-term customers, and investors frequented the Café because they knew they could find high-quality projects there.

Although these tangible benefits were a big part of the Garage Café's appeal to entrepreneurs, Sudi also emphasized the "intangible" and emotional support members provided for each other. Unlike most other coworking spaces I visited in China and elsewhere, Garage Café entrepreneurs were quite willing to engage in conversations with each other and with visitors like me. They spent their time not, just helping fellow coworkers refine and improve on their ideas and business plans, but also socializing with each other outside the café. As Shi, a longtime patron, told me, the Garage Café is "not only a café or an office, but also an emotional and spiritual shelter." It was common to see groups of entrepreneurs gathering together over lunch or a cup of coffee or tea to catch up on each other's projects, offer critiques, and share words of encouragement. To foster this collective sharing and tinkering, the café hosted daily "case shows" during lunch breaks and monthly "demo days." Case shows gave coworkers a platform to introduce their projects, share progress, and get community feedback, while on demo days, select teams with relatively mature projects pitched their business plans to groups of investors invited by the café.

According to many of my informants, the Garage Café pioneered a more transparent, dispersed, open model of business networking than the traditional Chinese style of cultivating connections (*guanxi*) from existing social ties. "The threshold of entry for business start-ups is lower, and the criteria that investors use to evaluate projects are more transparent," commented Wei, a coworker at the café who had secured series-A funding. "I learned so much about how to make it in the new economy by talking to people and by participating in open events."

This sense of empowerment was echoed by Jun, a young game developer and a former Garage Café member who moved into an office in 2014 that could accommodate his growing team. "Given my humble background, I would never have had the courage to strike out on my own in my twenties if not for the resources that the Garage Café provided me," he said. "The Garage Café offered me so many things: low-cost working space, collaborators, training, emotional support, free media publicity, and investment."

Benefiting from the rapid rise of China's domestic VC industry, and the labor of growing numbers of IT entrepreneurs, the Garage Café positioned itself as a social platform on the margins of state capitalism, a place where coworkers could experiment with a new vision of Chinese capitalism: one more tolerant, open, creative, and less hierarchical. Yet this "new social" vision was neither external to the market nor oppositional to the state. Instead, new social platforms like the Garage Café worked through the market and with the state to pioneer a new state-society-market relationship.[64] In the process, they reinvented existing state-capital relations to form new linkages and sites of innovation. This positioning achieved much success in the early 2010s but was challenged by market competition and shareholder profit imperatives, which eventually pressured the Garage Café to become more profit-driven. It was also complicated by the state's endorsement, and later co-optation under the mass entrepreneurship and innovation campaign that followed.

A Model Space for Mass Entrepreneurship and Innovation

The Garage Café's support of early-stage entrepreneurs of all backgrounds and its commitment to the ethos of participation, open sharing, and mutual support complimented the Chinese government's dual desires to restructure the economy through financialization and digitalization while boosting employment and redressing social inequalities via mobilization of grassroots entrepreneurship. In November 2011, the Garage Café became one of the first private companies officially recognized by Beijing's municipal government as an "innovative incubator." The label meant that the Garage Café would be eligible for subsidies and state support that, until then, was reserved for state-owned high-tech incubators like TusStar. The municipal government subsidized the Garage Café's rent and streamlined its bureaucratic processes to lower the threshold of entry for small-scale IT entrepreneurs, shorten the average time it took to register a business from two months to two weeks and reduce the registration fee from 15,000 to 10,000 yuan. The ZGC Administrative Committee also set up a special "fast track" business registration channel for entrepreneurs based at the Garage Café.

Sudi's idea of transforming "Haidian Book City" into a street of incubators for early-stage IT start-ups dovetailed with municipal government desires to gentrify ZGC by capitalizing on the central government's economic restructuring policy. The central state was responsible for launching the campaign, but Beijing officials had their own motivations for taking part in it, including a desire to boost real estate prices within ZGC. Beijing had embraced the high-tech sector to garner preferential treatment from the central state, thereby enhancing local revenues through real estate development. Despite state efforts to break from an unsustainable development model centered on fixed asset construction, real estate development remained important in ZGC's transformation, even after 2008.

It was in this context that interest arose, not just in the Garage Café, but in "the Garage Café model." The municipal government had built Haidian Book City, the two-hundred-meter-long street where the Garage Café was located, in 1992 as a "city cultural landmark." Twenty years later, most of its stores had closed due to competition from China's booming e-commerce industry. Only a few struggling bookstores and shops selling sundries like clothes, shoes, and eyeglasses remained. Given Haidian's struggles, it's no surprise that Sudi's model of cultivating start-ups would strike a chord with local politicians who had wanted to gentrify the area for years. Like the electronics mall transformation described in the previous chapter, Haidian Book City's gentrification soon joined the larger project of boosting IT entrepreneurship, innovation, and financialization. After two years of planning, relocating residents and renovation, the area reopened for business as "InnoWay" in 2014. The street featured café-style coworking space and incubators, a government start-up service center, and several investment firms and media start-ups. It was managed by Haizhi Kechuang (HK), a joint venture between a real estate SOE affiliated with Beijing's municipal government and an IT investment and consultant firm partially owned by Tsinghua University. From the beginning, InnoWay straddled China's commercial and political logics.

Appropriating the Garage Café model in InnoWay's design allowed the municipal government and the ZGC Administrative Committee to gentrify Haidian Book City by replacing unprofitable bookstores and small businesses with trendier spots. Equally important, the Garage Café's vision of a more communitarian, open, and tolerant economic development model converged with the state's new mass line campaign to promote grassroots entrepreneurship and innovation. Two officials from the ZGC branch of the Beijing Municipal Administration for Industry and Commerce visited the Garage Café and reported that its business model "has to a certain extent assisted the work of the government, helping to counteract the government's many shortcomings in managing the economy, such as excessive regulation, an ossified bureaucracy, and slow responses to market changes. In doing so, the Garage Café has contributed to facilitating business innovation."[65]

Departing from the radical socialist ideology of egalitarianism and economic redistribution, post-2008 China reinvented its socialist legacy of mass mobilization in order to accommodate the individualistic discourse of entrepreneurialization. Reimagining "grassroots" peasants and urban working-class youth as agents of IT entrepreneurship and innovation distinguishes the current moment from previous decades. The Garage Café became the state's model platform for advancing and showcasing grassroots IT entrepreneurship. In their 2013 book *The Garage Café*, Sudi and his coauthor, Wang Haizhen, a journalist from the state-owned *China Daily*, linked the Garage Café's ideals to a government report issued during the Eighteenth National Congress of the CCP. This report encouraged the development of small and medium-sized enterprises as a "more proactive employment policy," advocating for "more diversified channels for generating employment opportunities" and "using entrepreneurship to lead employment."[66]

The growing media coverage soon increased official visits to the Garage Café. Anyone familiar with the history of Chinese socialism will recognize these pilgrimages as the legacy of model- and hero-emulating campaigns captured in the Mao-era slogan "Learn from Dazhai in agriculture and learn from Daqing in industry" (*nongye xue dazhai, gongye xue daqing,* 农业学大寨，工业学大庆). After its opening, numerous local and national politicians, including the chairman of the China Banking and Insurance Regulatory Commission, Guo Shuqing, and Beijing's Communist Party Secretary, Guo Jinlong, stopped by the Garage Café. In China, these "inspection tours" (*zoufang,* 走访) are often laden with political meaning. Once marked as a "model site" in the state's economic restructuring agenda, the Garage Café and InnoWay became examples to be propagated nationally.

Media frenzy over InnoWay peaked on May 7, 2015, with Premier Li Keqiang's high-profile inspection tour of the street during his mobilization campaign for the "mass entrepreneurship and innovation" and "Internet Plus" initiatives. This much-publicized event made InnoWay the poster child for the regime's ongoing economic restructuring. As with Deng's famous Southern Tour in 1992, the symbolism of Li's tour was obvious. He spent a few morning hours at the Chinese Academy of Sciences, the socialist era "incubator," celebrating the institution's sixtieth anniversary and talking to staff about the importance of basic research. Then he visited Lenovo's iconic Legend Star incubator, the high-tech success story of China's post-Mao market reforms. Finally, he joined an enthusiastic crowd of selfie-snapping young entrepreneurs on InnoWay, who represented the future of China's state-championed, venture capital-backed entrepreneurial workers and enterprises.

Yet, state involvement in the form of policy support, subsidies, and campaign-style promotion of IT entrepreneurship had paradoxical effects. It promoted the Garage Café as a social platform, but also heightened the inherent tensions between social idealism and venture capital profit maximization in the Garage Café model.

After the Café was singled out as a model incubator space, the government heavily subsidized its rent and high-speed broadband internet. This kept it financially solvent without the need to go beyond selling food and drinks to coworkers, putting up ads in its hallways and at public events, and, later on, offering optional membership for a modest fee. Government political endorsement also provided intangible social support by boosting the national and international fame of the Garage Café brand. From this perspective, government involvement helped sustain its nonprofit communitarian character in the face of growing market competition.

Nevertheless, as time went on, the Garage Café began to lose its competitive edge. The number of MEIS infrastructures of all types ballooned after 2011 in the wake of the Garage Café's success, and more than quadrupled between 2013 and 2018 under the aegis of the mass entrepreneurship and innovation campaign. Some emulated the Garage Café model, but the majority were profit-driven from the get-go. Many were backed by wealthy investment firms, powerful SOEs, or private tech giants like Tencent and Baidu. Existing state-owned or university-run incubators like TusStar also went through marketization reforms. Many benefited from government subsidies and preferential policies, like the Garage Café. Yet, their profit-driven approach, meritocratic start-up selection, and financialized incubation model rendered the Garage Café's grassroots-friendly, low-threshold communitarian vision increasingly unviable.

After the mid-2010s, the proliferation of profit-driven, subsidized MEISs made the Garage Café less attractive to high-quality entrepreneurs and deep-pocketed VC and private equity funds. At the same time, government tokenization of the Garage Café, via financial and political endorsement in its mass entrepreneurship and innovation campaign, imposed new responsibilities on the business. The café's "model site" status and commitment to its founding ideals made it a hybrid platform juggling duties as a coworking space/incubator, a showcase for government initiatives, a popular tourist spot, and a hangout for precariously positioned flexible workers with unrealistic venture capital dreams. Its very openness to politicians, visitors, media, and researchers like me—the foundation of the Garage Café's national and international popularity—disrupted its working environment and distracted from its function as a coworking space and entrepreneur community.

Both Meng and Fu, the self-identified grassroots entrepreneurs introduced in the previous chapter, joined the Garage Café after 2013. In my visits between 2015 and 2016, I met numerous "wantrepreneurs" like them. Hailing from outside Beijing and motivated by media coverage, they join the ZGC entrepreneurial gold rush. Some hung out for a week or so, paying tribute to the entrepreneurship mecca. Others lingered at InnoWay for several months, trying their luck, only to leave after exhausting their savings. A few stayed and held on to their dreams despite repeated failures.

Sudi did not see this process play out at the Garage Café. Straddling China's commercial and political logics, the Café struggled to maintain its founding ideals in the face of external influences and internal divisions. Conflict arose as shareholders debated its future direction, but Sudi held fast to his original intentions and fiercely resisted pressure to proactively monetize and financialize the business. In an open letter in 2013, he wrote:

> We will not open a new branch, nor will we establish our own angel investment fund. We might just go with the flow and stay simple. We stick to the "no-branch" principle because we want to perfect the Garage Café and stay faithful to our founding philosophy: that is, to establish a gathering community for start-up entrepreneurs. We refuse to follow the financialization model, because we want to retain the Garage Café's purity as a platform. We don't want people to worry about competition. Just think: if the Garage Café has invested in your competitor and not you, would you still feel comfortable sharing your ideas with your coworkers? We hope all entrepreneurs at the Garage Café are friends.[67]

Overwhelming shareholder pressure to monetize and follow the mainstream meritocratic and financialized model drove Sudi to quit in late 2014. Peter Zhang, his successor, told me in 2016 that its shareholders were contemplating ways to diversify and monetize the Garage Café brand. When I talked to him again in the summer of 2019, the Garage Café had outsourced the management and operation of its coworking space on InnoWay to a real estate management company. The company agreed to keep the original space intact, but was renting additional offices in the same building, which had been renovated as a profit-driven incubator with an operational logic no different from that of any other profit-driven MEIS.

The rise and fall of the Garage Café as a space for social entrepreneurship demonstrates the contradictions of reinvention and reveals both the potential and limits of entrepreneurial labor to bring about social change. Instead of reinforcing the state-society dichotomy prevalent in China studies, the story of the Garage Café opens up and destabilizes conceptions of the Chinese state as merely developmentalist or nationalist to reveal the multiplicities and contradictions intwining state and society in the post-2008 era. Early on, the Garage Café, guided by Sudi's vision and bolstered by access to expanded domestic venture capital, evolved a new social platform and postulated a more equal, tolerant, accessible, and creative Chinese capitalism. Later on, these ideals clashed with venture capital's profit imperatives and were compromised by the close ties between capital and the state in contemporary China. At different points, the state appropriated the Garage Café's platform to promote the entrepreneurialization of its residual socialist mission and to reenergize its real estate–centered development model. The Garage Café's rise and fall speak to tensions between developmentalism and society in China, a conundrum that new forms of social entrepreneurship have not resolved. The entrepreneurial labor of reinvention produced some success stories, but rendered others more precarious. Eventually, marginalized grassroots entrepreneurs like Tu, the owner of a holdout property on InnoWay, would coalesce into a new generation of "entrepreneurial" migrant workers in ZGC, a "floating population" situated at the fringes of the new economy.

THE "NAIL HOUSE" ON INNOWAY

Tu's genealogy and biography business is hard to miss. The three-story building where the business is located occupies a strategic location near InnoWay's north entrance, right off Beijing's Fourth Ring Road. Tu's company compiles family genealogies and publishes personal and family biographies for its clients. When I first visited InnoWay in mid-2015, a year after its establishment, Tu's company was one of just four holdovers from the old days of Haidian Book City.[68] By the end of the year, the other three—a restaurant selling beef noodle soup, a business specializing in calligraphy tools, and another bookstore—were gone. Tu's business was InnoWay's last "nail house." To blend in, Tu and his business partner hung a poster in front of their building dotted with phrases like "Internet + Family Names" and "Internet + Social Networks Based on Families and Friends," along with a QR code for their official account on the messaging app, WeChat. Tu's struggle for survival on InnoWay speaks to the precarity of entrepreneurial labor and the limits of state-led, market-driven entrepreneurialism in redressing social inequalities and empowering grassroots individuals (figure 3.5).

FIGURE 3.5 Zhongguancun electronics vendors in the process of being evicted. Photo by author.

Growing up in a small county in central China during the Cultural Revolution, Tu had a difficult childhood. His family was classified as "rich peasants" and were targeted for persecution and reform. To protect him, his parents sent him to stay with his grandmother whenever they were forced to attend struggle sessions (*pidouhui*, 批斗会). His grandmother was a superb storyteller. From her, Tu learned about the folklore of his hometown and its traditional moral universe centered around family values and filial piety. When the national college entrance exam restarted after a decade in the late 1970s, Tu tested into a local teacher's college to study Chinese literature.

"I was probably too naïve at the time, but I truly believed in socialism and desired to sacrifice myself for this great cause," Tu told me, reflecting on his decision to become a schoolteacher in one of the poorest villages in his home province: "I went there feeling like a hero. Then, I was totally defeated by its sheer poverty in my first two years there. I felt hungry all the time, and for a while, I was one of just two teachers in the whole school." In his later years in the village, Tu found solace in literature. Reading and writing poems, short stories, and novels helped him cope with his poverty and loneliness. He also made friends with his students and local peasants and met his first wife there. He spent half of his twenties in the village before returning to his home county in the late 1980s to teach at a local middle school.

Amid the marketization wave that swept the country after 1992, Tu and his wife migrated to the southern coastal city of Shenzhen—China's first special economic zone and a land of abundant opportunities—to test the waters of business. Starting out as a journalist and writer outside of the established state-owned system (*tujizhe*, 土记者), Tu learned how to be entrepreneurial and business savvy. In 1995, he opened his own company specializing in writing and publishing bilingual Chinese and English biographic pamphlets for entrepreneurial villages eager to attract foreign investors. The business did well until Tu experienced a series of personal tragedies in the late 1990s: first, he lost his daughter in a car accident, then he and his first wife divorced. Devastated, he returned to his hometown to recover. In 2001, he returned to Shenzhen, reinventing himself as an insurance salesman at a time when the emerging private insurance industry was generating money-making opportunities. Due to his advertising and marketing talents, Tu quickly climbed the ranks. Within a few years he was a midlevel manager.

Tu's life trajectory shifted again with the rapid rise of the internet in China. In 2005, Tu reconnected with a friend from his hometown who ran a successful dot-com company in Beijing. Taking advantage of the industry's post-bubble recovery in China, his friend had made a fortune by creating and providing content to major portals like Sina.com and Sohu.com. He was expanding his business and invited Tu to join him in Beijing. Tu was reluctant at first: "I was already in my early forties, and I didn't know a thing about the internet. My secretary at the insurance company helped me type what I wrote into our company's computer. I didn't even know how to use [the instant messaging service] QQ!"[69] Tu recalled. "But my friend told me that the internet is the future. If I didn't learn how to do business using the internet soon, I would be done."

Driven by fear of being left behind, Tu forced himself to learn about computers and the internet industry in his spare time. This convinced him that IT was about to take over the world. In 2006, he decided to move to Beijing and remake himself as an internet entrepreneur.

Tu started by buying a health and medicine website from his friend. With no experience in operating an internet business, he exhausted his savings and had to close the site within a year. Struggling to make ends meet, he shopped for groceries at the end of the day and bought leftover vegetables from street vendors for next to nothing. One day he read a news story about a rich real estate developer who had self-published a collection of his own poems and thrown a lavish banquet to celebrate its publication. It suddenly hit him that he should reinvent himself based on his skillset—writing and publishing—and start an internet business targeting amateurs who want to publish their own work.

The next day he borrowed 5,000 yuan from his friend, spending 2,000 yuan to cover a few months' rent, 500 yuan to set up a website called "Publish Your Own Book" (*geren chushuwang*, 个人出书网), and the rest on advertising his new business. His website quickly took off, and in a few months he had made hundreds of deals. Most of his customers were senior citizens who wanted to document their life stories or the history of their families. Beijing was a particularly good market because of its concentration of retired cadres with good pensions and a strong desire to preserve their deeds and experiences. In addition to publishing biographies for seniors, Tu discovered a market for compiling family genealogies. His business went so well that within two years he had attracted several investors.

Supported by his investors, Tu rented a new space in a building in Haidian Book City in 2010, relocating his company there a year before Sudi set up the Garage Café across the street. Rent was affordable because booksellers were abandoning retail spaces in Haidian Book City and moving their businesses online. Tu sublet a second-floor space from the owner of a hairdressing business. His business soon became one of the most profitable on the street. In 2014, when Haidian Book City was being transformed into InnoWay, Tu rented and renovated the whole building. He was branching out, selling genealogy-related merchandise and hosting cultural events like public lectures, book launches, and guided tourist trips.

To his surprise, things went downhill almost immediately. First, HK, InnoWay's operation and management company, started pressuring him to move out. Tu was told that his business did not align with InnoWay's market positioning and brand image as a street for IT entrepreneurship and start-up incubation and financing. Later, delegates from the ZGC Administrative Committee knocked on his door with the same request. Yet, Tu refused to budge. Instead, he attempted to reinvent his company as an internet business.

When Premier Li Keqiang visited InnoWay in the summer of 2015, Tu took his employees out onto the street to greet him. As Li drew near, Tu pushed to the front of the sea of spectators to shake hands with him, telling him that he was digitalizing and modernizing traditional Chinese family genealogies on InnoWay. At the peak of the mass entrepreneurship and innovation campaign in the fall of 2015, Tu transformed part of his office space into an IT incubator but, he confessed, none of his incubatees obtained an investment, nor did they pay him any rent. His business cratered in December 2015 when his landlord—a private real estate company—quadrupled the rent with no prior notification, citing the dramatic increase in the value of InnoWay properties over the past year. Their real intention, Tu told me, was to pressure him to move out so they could rent the space to a deep-pocketed IT company for a higher price.

Tensions between Tu and his landlord escalated when Tu refused to leave and threatened to sue for compensation. That is also when Tu realized that the original owner of the property was not his landlord, but rather the state-owned Beijing Publishing and Distribution Group. His landlord was not the owner of the property but a tenant with no legal right to sublet it for profit. The situation escalated until one night, after Tu and his employees had left, a group of thugs hired by the landlord broke into the building. They confiscated all his books, boarded up the gate, and stationed a team of security guards in the lobby to prevent Tu and his employees from getting back in.

Eventually, Tu snuck in through a window, but the pressure didn't stop. After a string of confrontations with his landlord and various local government institutions, Tu found that he had reinvented himself as a rights activist when his business had become InnoWay's last nail house. The last time I met Tu, in the summer of 2019, he was still operating out of his store on InnoWay, but the toll on his personal life had been immense. After years of harassment and court hearings, Tu's hair was completely white, and he was deeply in debt. Meanwhile, as government control of media tightened, his self-publishing business had come under investigation for distributing politically sensitive content about historical events like the Cultural Revolution and Tiananmen Square. Worst of all, a fall down the stairs during a quarrel with his landlord had crippled him.

Dressed in the same traditional Chinese *hanfu* suit he had worn when we first met in 2015, Tu was cynical about China's IT entrepreneurship and innovation-driven economic restructuring. Over the past four years, he had seen numerous failures and bankruptcies on InnoWay. "Their stories usually don't get reported," he said, showing me a huge box of documents he'd gotten from a garbage collector: personal diaries, business proposals, business contracts, investment agreements, and more. "These are living records of this crazy time. Businesses come and go. People move on. No one cares about history." He paused for a few seconds before adding: "I've published so many biographies for other people. One day, I'll write a book about myself and my own experiences: my entrepreneurial journey from a village schoolteacher to a nail house owner and rights-defender in ZGC. I will show the darkness behind the light and all the social injustices. I already have a title: I will call it *The Passion of the Entrepreneur*" (*chuangye shounanji*, 创业受难记).[70] Stories like Tu's, and those of many other "grassroots" entrepreneurs I met in ZGC, often go untold. These entrepreneurs are invisible to mainstream media obsessed with finding the next big start-up and policymakers who, despite renewed attention to social disparity, remain more concerned about GDP and employment figures. Yet these people disproportionally bear the risks of entrepreneurialization and suffer what Silvia Lindtner calls the "slow violence" of displaced technological promises.[71]

The experiences related in this chapter highlight the creativity of entrepreneurial technocratic elites as they strive for technological independence and reenergize China's socialist technonationalist tradition via capitalist financial devices like venture capital and the stock market. China's new generation of social entrepreneurs and venture capitalists are borrowing from international experiences to experiment with new state-market relations and new forms of entrepreneurial participation as part of a broad pursuit of a more inclusive economy at home.

However, although venture capitalists and the state shower money and resources on MEISs, they remain contested spaces where winners take all and losers bear the risks and suffer the precarity of ongoing economic restructuring. Despite the state's declared intentions of promoting not just innovation but also social equity through entrepreneurship, its developmentalist logic continues to frustrate both aims. By looking beneath and beyond the science parks and coworking spaces dominating ZGC's urban core, we see the opportunities that have opened up and the contradictions and limits that have been revealed in China's entrepreneurial reinvention. As we shift attention to the countryside, we find that these lessons resonate with the experiences of rural e-commerce entrepreneurs who are closely linked with their urban counterparts in the national project of entrepreneurial reinvention.

PART TWO

Back to the Countryside

CHAPTER FOUR

The Platformization of Family Production

Reinventing Rural Familism and Governance
for the E-Commerce Era

On a cold winter morning in December 2013, I found myself in a huge conference hall on the top floor of a hotel in Lishui, Zhejiang Province. I had come to this small city in eastern China to attend the inaugural "Taobao Village Summit," an event co-organized by the Lishui municipal government and Taobao's parent company, the Alibaba Group. A quick Baidu search of "rural e-commerce" (*nongcun dianshang,* 农村电商) returns page after page of results related to "Taobao villages," a new rural development model pioneered by Alibaba that spread rapidly after 2011. According to AliResearch, Alibaba's in-house data analysis arm, China had more than seven thousand Taobao villages by early 2022—over one percent of the country's administrative villages.[1]

I first became interested in rural e-commerce through my cousin, a peasant e-commerce entrepreneur in Shandong Province. In 2010, he took me to visit the then-burgeoning e-commerce village of W in Shandong. Three years later, AliResearch hosted a press conference in W publicizing the release of its first report on the Taobao village phenomenon.

At the Taobao Village Summit that December, I was intrigued by Alibaba's ability to penetrate the rural Chinese market, and the evident eagerness of local governments to collaborate with the tech giant. Surrounded by journalists, academics, and government officials from all over the country, it was easy to be impressed by the network of agents promoting the Taobao village model. Three speeches left a deep impression on me. One given by Alibaba's vice executive director, Ye Peng, asserted that the Taobao village push was about more than Alibaba's business plans or China's economic restructuring. It was a moral imperative: Alibaba was serving its "peasant brothers" (*nongmin xiongdi*, 农民兄弟).

Then there was An, party secretary of W Village's Communist Youth League and a member of the village's developing bureaucratic-commercial elite. Equally at home speaking with rural entrepreneurs, national journalists, e-commerce platform representatives, and politicians, An represented W to the Summit's assembled guests. His talk opened with two photographs. The first was from when he accompanied a journalist from Shandong's provincial TV station to interview a peasant e-commerce entrepreneur. It captured a harmonious after-dinner moment in a rural family of three: the father taking care of the family's e-commerce business on a computer while the mother sat on the sofa near him, helping their son with his homework. The second picture, taken when An accompanied a professor from China's Central Academy of Fine Arts on a visit to an elderly village weaver, showed a similarly idyllic scene. The old woman was watching TV as she wove a grass futon; next to her on the bed her infant granddaughter was sleeping. "My two visitors were really moved by the scenes they saw in our village," An informed the audience. "In their imagination, rural life means hard labor. Instead, they found a harmonious and sweet family life that even urbanites like them might long for."

The third notable speech was given by the director of the Institute for Information Studies (IIS) at the Chinese Academy of Social Sciences. An expert on rural informatization, he ran through the state's previous, largely ineffective top-down approaches to digitalizing the rural economy, then declared that Alibaba's Taobao platform offered an effective bottom-up alternative. It revitalized the rural economy while drawing peasant migrant workers back home to build the countryside—another state goal. He likened the Taobao village campaign to a "genetic engineering project," where a new e-commerce "gene" was grafted onto the "old body" of rural China, and called for the model to be emulated nationwide.

Together, the three talks encapsulated the phenomenal rise of e-commerce entrepreneurship in rural China after 2008 and, particularly, the emergence of what I call "platformized family production."

This new rural production model has reenergized the rural economy through a synthesis of preexisting family-based labor organization with the e-commerce platform-based model of production, sales, and consumption. The speakers were representative of the types of agents—central and local governments, corporations, and rural entrepreneurs—involved in constructing rural entrepreneurialism in China. The summit's guest list hinted at the increasingly tight bonds forming between digital platforms and different levels of government, bonds that are reconfiguring state-business and state-society relationships and shaping new rural subjectivities. Along with the entrepreneurs themselves, they are advancing the Taobao village model as an alternative path to rural development and a new means of resolving tensions between sustained development and social equity in contemporary China.

Turning away from IT entrepreneurs in metropolitan centers, this chapter and the next follow migrant returnees and rural-to-urban entrepreneurs as they carve out space for themselves on China's rural periphery. After 2008, digital entrepreneurialism in the countryside grew out of a convergence of capitalism from above (digital platform expansion into rural areas) and capitalism from below (village and family-based e-commerce production). In the aftermath of the global financial crisis, both were sanctioned by different levels of the state as it sought to find a more economically, socially, and ecologically sustainable path to rural development. Reflecting global trends toward entrepreneurialization and platformization, the digital "entrepreneur" emerged in rural China as a self-employed, independent contractor who was his or her own boss. As is true elsewhere, mythologization of this figure is central to digital platform business models. Around the world, promoting entrepreneurialism makes financial and ideological sense: e-commerce platforms reduce costs by offloading their societal responsibilities onto workers and consumers, and they burnish their brands by claiming to empower ordinary people to make a living through flexible working arrangements. Concealed by the valorization of so-called digital entrepreneurs, however, is the role of platformized *labor* in the new rural economy. That includes *platform-based* labor, such as e-commerce platform customer service, website design, and online marketing teams, and *platform-mediated* labor performed by those who manufacture, package, and deliver e-commerce goods.

After 2008, China's entrepreneurial reinvention took a different trajectory from that of the United States. Building on and restructuring traditions of family-based production and centralized minimalist governance, the rural digital entrepreneur emerging in China is individualized, but also embedded in village society and central-local state relations. Thus, my central question in this chapter is why and how did platformized family production first emerge and proliferate in rural China following the financial crisis.

To answer this question, I use W Village as a case study to explore the broader Taobao village phenomenon and learn how, in attempting to reinvent rural China, the rural digital economy was co-constructed by e-commerce platforms, central and local governments, and rural entrepreneurs within an evolving system of centralized minimalist governance and proliferating entrepreneurialism. I pay particular attention to how digital platforms became agents of rural development and entrepreneurial labor, transforming political governance and central-local state relations.

Because platform technology and culture in W Village have been shaped and reshaped by historically and locally situated regimes of production and labor, background is needed to situate the rural entrepreneurial subject and emergent platformized family production in appropriate context. Whereas the intent was to rejuvenate rural areas, bring about social equity for peasants, and narrow China's rural-urban and intrarural economic gaps, contradictions inherent in this new regime of labor and governance problematized the entrepreneurial approach to development and social equity.

Throughout, I found a convergence of structural and personal forces that shape the hybrid labor practices and lived experiences of rural Chinese in different ways than their ZGC counterparts. While attendees at the Taobao Village Summit celebrated rural entrepreneurial labor as a silver bullet capable of doing away with the challenges of economic restructuring, this chapter calls such uncritical optimism into question by identifying unique risks as well as opportunities in the entrepreneurial reinvention of the countryside. Close analysis of corporate discourse, government policies, and entrepreneurial experiences reveals the broad grassroots appeal of rural entrepreneurial labor and the benefits Big Tech receives from this new regime of capitalist accumulation, sanctioned by the state, that thrives on the fodder of tradition and innovation.

RURAL FAMILY PRODUCTION GOES DIGITAL

Family-Driven Individualization Under a Centralized Minimalist State

One point the IIS director made at the Taobao Village Summit stuck with me. In his five-minute speech, he acknowledged that rural e-commerce, after 2008, represents the grafting of digital platforms onto rural traditions. He didn't address the substance and reinvention of those traditions via e-commerce, but An's two photos helped fill those gaps. Sociologist Fei Xiaotong described the traditional Chinese village as "a society of acquaintance": a close-knit, often isolated community based on kinship relationships. Almost everyone is connected to each other by blood or marriage. Economic anthropologist Hill Gates coined the term "petty capitalism" to refer to the Chinese small peasant mode of production and traditional familial division of labor. For centuries petty capitalism interacted with the tributary mode of production to support Confucian-agrarian society. Petty-capitalist households, according to Gates, were usually agnatic, patriarchal, and heavily dependent on family members for labor. They produced "for their own use," and maintained "non-capitalist exchanges with kin, friends, and fellow villagers."[2] The tributary mode of production operated atop this system, leveraging political and military authority to extract surplus value for state use.

At the root of China's imperial longevity is what Teijun Wen termed the "village rationale" (cunshe lixing, 村社理性), in which rural economic subjects were embedded in village-based family production and kindship-based traditional social structures.[3] Interactions between the "highly centralized imperial state" and the "peasant society-economy" mutually constituted a "centralized minimalist" structure of political governance, as both systems worked together to "guard against parcelization of centralized imperial power and to maintain governance at minimal cost to the state."[4] This interactive relationship between state and society, layered with internal and external "administrative subcontracting," set imperial

China apart from the "parcelized feudalism" and modern Weberian bureaucracy in the West.[5]

After the founding of the People's Republic in 1949, China collectivized its agriculture and family-based handicraft industries.[6] Unlike Western capitalist economies that relied on external primitive accumulation via colonialism, socialist China resorted to an internal accumulation model carried out at the command of the strong socialist state. This was largely achieved through Leninist party-state organization and the Chinese Communist Party (CCP)'s mass mobilization capacity, a configuration that allowed the socialist state to "effect a much higher degree of infrastructural penetrative power than in imperial times."[7]

This emerging "state rationale" (*guojia lixing*, 国家理性)[8] guided the party-state's direct participation in planning, organizing, and running the economy to ensure national security, promote industrialization and guarantee social equity. Soon it overpowered the ancient "village rationale."[9] State-implemented collectivization of rural institutions and economic production, along with other socialist campaigns, penetrated deeply into the social fabric of peasant society, supplementing kinship-based communal ties with a multilayered socialist administration and a bureaucracy of cadres.[10]

State grain production quotas, a hukou (户口) household registration system to prevent rural-urban migration, and elevated prices for agricultural machinery and fertilizer produced in urban factories, facilitated the party-state's efficient capture and transfer of rural surplus value to support urban industrialization. In addition to subsidizing the urban economy, the countryside served as a shock absorber to ease urban unemployment. During times of economic crisis between the early 1960s and the mid-1970s, the state mobilized three waves of young urban Chinese for its "Up to the Mountains, Down to the Countryside" (*shangshan xiaxiang*, 上山下乡) campaign, sending them to work on rural communes.[11]

The state-led "individualization" of rural society liberated peasants from their "ancestors' shadow" and traditional kinship networks, and reembedded them in a socialist individual-state relationship.[12] Peasants benefited from state investment in rural infrastructure, education, and public health care, and their sacrifices made possible the rapid industrialization of socialist China without imperialist expansion or the high external indebtedness hindering other developing countries. Yet, despite the state's top-down management and ideological control, a "family ratio-nale" persisted. The economic hardships peasants experienced due to deficiencies in the state's collective farming model and urban-centric pol-icies actually reinforced their reliance on the household for economic and cultural support.[13]

In the 1980s, post-Mao economic reforms restored family-based agri-cultural production under the aegis of the household responsibility sys-tem. Peasant households leased land and machinery from village collec-tives and could freely dispose of surplus production after they had fulfilled their quotas.[14] Communes and brigades of the Great Leap For-ward and the later years of the Cultural Revolution evolved into town-ship and village enterprises (TVEs).

During the 1980s, the central state adopted a laissez-faire approach to rural governance, allowing village communities to "self-capitalize" (*ziwo zibenhua*, 自我资本化) by using surplus rural labor and collective-owned land to make up for lack of capital investment.[15] Increased grain procurement prices and improved agricultural productivity helped diver-sify the rural economy and ease rural population pressure by generat-ing nonagricultural employment/entrepreneurship opportunities and enhancing rural standards of living.[16] Reviving the household as the basic economic unit in the countryside and redistributing collective land and property to households (on a contract basis) effectively sanctioned vil-lage and family economic rationales and revitalized China's "petty capi-talist" system.

Peasant familism reduced the cost of labor reproduction and helped TVEs keep wages down, but it also perpetuated intrafamily exploitation. Offloading reproductive labor costs onto rural families is an often-neglected dimension of China's global economic competitiveness, which has persisted until today. Decentralizing state power and responsibili-ties via internal and external subcontracting to local governments and enterprises also blurred boundaries between the state and the emerging market economy.[17]

Throughout the 1980s and early 1990s, China's state and village-based family rationales coexisted in relative harmony, facilitating rural develop-ment and narrowing rural-urban disparities. But this wouldn't last. After Deng Xiaoping's 1992 Southern Tour, the state prioritized the develop-ment of large coastal cities and adopted an export- and foreign direct investment (FDI)–driven economic model. In contrast to the "golden decade" of the 1980s and early 1990s, the countryside declined in the late 1990s. The recentralization of state power via the 1994 tax reform, the decentralization of fiscal burdens to local county and township governments, and the offloading of reform costs onto the countryside through commodification of education and health care, all contributed to GDP-centric developmentalism and the corporatization of local government.[18]

Faced with a looming budget crisis, local governments increasingly depended on FDI and real estate development to stay afloat. China's decentralized administrative subcontracting system pitted governments and politicians against each other to attract investors and developers. Local officials grew increasingly predatory and corrupt. Some formed informal ties with private entrepreneurs, local elites, and urban or over-seas investors, pursuing personal gain at the expense of the village com-munities they were supposed to govern. Facing increased competition, TVEs shed many of their social functions, including job guarantees for local residents. Many were privatized or went out of business. Rural land was sold to developers, and agriculture grew increasingly unprofitable. By 2000, the rural-urban gap was opening up once more.[19] Heavy agri-cultural tax burdens, rural poverty, and new urban employment oppor-tunities sparked unprecedented rural migration into China's cities.

Migration further individualized and disembedded peasants from village communities and kinship networks. The restrictive hukou system still barred migrant peasant workers from enjoying the same economic opportunities as their urban counterparts.[20] Migrants became a source of cheap urban labor, without welfare or social security benefits, even though their rural hukou entitled them to land in their home villages. Under this dual social structure, peasants were caught between a decay-ing rural society and an exploitive urban labor regime. Many had to leave parents and children behind in the countryside and find work elsewhere. This semi-proletarianization of the rural Chinese made Chinese labor costs globally competitive and reduced problems like urban ghettoiza-tion and unemployment, but it subjected peasant migrant workers to a "partial and incomplete process of individualization."[21]

Thus, Chinese peasants went through a distinct process of individ-ualization in the post-Mao years as China's centralized minimalist gov-ernance evolved. Dismantling traditional and socialist institutions set

Chinese peasants "free" without reembedding them in new social systems of care, security, and protection. Atomized peasants and peasant workers relied on families, relatives, and people from the same hometown (*laoxiang*, 老乡). Despite trends toward individualization, this reliance preserved family and lineage networks as both economic and cultural institutions.[22] By the early 2000s, contradictions between the small peasant familism of villages and state developmentalism—and the widening gap in urban and rural wealth—were harder to ignore. The deterioration of villages and plight of peasants and migrant workers prompted advocates of rural development to warn that life in the countryside was becoming "bitter," "impoverished," and "precarious." The later discourse of the "three rural problems" (*sannong*, 三农) articulated this as rural communities, rural people, and agriculture.[23]

The Post-2008 Rise of Platformized Family Production

Faced with an intensifying rural crisis, the new Hu-Wen administration augmented pro-social and pro-rural policies. Following its announcement of the "building a new socialist countryside" campaign in 2005, the central state had invested roughly US$1.2 billion into rural areas. Much of this money went toward integrating rural China with the rest of the country by building roads, water systems, electricity and telephone lines, and broadband services: known collectively as the "five connections" (*wutong*, 五通).[24] By 2008, the central state had abolished agricultural taxes, initiated a rural pension scheme, and opened a rural cooperative medical insurance system.[25] During the 2000s, voices in scholarly, policy, and activist communities began advocating for a uniquely Chinese rural development path that would build on and strengthen rural China's family-based village economic rationale and village-based collective land ownership as an alternative to American-style agribusiness and urbanization.[26]

Yet, under the persisting administrative subcontracting system, local governments, especially at county, township, and village levels, struggled to break free from the old path of GDP-driven developmentalism. Loss of local revenue from the rescinded agricultural taxes forced them to double down on debt-financed real estate development and FDI investment to close the gap.[27] Meanwhile, the pro-social, pro-rural "investor state" encouraged the flow of capital and urban businesses into the countryside, thus facilitating "elite capture," tightening ties between rural officials, urban businesses, and local elites while marginalizing ordinary peasants and peasant workers. As a result, the state's pro-rural policies improved rural incomes, welfare services, and basic infrastructure, however, they also intensified differentiation and inequality within the countryside.[28]

The 2008 global financial crisis further complicated the situation. Within a year, overseas consumer demand for Chinese goods contracted, many export-oriented factories went bankrupt, and the country lost 25 million jobs.[29] Unemployed migrant workers, locked out of the urban welfare system without the proper hukou, returned to their villages en masse. The central state responded quickly with a four-trillion-yuan stimulus package to stabilize unemployment. A portion of this was allocated to the construction of rural infrastructure.[30] To offset weak foreign demand, the state offered subsidies to increase rural consumption of consumer goods like home appliances.[31] Eager to restructure the economy and find new markets for surplus production, China accelerated the capitalization and the urbanization of the countryside. This involved cultivating "new-style agriculture subjects" (*xinxing nongye jingying zhuti*, 新农业经营主体), which included commercial household farms, entrepreneurial farms, and collectives of small subsistence farmers coordinated by specialized cooperatives or led by "dragon head" firms (*longtou qiye*, 龙头企业) with ties to local government and heavily subsidized by the state.

This is the context in which platformized family production emerged as a hybrid regime of production and labor. Benefitting from the rise of e-commerce platforms, it took advantage of and reenergized rural China's village-based familial division of labor. For rural entrepreneurs, platformized family production was a culturally appealing and economically productive way to keep business costs down while boosting rural employment.

It also promised a more autonomous, respectable, and flexible form of self-employment that, unlike many other opportunities in the digital economy, was actually accessible to rural Chinese. Whereas peasants embraced temporary urban employment as way out of rural poverty and a means to provide for their families prior to the early 2000s, their children tended to be better educated and more interested in pursuing self-fulfillment and material comfort. Many were born in cities to migrant-worker parents. They no longer identified with traditional agriculture or the limited employment open to China's migrant underclass. As generations of migrant workers aged, they, too, found urban work increasingly demanding and exploitative, and grew frustrated with its inability to guarantee them security and comfort in old age.[32]

Rural IT entrepreneurship and e-commerce also aligned with the interests of a wide variety of nonrural agents. They complimented the central state's economic goals of boosting domestic consumption and urbanization; modernizing agriculture; promoting the digital, service, and cultural sectors; redressing inequalities in rural-urban development; and rural poverty.[33] Even local governments, which were initially indifferent to platform-based e-commerce because it didn't generate taxable revenue, embraced digital platforms after the central government endorsed the model.

As for the tech companies running the platforms, by the late 2000s they faced an increasingly oversaturated domestic urban market and fierce competition from new firms. In response, Alibaba announced plans in the late 2000s to simultaneously expand abroad and into rural China, integrating peasants into its platform-based empire as workers and consumers. Together with rivals like JD.com and Pinduoduo, Alibaba assumed a central role in the Chinese state's economic and social restructuring campaigns. In the process, platforms became external subcontracting agents of the state under the evolving centralized minimalist governance regime.

The digital entrepreneurialism that proliferated in rural China post-2008 was part of a state effort to entrepreneurialize rural development and social equity. This required reinventing both the village-based family production rationale and the state rationale of centralized minimalism.

PLATFORMIZED FAMILY PRODUCTION IN W VILLAGE

From Straw Shoes to Digital Storefronts

In the spring of 2015, about a year after the Taobao Village Summit, I returned to W Village for fieldwork. Located in northern Shandong

Province near where the Yellow River meets the Bohai Sea, W was an established Taobao village at that time. To immerse myself in the rhythms of village life and e-commerce production, I rented a small room in the home of a local middle-aged couple. My landlords, the Wang family, specialized in wholesaling handicrafts. "Auntie Wang," an illiterate woman in her mid-fifties, had woven all her life. "Uncle Wang," a former village electrician, got involved in business in the mid-2000s, at the height of the village's pre-internet boom in family-based handicraft firms. The couple owned a small home handicraft workshop that employed four weavers and two carpenters, all of them relatives or neighbors. By 2015, their workshop had been supplying export companies across North China for more than a decade. Since the late 2000s, however, local e-commerce shops servicing the domestic market increasingly snapped up their products.

B County's "Hubin Strip" is an area surrounded by marshes, called "along the riverbank" in Chinese (figure 4.1). For millennia, residents of

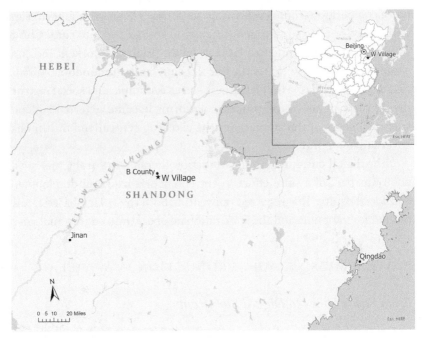

FIGURE 4.1 Map of W Village, B County, Shandong Province. Credit: Tu Lan.

W and the other thirty-two villages on the Hubin Strip have woven hand-icrafts from the native bulrushes, everything from straw sandals and fans to cushions.[34] In the self-sufficient, small peasant economy, most of this work was done by women. A ninety-eight-year-old villager who had sold hand-woven goods in the Republican period told me that surplus products were bartered at village or town fairs or sold to peddlers who marketed them elsewhere in North China. A study of county annuals and books on local handicraft history suggests that Hubin's family-based, small peasant handicraft production showed signs of industrialization and integration into the world economy by the late nineteenth century. In the 1920s, straw shoes made by women in B County were regularly exported to Japan.[35] Because arable land was scarce—plots averaged about one acre per person—exported handicrafts supplanted grain production in B County's decidedly mixed economy. During the heyday of the prewar handicraft industry, B County artisans and traders even formed a local guild, "The Willow Leaf Industry Society" (liuye she, 柳叶社), to organize production.[36]

In conversation with village elders and former employees of B County's two handicraft factories, I learned how family-based handicraft production continued into the early socialist period. The nascent socialist state prioritized grain production but also sought to collectivize the handicrafts industry. In the 1950s, handicrafts were put under direct supervision of the Provincial Native Produce Import-Export Bureau (sheng tuchan jinchukou ju, 省土产进出口局). Output remained limited. The move was mainly driven by need for foreign currency to support China's urban industrialization. In 1965, a bulrush weaving factory established in W Village primarily functioned as an intermediary between the provincial import-export bureau and village weavers. The factory closed during the Cultural Revolution. Between 1966 and the early 1970s—the peak of the planned economy era—market-driven handicrafts were discouraged as "petty-bourgeois" and a distraction from grain production. Villagers continued to weave for personal use after finishing their work for the commune, but the weaving industry only recovered near the end of the Cultural Revolution when collectivization and centralized control began to weaken. In 1974, the B County Handicraft Factory opened as a commune enterprise. By 1977, a second factory opened, the No. 2 Hand-icraft Factory (hereafter "No. 2") specializing in bulrush products.

After the reform and opening-up policy of the late 1970s, township and village workshops began replacing commune and brigade enterprises nationwide. B County's handicraft factories soon became TVEs ramping up production for export. Over the course of the 1980s, No. 2 spurred the development of a mature, export-oriented industrial supply chain in B County. Older women weavers recalled spending most of their agricultural downtime weaving. On a weekly basis, they delivered finished products to village collection sites operated by No. 2, whereupon their products were sorted, packaged, and transported to the nearby port of Qingdao. From there, they were shipped overseas to countries in Asia, Europe, and North America. By the late 1980s, weaving had become a major source of peasant wealth and tax revenue in B County.

After the central state withdrew support for TVEs in the early 1990s, the local handicraft industry was swept up in TVE privatization. According to interviews with former workers and the head of No. 2, profits began to fall in the mid-1990s even as overseas demand grew. As marketization and privatization took root, many former factory workers—some with direct connections to foreign importers—quit to start their own private businesses. Market competition increased production but cut profits, and the two collective handicraft factories went bankrupt in 1998. Those who adapted to the market economy grew rich. Others were laid off and had to find alternative employment.

Private export businesses boomed between 2001 and 2006, building on production chains established during the TVE era. Growing overseas and domestic demand for woven products of all kinds stimulated production and encouraged more diverse designs. New private handicraft factories and retail shops thrived in B County. Female weavers kept busy at home at a time when many of their husbands had to work in the cities. As farming became less profitable compared to other professions, a new labor structure formed in the Hubin Strip in the early years of the millennium: Women stayed home weaving and taking care of the family. Entrepreneurial men ran handicraft or other sideline businesses, while other men found work in nearby cities, mainly as construction workers. Unlike villages in less-developed areas, the dynamic economy in B County and its adjacent cities kept most migrant workers close to home.

The 2008 financial crisis disrupted this system. Handicraft exports suddenly shrank due to contracted overseas demand. Local handicraft export factories and retail businesses became less profitable. Meanwhile, dismal urban job markets drove migrant workers back home, where some began selling handicrafts online to domestic consumers. As early as 2002, business owners in W started to experiment with selling goods online. They began by listing their products on 1688.com, Alibaba's early business-to-business (B2B) platform connecting small and medium-sized enterprises with domestic and overseas wholesalers. After its consumer-to-consumer (C2C) site, Taobao.com, was launched in 2003, some young villagers opened virtual shops targeting domestic consumers via the platform. At first, business was sporadic, but it picked up in 2006 with the rise of platform-based e-commerce. The exponential growth of internet users and the popularity of online shopping in China opened new opportunities for the handicraft industry in B County. In 2008, when offline export sales collapsed, the domestic e-commerce economy flourished as a low-cost alternative market for consumption, trading, and (self)-employment. The stage was set for the surge in platformized family production.

The Return of the Migrants

In W Village, as in other early Taobao villages, e-commerce began to take off in 2007, just prior to the financial crisis. Its popularity was sparked by the return of a few entrepreneurial urban migrants who "had seen the world" (*jianguo shimian*, 见过世面). They had worked or attended college in the city and were not only more technically and commercially savvy than their elders, but also better attuned to urban consumer tastes. Rural e-commerce provided them with alternative self-employment opportunities accessible from the comfort of their homes: an important advantage for dissatisfied members of China's migrant underclass.

Wei and his wife Yunyun were born in a Hubin village not far from W. Before moving to W to become full-time e-commerce entrepreneurs in 2007, the couple had run a small motorbike repair shop in the B County seat and sold Hubin handicrafts on Taobao in their spare time.

This side gig led Wei to a chat group for Taobao sellers on the popular messaging service QQ. "We didn't just talk about business but also about life," he recalled. "It made me feel hopeful that starting a business on Taobao might change people's lives for the better." One day, he opened a link shared by a fellow member. It was a video of Jack Ma, CEO and cofounder of Alibaba, Taobao's parent company, giving a motivational speech. "The speech was addressed to young people born in the 1980s or 1990s," Wei recounted. "I still remember what he said: He told the audience life is not fair, and society can never be equal. How could someone born into a Chinese peasant family compare himself to Bill Gates's son? He said to stop complaining and start your own e-commerce business. E-commerce is the future of the world. Only you can change your fate."

Ma's words kept playing in Wei's head. The couple's online handicraft store was doing well, but the time they spent running the repair shop kept them from expanding their e-commerce business. It also tied them to B's comparatively expensive county seat. After some deliberation, Wei made up his mind to devote himself to e-commerce full-time. To stay close to the county seat, which had urban conveniences that he and Yunyun were accustomed to, they decided to rent a house in W—the Hubin village closest to B County. By the end of the month, Wei and Yunyun had closed their repair shop, bought a new desktop computer with money from the sale of his repair kit, and moved to W Village. Wei compared the early days of e-commerce in W to a "gold rush." "It was really easy back then to sell products on Taobao," he recalled. "You uploaded a picture and boom, orders started to come in. There were so few sellers compared to the rapidly growing number of buyers."

Inspired by Wei's success, many young villagers in W opened their own shops. By late 2008, when Xiao and his wife Ling returned to the village, there were more than thirty Taobao shops in W. Xiao and Ling had met in the oil-producing city of Dongying, in Shandong Province. At the time, Ling was an accountant and Xiao worked as a clerk in a hotel affiliated with a state-owned oil company. Both were well-educated. Ling had an associate degree in accounting, and Xiao had majored in computer science in college. Despite their educational qualifications, their rural hukou made it almost impossible for them to become permanent employees of a state-owned enterprise.[37] Without a Dongying hukou, they could find only temporary work and were barred from the benefits enjoyed by permanent staff, like subsidized housing and yearly bonuses. Seeing no future in their low-paying temporary positions, the couple quit to try several small business ventures. They sold breakfast on the street and operated a small restaurant, yet none of these gigs lasted long. When

Ling became pregnant with her first daughter in 2006, the family was desperate for a stable life and income.

A lover of books, Ling kept busy reading while she prepared to give birth. Because she couldn't afford books at full price, she relied on sales or purchased used copies online. This was before online shopping had caught on in small cities like Dongying. One day, it suddenly occurred to Ling that she could open her own online bookstore. Her research took her to a forum for shop owners on Taobao. There she learned that she could open a bookstore on Taobao for free. She also found stories, compiled by forum administrators, about ordinary people whose lives had been transformed by the platform. "It was like a burst of light on a dark night," Ling told me. A couple of months after giving birth, Ling opened her online bookstore. Business was slow in the beginning, but whenever she lost hope, she returned to Taobao's online forum and read the stories of other entrepreneurs. She also made friends with her fellow sellers, forming a community for mutual support and advice. "Back then, Taobao was more like a community for forward-looking young people," Ling explained. "I felt so empowered and proud as an e-commerce entrepreneur. I felt that I was part of a revolution that was going to change China's economy and society."

Within a year, Ling's online book business began to pick up. By the end of 2007, the monthly profits from her Taobao shop were more than double the couple's combined state-sector salaries. Xiao had gone back to temping at the hotel during Ling's pregnancy, but he began to feel restless after learning about the burgeoning e-commerce industry in his home village of W. Armed with Ling's experience selling books online, the couple went back to W and opened a new Taobao shop selling village-made handicrafts. Xiao's father, an army veteran, and mother, a skilled weaver, helped them collect handicrafts from village weavers and package and ship products, and they shared chores like cooking and childcare. Better educated and more business-savvy (*you shangye tounao*, 有商业头脑) than most of their fellow villagers, within a year the couple turned their online shop into one of the village's biggest and most successful e-commerce businesses.

The majority of e-commerce businesses in W were family affairs. The distinction between work and life was fuzzy for local entrepreneurs, but village ventures could generally be divided into two types:

husband-and-wife stores (*fuqi dian*, 夫妻店) and family workshops (*jiating zuofang*, 家庭作坊).

Chun and his wife Le started their husband-and-wife store to sell furniture braided from grass. Before becoming a full-time e-commerce business owner, the thirty-seven-year-old Chun worked at the B County seat as a contract construction worker, the most common type of employment for poorly educated male migrants from W. Le, thirty-five, stayed in the village, farming, weaving, and raising the couple's ten-year-old daughter.

I visited the family's house/office in the summer of 2015. Arriving around 8:00 a.m., I found the couple already hard at work, Chun on a desktop computer and Le on her smart phone. A three-wheeled electric mini-truck was parked in their front yard. These trucks are prized for their size and maneuverability—e-commerce entrepreneurs use them to roam W Village's narrow alleys and reach the homes of local weavers. As I stepped into their living room, I noticed that it seemed split in half. To my left were the trappings of domesticity: a coffee maker, sofas, and a flat-screen TV. To my right, the house was all business: a DIY photo studio equipped with a tripod, photography umbrella, and newly arrived handicrafts waiting to be photographed. A huge wedding photo of the couple decorated the studio wall. The rest of the living room was storage area for their wares. Walking past the living room, I entered a small office with two desktop computers and a TV. The second floor contained the couple's private living quarters.

Although husband-and-wife stores were the most common type of venture in W, many younger couples, especially those with healthy parents, preferred the family workshop model. Kang's family fell into this category. Kang's parents used to run an export-oriented handicraft workshop in the village. After leaving W in his early twenties and studying graphic design in college, Kang worked for a time as a technician for a state-owned oil company in Dongying. In 2012, Kang returned to the village to bring his parents' family business into the digital age. Before getting married and giving birth, Kang's wife Qing worked at a jewelry shop in a big shopping mall in B County. With Kang's parents and some of Qing's relatives, they started one of the most successful e-commerce ventures in the village, with two Taobao shops and a third storefront on Taobao's higher-end sister platform Tmall.[38]

Just thirty-one years old, Kang managed the business and oversaw the operations of its three shops. Qing, twenty-seven, and her younger brother Dong, eighteen, were in charge of online sales. To keep up with demand, Kang's parents' old weaving workshop hired five women weavers to work on-site, three of them distant relatives. Kang's father supervised the team as they produced specialty products for the family business. Kang's mother was responsible for cooking, cleaning the house, and helping Qing watch the couple's grandchild.

In my conversations with migrant returnees, I found that the decision to return home is both economic and cultural. Its well-established handicraft industry supply chain makes W Village unusually attractive. Still, recent state investment in rural infrastructure—roads, high-speed broadband internet, and so on—and wider access to social benefits like low-cost health care and expanded social security have made rural e-commerce more viable and desirable nationwide.

The rise of e-commerce has also highlighted the advantages of small family-based production. Previously underemployed villagers, including women with young children, aging parents, and teenage children, can participate in family businesses as free labor or as low-cost hired labor. Parental assistance in cooking, childrearing, or other household chores reduces the cost of labor reproduction. A family firm's small size and flexible labor arrangements make it more adaptable while allowing it to benefit from low real estate and living costs in the country.

China's entrenched rural-urban divide generally puts young people of rural origin at a disadvantage in terms of financial, social, and cultural capital. In this context, heading to the countryside to become an e-commerce entrepreneur can be a shortcut to middle-class status. Xianglan and her husband arrived in W Village in 2009. The pair had just graduated from college, after which Xianglan spent a year interning at a local elementary school while her husband worked as a sales agent for an insurance company. In W Village, they set up two Taobao shops selling small furniture items made from rubber tree leaves. When I interviewed Xianglan in 2015, the couple had a car, a new house, and a combined income of more than 100,000 yuan, roughly equivalent to that of an urban middle-class couple. Xianglan told me that if they had stayed in the city, they probably could not have bought their own home. She believed that e-commerce helped narrow the rural/urban gap at a time when many young rural people lacked the channels to achieve social mobility. "Unlike in the 1990s, when people could get rich quickly by working hard, nowadays you need your dad to get ahead" (*pindie de shidai*, 拼爹的时代), Xianglan told me. "As children of the peasant class, our fates would have been sealed if not for this [e-commerce]. Compared to when we first came back, it's not as easy to survive in the industry, but we're sticking with it because it's the only option."

Not all migrant returnees are motivated by economic considerations. For some, the decision to "go back" is cultural. Though many of the entrepreneurs I interviewed said they liked the convenience and excitement of modern city life, they felt nostalgic for the "rural way of life," with its slower tempo and greater degree of interconnectedness. The proximity of W Village to the B County seat attenuated the rural/urban difference, making it possible for returnees living in W to enjoy some urban benefits. A feeling of community and the chance to reunite with family were among my informants' most commonly cited reasons for going back to the village. Many left their children in the countryside with their parents when they migrated to the city. Even those who once commuted between W Village and the county seat complained of having little quality time with family after an exhausting day's work. Tears welled in Ling's eyes as she recalled separating from her daughter each week when she and her husband worked in Dongying. "We were too busy, so we had to leave our two-year old daughter with my in-laws," Ling told me. "She would cry loudly every time I left, so I always asked my mother-in-law to take her to the playground. That way she wouldn't see us leave. I still remember watching her playing on the swing from the back seat of our motor-truck and thinking how upset she would be when she found our room empty. Now our family has settled down together and we work under the same roof every day. We feel busy, but complete."

I paid several visits to the office she had rented on the village's main street. Strategically located, the office was only ten minutes' walk from her home and close to both shipping company offices in the village, as well as to the new road connecting W to the B County seat. During the day, Ling and her husband divided their time between work and taking care of their children. She took frequent breaks from the computer to feed the baby or help her older daughter with her homework. After finishing their work for the day, the four would go to her in-laws' house for dinner. Both Ling and Xiao believed strongly in the importance of family values and felt grateful that their rural e-commerce business allowed them to spend more time with their children and parents.

Another young e-commerce entrepreneur, Yingchun, echoed this emphasis on the benefits of rural life. Although he owned an apartment in B County seat and a house in W, in 2014, the twenty-seven-year-old Yingchun closed his small clothing store in the county seat and returned to the village with his wife to become a full-time e-commerce entrepreneur. He told me that he preferred village life because of the stronger bonds between residents. On the difference between his urban apartment and his village house, Yingchun said: "There was little sense of community in city apartment buildings. People don't even say 'hi' to their neighbors. They've just walled themselves up inside small concrete matchboxes. The village house is a more open structure. Though it's not as common as it once was, it's still customary for friends and relatives to drop by each other's houses just to catch up. I grew up in this kind of environment, and I feel more comfortable coming back to it."

In general, returnee entrepreneurs were eager to tell me the benefits of living and working in rural areas, though many of them, like their fellow villagers, believed that the best and brightest would stay in the city. Those who came back were seen as "less competitive." I sensed in my interviews that country life still carried a certain stigma. Still, the returnees rationalized their decisions by focusing on the positive. For many entrepreneurs who had made the passage back to the countryside, the village was both an economically competitive site for entrepreneurship and a culturally appealing place to live (figures 4.2 and 4.3).

The Arrival of the Urbanites

The competitive advantages of rural e-commerce have even attracted some young urbanites to decamp for the countryside. Marginalized in the cities, the few urban-to-rural migrants I met in W were among the most successful entrepreneurs in the village. Hai's parents had spent their lives working for urban SOEs in Jinan, the capital of Shandong Province. When we spoke, his father had recently retired; his mother had been laid off a decade earlier and worked night shift at the front desk of a small hotel to make extra cash. After graduating from a local college with an

FIGURE 4.2 The courtyard of an e-commerce entrepreneur's family, where products were stored. Photo by author.

FIGURE 4.3 Women weavers working outside their house while chatting. Photo by author.

associate degree in computer science, Hai dabbled in several small businesses. He sold men's clothing in a wholesale market and hawked roasted lamb on the roadside. One day in 2007, a college friend from Hubin told him about the area and its handicraft products. Hai's business sense told him that opportunities were there for someone like him. He immediately traveled to W Village and decided to start his own business.

At first, Hai opened a small brick-and-mortar store in downtown Jinan, renting space in a marketplace and traveling between W and Jinan every week to restock his wares. The business did well, but the rent was too high. He moved his business online and opened a shop on Taobao, but quickly realized that costs in Jinan were still too high for him to be competitive with entrepreneurs in W. He did some rough calculations and concluded that he could cut his business costs in half by moving to the countryside. By the end of 2007, Hai had relocated to W—over his parents' objections—and rented a space on the village's main thoroughfare. "My parents were against the idea at the beginning," Hai told me. "My dad was born in the countryside, and he worked so hard all those decades ago to get a job in an urban, state-owned enterprise so that I could become an urbanite." But as Hai saw it, he didn't have a choice: "I tried many different things in the city, only to realize that the odds of improving my life are low without capital or personal connections. My parents are old, retired workers who can't afford to buy me an apartment in Jinan. Without an apartment or a car, I'm worth little on the marriage market. I had to face reality and pursue a different path if I wanted to change my fate. Going to the countryside was the right thing to do."

Like other urban-to-rural migrants I met in W, Hai saw rural e-commerce as an alternative path for achieving social mobility. Once he settled down in W, Hai's urban background, prior business experience, and networks gave him an advantage over most rural-born entrepreneurs. His Taobao shop quickly became one of the most profitable in the village. As the scale of his business expanded, he invited his close friend and college roommate Zheng to be his business partner. Like Hai, Zheng was born to an ordinary lower middle-class family in Jinan. He went to the same college as Hai and also majored in computer science. Unable to find a suitable job after graduation, a distant relative helped him get a position as a personal driver for a municipal government official. In China's guanxi-based society,[39] being a personal driver to a high-ranking government official is considered respectable work. Though the salary is low, it's a stable position with benefits and the chance to build a close relationship with someone in power. But Zheng felt stuck. He couldn't stand the constant bowing and scraping in front of his boss, and he hated the frequent long-distance trips. The low pay also meant it would take him and his wife at least a decade to save enough to purchase an apartment in Jinan. After the birth of his son, his anxiety and sense of hopelessness intensified. So, Zheng jumped on Hai's offer and moved to W in 2012.

The partners rented an office attached to a large warehouse in what used to be the village theater. Their landlords were an elderly couple whom Hai and Zheng referred to as their "godparents." The "godfather" was a powerful, well-respected member of the W community. A former village head, he had leveraged his authority to rent several strategically located, collectively owned properties at a low price. When the village's handicraft e-commerce industry took off, he reaped huge profits through his own wholesale business and by subleasing these properties at a markup. To better integrate into the village's lineage-based society, the young partners carefully cultivated a good relationship with their land-lords. The old couple in turn took Hai and Zheng under their wing and helped them navigate and maintain the intricate relationships with villagers and the village government they needed to succeed. They were especially useful when Hai and Zheng found themselves in conflict with a villager: The old man always bailed them out by playing the role of mediator and advisor.

At times, Hai and Zheng felt bored with village life. To stagger their country shifts and spend half of their time with family and friends in Jinan, they hired a customer service assistant—a young man from a nearby village eager to learn more about e-commerce—and two middle-aged women from W to help them with product packaging and shipping. Their unusual reverse migration helped the partners accumulate a small fortune, something they never could have dreamed of, if they had stayed in the city. With his share of the money, Zheng bought an apartment for his wife and son in Jinan. Hai bought a new car and a motorbike. Over the years, other urbanites settled in W. Like Hai and Zheng, many of them shuttled back and forth between the city and countryside, but W Village was their business base and temporary home.

As these stories of migrant returnee and reverse migrant entrepreneurs suggest, platformized family production was ubiquitous in W Village by the mid-2010s, and most e-commerce businesses in W were family-based. Rural entrepreneurs could take advantage of the Chinese countryside's reserve army of labor, including the elderly and teenagers, and cheap or even free real estate, while enjoying more flexible and autonomous working arrangements. Even outsiders like Hai and Zheng adapted to this regime by forming quasi-familial relationships with villagers. The renewed importance of rural families as a competitive economic unit and a source of cultural meaning echo in studies of Taobao villages elsewhere in China.[40] Between 2008 and 2013, a period considered by locals to be the golden age of W Village's handicraft e-commerce industry, a host of young people either returned to the village or migrated there from cities to start handicraft e-commerce businesses (figure 4.4). While the majority of entrepreneurs in W were former migrant laborers with middle or high school diplomas, a small number of college graduates who felt stuck or marginalized in the cities were involved in the industry as well.

At the peak of e-commerce in W, platforms like Taobao lowered the barriers to starting an e-commerce business and provided opportunities for rural and marginalized urban young people to achieve upward social mobility. But if "digital empowerment" was a powerful draw in the lives of W Village entrepreneurs prior to 2013, Taobao and Alibaba were remote entities. This changed as the Taobao village campaign swept W Village into the national spotlight.

REINVENTING STATE-CAPITAL-VILLAGE RELATIONS UNDER PLATFORMIZATION

After Taobao was founded in 2003, it quickly became one of China's most successful e-commerce platforms. Both Taobao and Alibaba benefited from the central government's laissez-faire approach to the industry, which allowed Chinese tech companies to access global venture capital funds.[41] Yet, it was the entrepreneurial labor of numerous small platform-based sellers that really fueled Taobao's expansion and helped it dominate market share by fending off eBay and other foreign and domestic competitors.[42]

FIGURE 4.4 An urban-to-rural migrant entrepreneur packaging products for shipping. Photo by the author.

Alibaba's socially progressive brand image is at the heart of its global digital empire. Through strategically orchestrated media campaigns that tout the merits of "being one's own boss," Taobao has positioned itself as a patron of grassroots entrepreneurial dreams and a benevolent provider of self-employment opportunities. Taobao's cofounder, Jack Ma, embodies this brand. Ma has been lionized as a Steve Jobs–like figure, a rebel executive who climbed up from a humble English-teaching job to become CEO of one of the most successful internet companies in the world.[43]

The widely circulated rags-to-riches story of how Ma achieved the "Chinese dream" has become a powerful inspiration for millions of young Taobao entrepreneurs who want to emulate his success and earn their "first bucket of gold." Ma has carefully cultivated this mythos. In 2018, he was quoted as saying, "If people like me can succeed, then 80% of [the] young people in China and around the world can do so, too."[44] Like Wei, the W Village entrepreneur who was inspired by Jack Ma's speech, many rural e-commerce sellers told me that Ma's words and stories influenced their decisions to become entrepreneurs. Posters featuring Ma's image and business mantras were fixtures in the homes and offices of the rural entrepreneurs I visited.

Ma had good reason for pushing this narrative. Taobao's success as a C2C platform can be attributed to the large number of small-scale entrepreneurial sellers it attracts, who help build its platform and supply chain. Just three years after its founding, Taobao drove eBay out of China and secured a virtual monopoly over the country's C2C e-commerce market.[45] It's no coincidence that Taobao first broke even in 2009, following the global financial crisis, when urban unemployment soared in China and large numbers of migrant workers returned to their home villages. The emergence of rural consumers and sellers, and the partition of Taobao's platform into two branches separating C2C and B2C sales, drove much of its growth that year.[46]

As a key private sector agent of China's post-2008 economic restructuring, Alibaba turned the crisis into new opportunities for commercial expansion. With the country's urban markets increasingly saturated, Alibaba began to court rural consumers and producers in a strategic bid to integrate China's "underdeveloped" countryside into its platform-based commercial empire. In this, Alibaba's corporate ambitions aligned with the central government's desire to recalibrate the economy and redress rural-urban wealth disparities.

Platformization of the Chinese countryside, led by private tech companies like Alibaba, helped restructure relations between the state, villages, and capital, thereby reinventing China's centralized minimalism. Emerging as a new private-sector "external subcontractor" for the central state, digital platforms have not only assisted state efforts to entrepreneurialize development and social equity, but they have also shaped its policy agenda.[47] Beginning in the late 2000s, Alibaba formed strategic alliances with various government agencies to advance rural expansion, fueling growth in entrepreneurialism in the countryside and boosting its own bottom line. Its statistical and analytical division, AliResearch, played an instrumental role in weaving a web of journalists, scholars, government agencies, and peasant entrepreneurs to manufacture the national "Taobao village" phenomenon. Yet, while these platforms helped the central state advance its economic restructuring goals and mobilized local officials to participate in these efforts, they also rendered rural residents and governments increasingly dependent on them.

The term "Taobao village" was coined by AliResearch in 2010 to describe three villages where e-commerce self-employment had become a leading occupation. Attention-grabbing stories of Chinese peasants on computers were soon picked up and widely circulated by domestic media outlets. In September 2010, the Alibaba Group named Shaji Village in the relatively well-developed Jiangsu Province the "World's Greatest E-commerce Cradle" (*Quanqiu Zuijia Wangshang Wotu Jiang*, 全球最佳 网商沃土奖). Three months later, a research team at the Institute for Information Studies released a report on Shaji that was published on the AliResearch website. Titled "The Shaji Model and Its Significance," the report compared Shaji to Xiaogang Village, widely known as a cradle of China's post-Mao economic reforms, and celebrated rural e-commerce as a triumph of information technology and market forces in the countryside: a grassroots "bottom-up" path to informatization.[48] On December 18, immediately following the IIS report release, a group of "high-level experts" from various central-level ministries and academic and policy think tanks, including the Development Research Center of the State Council, the Ministry of Agriculture, and the Ministry of Industry and Information Technology, convened in Shaji with representative entrepreneurs and journalists to "discuss the significance of the Shaji model" as "a new path for rural development."[49]

In a more detailed 2014 report, the IIS embraced the Taobao village model as a potential solution to China's "three rural problems" and an alternative to universal urbanization.[50] The report argued that the internet made it possible for small household-based producers to directly reach global markets without the mediation of big companies. Compared to TVEs in the 1980s, e-commerce was more effective at absorbing rural surplus labor, driving modernization, and democratizing economic opportunities. It was helping restructure the rural economy to make rural society more just and "harmonious" (*hexie*, 和谐)—a key policy goal since the Hu-Wen administration. This endowed the Taobao village phenomenon with the same significance that TVEs enjoyed during the post-Mao market reforms two decades earlier.

Back in W Village, although local e-commerce had expanded rapidly since 2007, none of the villagers I interviewed remembered hearing W called a Taobao village before early 2013, when a researcher from Ali-Research got in touch with An, the village's Communist Youth League Secretary. The researcher introduced Secretary An to a journalist from the Chinese IT magazine *CEOCIO*, who wanted to profile a Taobao village. This profile catapulted W to national renown as one of China's leading Taobao villages. Soon, journalists from around the country were pouring in. That June, AliResearch sent researchers to gather information about e-commerce development in W. The trip resulted in an August press conference, where AliResearch released its first report on the "Taobao village phenomenon" to a crowd of researchers, local officials, and hundreds of reporters the institute had invited from across China.

According to my interviewees in W, Alibaba began channeling advertising traffic to selected peasant businesses in the village around that time. Sometimes this was achieved through technical means, by bumping up the businesses' product rankings or offering them more opportunities to participate in promotional activities on the platform. As one entrepreneur told me: "They will help a few get rich quickly, get a car, and buy a new house. Then villagers will follow in their footsteps in the hopes of replicating their success. It's all the same pattern if you observe the other Taobao villages."

This algorithmic cherry-picking was complemented by lavish media coverage of the successful e-commerce entrepreneurs, which spread their success stories far and wide. As I describe in the next chapter, the most articulate, outgoing, politically savvy peasant sellers were recast as "model" entrepreneurs via self-selection and selection by platform companies, journalists, and local cadres.

The observations of my village informants echoed in my interviews with former employees of Alibaba's government and public relations departments. Alibaba cultivated representative villages and individual entrepreneurs through data aggregation and media management. The firm's big data team generated visualizations of e-commerce businesses on its platform by tracking store owners' IP addresses. Once they identified a heavy concentration of businesses in a given area, they dispatched a team of Alibaba employees to cultivate relationships with the local government and shop owners.

To bring visibility to the selected village, the company would invite journalists from various media outlets to file reports on the village and its peasant entrepreneurs. To bring more peasants into e-commerce, Alibaba would form a collaborative relationship with a representative peasant in the village and create a "success story." This model entrepreneur, often a local industry leader, would then offer a helping hand to fellow villagers eager to join the e-commerce gold rush. In many ways, these entrepreneurial village representatives resembled the unsalaried semiformal *xiangbao* village officials and rural gentry in traditional Chinese society, who operated as grassroots subcontracting agents in the space between the state and rural society.

What really put W on the map was a visit in 2013 from Guo Shuqing, then governor of Shandong Province, and his seven vice governors. Such an occurrence is extremely rare for a small village like W, where few residents ever meet the county chief. One well-connected W Village entrepreneur told me that Guo, who in 2017 became chairman of the China Banking and Insurance Regulatory Commission, learned of W's e-commerce industry from internal government materials (*neican*, 内参) that cited AliResearch's reports on rural e-commerce.

Like Li Keqiang's tour of Zhongguancun in 2007, Guo's inspection tour represented a high-level political endorsement for Shandong's Taobao villages and Alibaba's rural expansion. The heavily publicized visit brought W not only more media attention but also an opportunity to demand more state investment and policy support. Most important, this symbolic gesture awakened municipal and village politicians to the significance of the Taobao village phenomenon. Before Guo's visit, local officials had been lukewarm to Alibaba's initiative. Guo's visit and other high-profile inspection tours of e-commerce villages finally convinced local officials in B County and across the country to enthusiastically promote rural e-commerce and peasant digital entrepreneurship.

It was a virtuous cycle: As Taobao villages drew more attention from media outlets and experts, rural e-commerce initiatives garnered greater policy support from different levels of government. In 2012, Alibaba proposed a new "Suichang Model" for Taobao villages, based on collaboration with the Suichang County government in Zhejiang Province. Emphasizing the important role played by local governments in fostering the industry, the tie-up hinted at tightening bonds between the e-commerce giant searching for new markets and officials eager to boost economic growth and bolster their political résumés.

This marriage of corporate goals with local governmental interests within a web of media coverage and academic endorsements was key to getting the Taobao village initiative off the ground. The system had reached maturity by late 2013, when the "Taobao Village Summit" was held. The event brought together the forces that had created the Taobao village phenomenon, and it was there that W officially became one of China's thirteen national-level Taobao villages.[51]

Since then, continued decline in China's export industries—a major engine of economic growth prior to 2008—has further incentivized local governments to seek alternative pathways to rural development. Coupled with aggressive, targeted promotional campaigns by the central government and e-commerce platforms, the Taobao village phenomenon reached a fever pitch between 2014 and 2016. Proposals from scholars, ministries, and politicians called on the Chinese state to spearhead rural e-commerce at the annual National People's Congress and People's Political Consultative Conference. Facing slower economic growth, the state issued documents encouraging peasant digital entrepreneurship and rural e-commerce. The most prominent of these was the State Council's "Opinions Regarding the Active Promotion of E-Commerce Development and Accelerated Nurturing of a New Force of Economic Development." Published in 2015, it came out the same year the mass entrepreneurship and innovation campaign first appeared in the central government's annual work report.[52]

The previous November, Chinese Premier Li Keqiang had visited Qingyanliu, the "No. 1 Taobao village" in Zhejiang Province, prior to making an appearance at the World Internet Conference. Li's visit showed support for his major policy initiatives—Internet Plus and the mass entrepreneurship and innovation campaign—which aligned with Alibaba's focus on rural internet entrepreneurship and the digitalization of traditional industries and agriculture. Rural e-commerce was positioned to become a central plank in the state's strategic polices of "new-type urbanization" (*xinxing chengzhenhua*, 新型城镇化), "targeted poverty alleviation" (*jingzhun fupin*, 精准扶贫), and "rural revitalization" (*xiangcun zhenxing*, 乡村振兴).[53]

For Alibaba, widespread political support for rural, bottom-up entrepreneurship couldn't have come at a better time. In September 2014, the company presented the biggest IPO in U.S. history. Seeking to burnish its brand image as a champion of global grassroots entrepreneurship, Alibaba invited eight entrepreneurial workers to represent the company at the bell-ringing ceremony: a rural Chinese Taobao shop owner, a self-employed e-commerce model, a delivery courier, a cloud-based customer service contractor, and an American cherry farmer from Washington State who started selling produce to Chinese customers on Taobao. This stratospheric IPO launched Alibaba on a new stage of growth focused on rural expansion, cross-border e-commerce, and big data.

Faced with competition from rivals like JD.com and Suning, which were eager to siphon off its rural partners and consumers, Alibaba announced a new rural campaign in the month following its IPO. The "One Thousand Counties and Ten Thousand Villages" (*Qianxian Wancun*, 千县万村) initiative sought to form public-private partnerships with local governments to build rural e-commerce infrastructure such as village and county-based service stations and logistics companies.[54] Alibaba also worked closely with the state on key national priorities like poverty alleviation, identifying households in need of assistance using big data, and investing in rural e-commerce programs.[55] In March 2016, the company's fintech arm, Ant Financial, launched a rural microfinance campaign titled "One Thousand Counties, One Trillion" (*qianxian wanyi*, 千县万亿). Leveraging its vast pool of consumer data and unrivaled data management capacity, Ant formed collaborative relationships with local state-owned banks to popularize its payment and microlending apps in the countryside.[56]

The rapid expansion of rural e-commerce and digital entrepreneurialism in China's countryside epitomizes the country's post-2008 entrepreneurial reinvention. Digital platforms and rural entrepreneurs joined with various levels of government to reinvent longstanding traditions of village-based family production and centralized minimalist governance to turn a structural economic crisis into new opportunities for rural rejuvenation and commercial expansion. Especially in its early days, rural e-commerce offered rural residents and disadvantaged urbanites entrepreneurial opportunities with low entry thresholds, thereby democ-ratizing entrepreneurship. This allowed rural residents and urban-to-rural migrants to join China's rapidly expanding army of online entre-preneurs, who formed a new entrepreneurial class with shared interests, aspirations, and concerns (figure 4.5).

In 2014, Duncan Clark, chairman of the Beijing consulting firm, BDA China, spoke on this issue to the *New York Times*, calling Alibaba's "Tao-bao Empire" a new "constituency" in China, one that was represented by its CEO, Jack Ma, whom Clark called "a politician with a small 'p.' . . . [Ma] effectively represents millions of people who now depend on Alibaba for their livelihood."[57]

FIGURE 4.5 The dorm/office of an urban-to-rural migrant entrepreneur. Photo by author.

Alibaba's ability to leverage its economic power and technological prowess to cultivate intimate ties with central and local governments helped it beat back challenges to its market dominance and consolidate and strengthen its monopoly.[58] In an interview that year with Lara Logan of *60 Minutes*, Ma himself did little to dispel Clark's characterization. "They [Chinese politicians] care that I can stabilize the country. . . . I tell the government, if people have no jobs, you are in trouble. Government will be in trouble. My job is to help more people have jobs."[59] Subsequently, the numbers of urban-to-rural and rural entrepreneurs have steadily increased, reaching 8.5 million and 31 million, respectively, in 2020.[60] That year, 1 percent of the China's 5,425 administrative villages and 5.8 percent of its 1,756 townships were listed in AliResearch's annual report of Taobao villages—which, together, were said to have created 8.28 million jobs (figure 4.6).[61]

Yet, the question remains: Has the rise of rural e-commerce and platformized family production really addressed the challenges rural Chinese face in the post-taxation era? Rural digital entrepreneurship and platformized family production have indeed provided desirable business and self-employment opportunities to peasants and disadvantaged

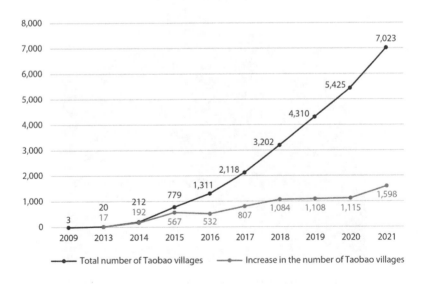

FIGURE 4.6 Number of Taobao villages (2009–2021). Source: AliResearch.

urbanites, especially prior to the mid-2010s. The transformation of W Village highlights the network of state, commercial, and grassroots agents that co-constructed the Taobao village phenomenon. My respondents outlined the varying appeals of rural e-commerce to peasants, e-commerce platforms, and officials up and down the state apparatus. However, the emergence of digital platforms as new agents of the state, and the rural digital entrepreneur as a new subjectivity are beset by the contradictions inherent in this hybrid regime of labor, which spur the development of a new regime of value and rural differentiation centered on entrepreneurialism.

Even as rural e-commerce production was hyped as a glittering solution to China's restructuring and rural development needs after 2008, the orchestrated techno-entrepreneurial optimism for the Taobao village phenomenon masked an emerging commercial-political nexus between platforms and local officials and obscured contradictions resulting from the specific ways in which rural Chinese peasants were being integrated into the digital economy. Contradictions inherent in the hybrid model of platformized family production—between manual and mental labor, individual interests and collective organizing, copying and innovation— grew sharper as rural entrepreneurs strove to sustain, expand, and upgrade their e-commerce businesses in an increasingly saturated market. The resulting conflicts and emerging hierarchies of entrepreneurial labor are the focus of the next chapter.

CHAPTER FIVE

Moving Beyond *Shanzhai*?

The Contradictions of Entrepreneurial Reinvention in Rural China

The winter of 2012 was an eventful one for the e-commerce entrepreneurs of D Village. Located in Jiangsu Province, near the border with Shandong, D had long been impoverished by lack of arable land. Things started to change in 2006, when Sun Han, a college-educated local, returned to the village. Inspired by Ikea's self-assembled furniture business model, Sun started selling locally produced Ikea knockoffs on Taobao, and other villagers quickly copied his successful business model.

In 2010, AliResearch designated D one of Alibaba's first three Taobao villages. Journalists, researchers, and politicians soon descended on the village to explore the phenomenon. As was the case with W, D shot to fame almost overnight, and migrant workers from the village began to return home to start their own furniture e-commerce businesses. As the market became increasingly saturated, however, competition among family businesses grew fierce. Entrepreneurs copied the most popular designs and tried to undercut each other on price. This *shanzhai* (山寨, colloquial for "knockoff") production logic led to mounting social tensions.

Reckoning came after the 2012 Spring Festival, when Taobao took down popular products from many e-commerce entrepreneurs in D for copyright infringement. The individual who reported them wasn't affiliated with Ikea, but a D native named Xu Song, who owned an e-commerce business called "Win the World E-commerce" (*yingtianxia wangshang*, 赢天下网商). Xu was a relative outsider in the village. Though born in D, his family went to live in a nearby town when he was just eleven years old. Xu was a shrewd businessman who made his first fortune running a wine factory before returning to D in 2010 to join the e-commerce gold rush.

Then twenty-seven years old, Xu learned his first lesson in intellectual property value in 2011, when one of the village's best-selling products, a TV stand, was taken down by Taobao. Villagers later learned that an e-commerce business in nearby Suzhou had copyrighted the product. The incident awakened Xu to the enormous consequences of lack of what he called "intellectual property awareness" in rural entrepreneurs. To avoid another legal debacle, Xu tried to persuade others to work with him to protect their intellectual property (IP), but none of his fellow villagers were interested. Xu felt marginalized within the village. Disappointed by their lack of organization and his inability to convince them, he decided to use his own money to copyright all of D Village's extant furniture designs. He would teach the village entrepreneurs a lesson by forcing them to pay to use their own intellectual property.

To copyright the two-hundred-some eligible village designs cost Xu more than 300,000 yuan. He had to sell his apartment in town to cover the cost. D villagers interpreted his behavior as profit-driven and selfish, calling him a "pot stirrer" (*jiaojuzhe*, 搅局者). In February 2012, hundreds of angry people gathered in front of Xu's furniture factory. Some threw stones at the windows; others threatened to "chop his hands and feet off and throw his body into the [nearby] East River."[1] The crisis made national headlines, and local township officials eventually persuaded Xu to drop his claims.[2]

One evening in 2016, I sat down with an e-commerce entrepreneur at a roadside barbecue stand in W Village and asked him what he thought of the "copyright crisis." Familiar with the media reports, my informant identified with Xu's frustration and also with the villagers' anger toward him. "Like D, we are trying very hard to upgrade the industry here and move beyond the *shanzhai* logic of production," he explained. "E-commerce indeed made some of us rich, but vicious competition has also threatened community solidarity and caused more interpersonal conflicts."

By way of explanation, he pointed to a dispute between two W Village entrepreneurs in early 2015. Bin was an e-commerce early bird, relocating to W from a nearby city in 2011 to sell village handicrafts and hand-woven futons on Taobao. By 2015, his Taobao shop had become one of the most profitable businesses in the village. That same year, Sen quit his job as a factory salesman in a nearby town and relocated to W to open his own Taobao shop. Like most latecomers, he began by getting to know successful village entrepreneurs—in this case, Bin—hoping to get tips and help from an experienced seller. Many nights, after shipping the day's orders, Sen would drop by Bin's home for a chat. The two urban-to-rural migrants were close in age and quickly bonded. A few months into the friendship, Sen's sales started picking up. At the same time, Bin noticed a drop in sales of his popular futons. It turned out that Sen was competing with him for customers by offering the same futons at a slightly lower price.

Of all the products sold in W, hand-woven futons are among the most labor-intensive. Still, their profit margins are above average. By 2015, however, the shortage of weaving labor had made labor-intensive and time-consuming products like futons increasingly hard to come by. Few young women in the Hubin Strip villages want to become stay-at-home weavers, hence the local weaving workforce is graying and shrinking. As Sen's futon sales shot up, Bin not only saw his sales drop, but he found it more difficult to fill his orders for futons in a timely fashion. The women weavers who used to supply him with products were weaving primarily for Sen. Bin was infuriated when a village woman who specialized in collecting products for sellers told him that Sen secretly offered her a slightly higher piece rate if she collected exclusively for him. That evening, Bin ignored Sen's text message inviting him to hang out and play basketball after dinner. The two friends had become business rivals.

These two stories, one from D and the other from W Village, encapsulate the ways in which rural China's ongoing IT-driven entrepreneurial reinvention, and its contradictions, have enflamed interpersonal conflict in e-commerce villages. These contradictions are embodied in shanzhai production logic, which can be traced back to the early days of post-Mao reform. Opening up the export-oriented subcontracting market in the late 1970s and early 1980s revitalized small family-based, family-run manufacturing businesses, while also fostering competition between them. In W Village, privatization and commercialization of collective and socialist handicraft practices boosted the local economy, but also created new tensions by reshaping the existing village economy and culture to better suit the needs of global capitalist production. Market competition heightened tensions between the market-based entrepreneurial self and the collective interest of the village community. Nascent intellectual property rights awareness coexisted with the proliferation of shanzhai practices. Opportunities for commercializing handicraft weaving labor expanded, even as the cultural and financial value of manual weaving depreciated relative to the value of entrepreneurship.

Building on the previous chapter's description of emerging entrepreneurial labor and changing state-capital-village relations under platformized family production, we now focus on how the labor of entrepreneurial reinvention in rural China produces hybrid subjectivities, generates contradictions, and creates new systems of value and valuation. The central question I seek to answer here is whether, and to what extent e-commerce, the specific form of platformized family production found in W Village can contribute to rural revitalization and improve social equity. My analysis highlights the experiences of villagers struggling to "upgrade" their local e-commerce handicraft industry in an increasingly competitive digital marketplace. Of particular importance is how changing subjectivities and regimes of value become entangled with existing systems of differentiation according to gender, age, wealth, education, and migration experience to create new opportunities for empowerment and new forms of inequality.

IT-driven entrepreneurialization in rural China privileges the individualized e-commerce entrepreneur as its ideal subject; fetishizes and instrumentalizes innovation and creativity in line with the global intellectual property rights (IPR) regime; and valorizes intellectual and digital labor by disguising it as IT entrepreneurship. These tendencies are out of step with the reality of collective labor organization within Chinese villages and even on e-commerce platforms themselves. They also occlude the indispensable role of manual labor in the production process.

Although such contradictions are immanent in digital capitalism and, thus, not particular to W Village or to China, they are accentuated and complicated by the overtly hybrid nature of platformized family production in the Chinese countryside in general, and in W Village in particular. There—coexisting in the same geographical and temporal space—are gendered, traditional handicraft labor and the "immaterial" labor of e-commerce; village-based family production systems and plat-formized e-commerce networks; and residual small peasant or socialist collective subjectivities and the individualizing forces of the entrepre-neurial economy.

This chapter analyzes these contradictions in the specific context of W Village's e-commerce industry. Tracing the genealogy of shanzhai pro-duction in W shows how—despite the avowed desire of entrepreneurs to transcend the model—the village's entrepreneurial reinvention through e-commerce builds on shanzhai production logic and magni-fies its contradictions. W Village's struggle to move beyond shanzhai exemplifies the hybridity of China's emerging regime of entrepreneurial labor, and the nation's challenges in reinventing and restructuring its economy. Over the past decade, villagers have learned how to "inno-vate;" to capitalize on their rural identities; to adapt to the declin-ing cultural and financial value of manual labor; and to self-organize into industry associations. Instead of a victory over inequality, rural e-commerce has fostered the development of a new regime of value and valuation.

SHANZHAI PRODUCTION AND THE CONTRADICTIONS OF ENTREPRENEURIAL REINVENTION

Shanzhai literally means "mountain stronghold." The term first appeared in ancient vernacular Chinese novels to describe the military fortresses of Robin Hood–like martial artists and bandits exiled by the imperial court. Most recently, it was appropriated for post-reform China's hybrid production regime, which disrupts the boundaries between global and local, copying and innovation, and manual and intellectual labor. This contemporary usage of shanzhai is usually traced to a cottage industry of family-owned manufacturing plants emerging in Hong Kong in the 1950s. These businesses grew out of shifts in the networked global divi-sion of labor and helped to revitalize traditional Chinese family produc-tion practices. In the process, Hong Kong, along with a few other regions in East and Southeast Asia, became a new frontier for global capitalist accumulation. Beginning in the late 1970s, shanzhai industries expanded onto the mainland as China embraced its new role as a global manufac-turing hub.

Arguably, shanzhai is most closely associated with Shenzhen's industrial ecosystem—particularly, its mobile phone production and sales industries.[3] These industries repurposed the informal, flexible, but sophisticated and networked division of labor found in Shenzhen's contract export manufacturers, and deployed it in the service of global brands like Apple and Samsung to create affordable alternative products for less affluent consumers in China and other developing countries. More recently, South China businesses have evolved from producing cheaper knockoffs of foreign brands, to manufacturing for globally competitive Chinese brands like Huawei and Xiaomi, and finally to cultivating a vibrant incubator ecosystem of cutting-edge tech start-ups from around the world.[4]

Public perceptions of shanzhai run the gamut from outright condemnation of the practice as an obstacle to Chinese innovation, to enthusiastic celebration.[5] Critics tend to idealize the trajectory of capitalist development in Western societies as universal, dismissing alternative non-Western experiences, or deviations within Western societies as evidence of a "lag" or a "lack" of something. For them, the hybrid shanzhai regime is merely a "transitional" stage on the path to a more "developed" and "modernized" state of Euro-American capitalism. As Lars Eckstein and Anja Schwarz put it with regard to mainstream perceptions of non-Western piracy practices, it is seen as "a crucial phase in the establishment of peripheral markets which will, if not criminalized and more fully 'developed,' naturally grow into the modern domain of copyright."[6]

At the other extreme, shanzhai is praised for its revolutionary potential to build a more democratic, effective, creative, and competitive alternative innovation system. Running counter to the established practices of Silicon Valley and the global international property rights system, it is celebrated for its seamless integration of manufacturing labor, design, and marketing.[7]

The experiences of W and other rural e-commerce entrepreneurial sites in China contest both the universalism of Western-centric IPR, and celebratory accounts of shanzhai's boundary-crossing, dichotomy-defying potential to resist Western hegemony. My observations in W and other Taobao villages suggest that, as a hybrid model arising from China's negotiated positioning in global digital capitalism, shanzhai is simultaneously productive and frustrating for its practitioners. China's rural e-commerce industry and platformized family production both build on and perpetuate the shanzhai logic of production, even as rural entrepreneurs seek to transcend it. If anything, the rise of rural e-commerce has heightened such contradictions in places like W by encouraging counterfeiting and further devaluing gendered weaving labor.

Shanzhai production first appeared in W in the early reform years as the area's collective handicraft production regime was privatized. This was part of China's transition from agrarian familial and socialist production systems to integration within the global capitalist division of labor. I first learned the history of W's handicraft industry from Shu, former director of the B County Museum, who had studied and documented B County's handicraft tradition since the mid-1970s. "Unlike nowadays, when you have to distinguish your products from others on the market, there was no pressure for innovation," Shu explained during our first interview in 2015. "My sense is that the more adventurous villagers might experiment with making new items to meet their practical needs. If their relatives or friends found a new design useful, they would ask for instructions or just pick it up by themselves through observation. Along the way, they might make some minor modifications here or there to better serve their own purposes."

Boundaries between innovation and copying, like those between mental and physical labor, were blurred in the village's family-based, subsistence-driven collective production system, and also in the handicraft commune and brigade enterprises of the late socialist period, when the state organized and coordinated handicraft production in the area.[8] Sun, the eighty-year-old former head of the No. 2 handicraft factory, helped found the plant in 1977, after the end of the Cultural Revolution, but before the start of the reform period. He served as its manager until he retired in 1998, the same year the plant closed for good. A county-level collectively owned TVE (*dajiti*, 大集体), No. 2 was one of two officially designated handicraft production units in B County under direct supervision of the provincial export bureau. Since the bureau had a monopoly over the province's export channels, there was little market competition. Instead, the aim of export-driven handicraft production in TVE system's early years was to generate county tax revenue, drive the local economy, and create new employment opportunities.

China's relative isolation from the capitalist world system, despite its gradual, negotiated integration after the late 1970s, had yet to generate the need for an IPR system to ensure profit and incentivize innovation. The incentive to create new products came from the foreign businesses sourcing goods from No. 2. Meeting their demands was the responsibility of the factory's "innovation unit" (*chuangxin xiaozu,* 创新小组)—a team of six experienced weavers. As Sun and other retired workers recalled, the innovation unit would come up with new designs based on product catalogues sent regularly by the export bureau. They would bring samples to Guangzhou's annual China Import and Export Fair—better known as the Canton Fair—the only place where producers could directly communicate with representatives of foreign companies or interact with other Chinese factories making similar products for export. Thus, the fair provided inspiration for new designs. Once an export order for a new design was confirmed, members of the innovation team made product samples and distributed them to No. 2's home-based subcontractors.

In other words, W Village's handicraft production system grew out of the small peasant economy, which, in turn, was based on the village lineage system. Under TVE, this system was repurposed to serve the state. Later, it underpinned the shanzhai production regime that emerged in the 1990s when B County's handicraft TVEs were swept away by nationwide privatization.

Growing overseas demand for handicraft products and new channels for international trade necessitated more frequent direct communication between foreign business representatives and Chinese TVEs. Gradually, some more entrepreneurial factory workers and their relatives formed cordial relations with foreign business representatives looking for subcontractors. This led to an explosion of small, family-run private handicraft export firms in W. Market competition bankrupted No. 2 in the late 1990s. Yet, almost all the owners of the new private export firms had accumulated experience, skills, and connections working for the two collective TVEs, until the lure of personal enrichment led them to bypass the collective and compete with each other directly on price, turnaround speed, and service.

Only then did they become aware of issues like "piracy" or the need to criminalize "copying" to protect intellectual property. Export business owners and villagers told me that it was common for producers to copy or appropriate competitors' designs and sell the same or similar products at lower prices. Interpersonal conflicts escalated as trust among villagers declined. Underlying the growing tension between copying and innovation in places like W was mounting national anxiety over China's inferior position in the international division of labor, a weakness made more acute by international pressure to conform to the global IPR system after the country entered the WTO. In the late 1990s, China invested heavily in cultivating creative citizens and entrepreneurs and in promoting its creative and cultural industries.[9] It became common for policymakers and the general public to debate the causes of the China's supposed lack of creativity and propose solutions to the problem. B County's handicraft industry was inevitably drawn into this national project of entrepreneurial reinvention.

Two competing local narratives explain the privatization of B County's handicraft industry. One celebrates neoliberal values like individual success and the entrepreneurial pursuit of self-betterment and personal enrichment. This narrative is closely intertwined with the reform-era discourse of *suzhi* (素质), an indigenous concept inspired by the neoliberal "human capital" theory.[10] In this discourse, people with "low suzhi" are doomed to a life of manual labor and stagnation in the declining countryside. This made it incumbent on individual peasants to improve their suzhi through education and entrepreneurial labor, thereby increasing their value as entrepreneur-workers.[11] Sun's son, a former employee of No. 2 who left the factory in the late 1990s to launch a private firm with a local investor, was a proponent of the neoliberal narrative. I met him briefly during one of my interviews with Sun, as he paid his parents a weekend visit. He overheard our conversation about the privatization of No. 2 while adding hot water to our teapot and volunteered his view that privatization was "economically democratic" and "antimonopolistic." "Privatization offered opportunities for people who were willing to work hard and had what it took to be successful," he informed me. This perspective is shared by many in B County and W Village who also benefited from the privatization process. They generally emphasized how the boom in private handicraft businesses since the late 1990s transformed their personal lives for the better and stimulated the local economy by bringing in more export orders.

The other narrative denounces privatization as selfish and detrimental to collective interest and social harmony.[12] Locals who hold this view believe that market competition created new social and economic disparities and tensions. "Some people did get rich first," Sun told me, referencing Deng Xiaoping's famous saying. "But the majority were left behind and had to swallow the bitter consequences," he added. In fact, Sun was so irritated by his son's remarks that he ordered him to mind his own business and stop interrupting our conversation.

My interviews with retired No. 1 and No. 2 workers suggest that, apart from a few workers turned export firm owners who made fortunes overnight, the majority stayed in the factories until bankruptcy forced their closure. Increased demand for handicrafts has since generated more subcontracting work for women weavers. Still, competition among export firms and the abundance of women weavers before the e-commerce takeoff in the late 2000s kept piece rates low and subjected weavers to the heightened discipline and demands for speed characteristic of global capitalist production. Income disparities between well-connected entrepreneurs and village weavers widened as weaving and other forms of manual labor became increasingly commodified.

PLATFORMIZED FAMILY PRODUCTION AND THE TENSIONS OF SHANZHAI

Platform-mediated e-commerce labor, when grafted onto family handicraft production networks in W, exacerbated existing tensions in the shanzhai logic of production. Emerging in the mid-2000s, this hybrid entrepreneurial labor regime opened up opportunities for young peasants and disadvantaged urbanites to become entrepreneurs. They would reap the financial and lifestyle benefits of performing mental as opposed to manual labor, while rendering product innovation both easier and culturally imperative. At the same time, it increasingly incentivized copying, strained community and interpersonal relationships, and devalued manual labor.

We have seen how the expansion of e-commerce in the countryside, especially via Alibaba platforms, connected village handicraft production to the rapidly expanding domestic market. E-commerce platforms lowered the entry threshold for small businesses and facilitated family-based individualization of labor through digital entrepreneurship. Rural entrepreneurs, E-commerce platforms, and different levels of government all participated in constructing the Taobao village phenomenon. Together with the global post-2008 trend toward platformization and China's state campaigns to restructure its economy and society, these efforts further valorized digital entrepreneurialism and internet-based self-employment. For peasants, the rural e-commerce campaign not only promised the democratization of business entrepreneurship opportunities but also offered a chance to participate in cultural and digital capitalism as autonomous self-enterprises and intellectual workers.

Corporate-state efforts to integrate peasants into the e-commerce regime of accumulation encouraged them to take part in the dual project of nation-building and self-remaking, to transcend their status as perpetual manual laborers, enhance their suzhi, and become their own bosses in the new digital economy. The hegemonic status of immaterial labor in the new economy helps explain the cultural and financial elevation of digital or mental labor over manual labor in W, and e-commerce's revolutionary power to restructure local handicraft-making.[13]

The reality of China's experiences with digital entrepreneurship, and those of W Village as a site where different labor regimes and subjectivities—the manual and mental, the entrepreneurial and familial, and the residual socialist—coexist and compete, tells a different story. Rather than erase the boundaries between these realms, the digital economy has intensified their contradictions.

Instead of competing to manufacture high-quality, low-cost products for foreign brands like Walmart and Ikea, e-commerce entrepreneurs began competing with each other on branding, pricing, and innovation as they adapted to the tastes and needs of China's domestic e-commerce consumers. In the process, they "moved up" the value chain by designing, producing, and selling directly to customers. It's true that small online businesses, equipped with a nearly limitless pool of product prototypes, easy access to online sales channels and data, and the ability to interact directly with customers through instant messaging apps and customer rating and review functions, have lowered the cost of innovation in W. Intensified competition in the e-commerce marketplace and the open-source nature of the internet made it convenient, and also imperative for entrepreneurs to come up with new designs to distinguish themselves from their competitors.

On the other hand, the search rankings and profit-maximizing algorithms of e-commerce platforms like Taobao have discouraged rural entrepreneurs from investing labor and time in designing and testing new products or improving the quality of existing products. One example of how Taobao's algorithm encourages the shanzhai production logic is its promotion of "best-selling products" (*baokuan*, 爆款). A baokuan is born when a particular product, and its many shanzhai variations, is embraced by consumers across the country and sold by numerous vendors online and offline.[14] E-commerce platforms like Alibaba implicitly encourage the creation of baokuan by turning a blind eye to copycats. This was especially true in the company's early years, when the platform's profit-maximization imperative and its role as a digital landlord extracting rents from platform-based entrepreneurs actually inhibited innovation and perpetuated shanzhai production.

After Alibaba consolidated its monopoly, it became more proactive in collaborating with local law enforcement to combat counterfeiting.[15] In 2017, under pressure from global brands that Alibaba courted as part of its expansion plans, Jack Ma published an open letter to China's National People's Congress calling for stricter punishments for manufacturers of fake goods.[16] However, Alibaba's own business interests continued to undermine the enforcement of China's fraud prevention rules.[17] This problem has grown worse in recent years with the rapid expansion of Pinduoduo—a competing e-commerce platform targeting sellers and users in smaller cities and the countryside. Despite China desire to move beyond its status as a shanzhai nation, the centrality of e-commerce to China's new economy, especially small business-dominated platforms like Taobao and Pinduoduo, helps perpetuate shanzhai production.

Taobao's complicated and evolving search ranking algorithm, together with profit-maximizing marketing plug-ins like Zhitongche (直通车), also discourage product innovation. Zhitongche is a paid search ranking system that charges shop owners a per-click fee to help them improve their product listing ranking on Taobao.[18] Village entrepreneurs like Li, an art school graduate and urbanite who migrated to W, told me that investing money and time in designing and prototyping a new product usually does not generate commensurate profits for innovators. Instead, it is much more profitable and cost-efficient to copy or appropriate existing products, especially baokuan designs, while redirecting the capital saved to Taobao's paid marketing tools. "People who invest in producing new designs often suffer," Li explained, adding:

> people are constantly monitoring each other's sales figures online. Once they notice a new product that sells well, they will ask around, locate the weavers, and ask them to supply the same product to them. Alternatively, they will show some weavers they trust a picture of the new product and have them produce copies, sometimes with minor modifications. For example, they might change the color of a futon's decorative cloth or add a cover to a storage basket. Then, when they create a new listing on Taobao, they will tag their shanzhai product with the same keywords as the original and sell it at a much lower price. Sometimes the profit margin is so thin that they have to cut corners here and there to outcompete other sellers with similar products. Why waste time designing and making new products when your efforts only enrich your competitors' pockets?

Even when W entrepreneurs have new designs, they are reluctant to invest capital and resources into R&D, for fear that imitators will steal their intellectual property and their profits. The prevalence of design copying and appropriation in W reflects broader tensions within platformized social production. The internet and other networked digital tools have energized nonproprietary production, but they have also made it cheaper and more convenient to profit from social production via applications like peer-to-peer sharing software. Consequently, distinctions between creativity and copying or between individualistic profiteering and community-based collaboration have become blurred.[19]

The nature of village-based family production networks further exacerbates these tensions. W Village's e-commerce industry was built atop collective, open production networks. That is, any e-commerce entrepreneur could source a particular product from any weaver, albeit sometimes with the assistance of an intermediary "product collector." According to local e-commerce entrepreneur Xiao, W's collective, open production regime inadvertently made it easier for villagers to steal or copy others' new designs. Instead of being governed by legally binding contracts, village production networks overlap with the traditional lineage system.[20] "I can't keep my design away from my cousin, and he has to tell his wife about it," Xiao explained. "Then his wife's sister knows it too . . . and in no time, you see my design listed on every village shop's front page" (figure 5.1). Though the platform benefits from pitting sellers against each other to offer high-quality products at a lower price, such competition devalues the labor that goes into making handicrafts.

Tensions generated by the platformization of *shanzhai* production are so thorny that they triggered heated debate at the otherwise celebratory 2013 Taobao Village Summit. In a panel discussion on common issues facing Taobao villages, shanzhai was the subject of the first question posed by panel chair Chen Liang, a senior researcher from AliResearch. "Let's start with the biggest challenge facing the upgrading of Taobao villages," Chen began. "How do we deal with product homogenization (*tongzhihua*, 同质化)?" One Taobao village entrepreneur argued

FIGURE 5.1 Pictures of the same handicraft products taken by different entrepreneurs in W village. Source: Taobao product website, www.taobao.com.

that shanzhai served a necessary function in the platform-based, algorithm-dominated e-commerce marketplace. "Taobao is a bottomless sea of commodities," he stated. "If I am the only shop selling a particular product, few customers will notice me. Through copying and repeated sales of the same and similar products, we are able to attract customer traffic toward these products, raise their platform ranking, and work together to create a baokuan. However," he added, "this always leads to price wars (*jiagezhan*, 价格战) and other forms of vicious competition (*exing jingzheng*, 恶性竞争)."

His comment resonated with village entrepreneurs sitting in the audience. A few jumped in to offer impassioned stories of vicious competition in their villages. Nevertheless, the panelists ultimately concluded that shanzhai production was just an expediency: a temporary and "immature" phase in the development of rural e-commerce, which will soon be transcended by the expansion and upgrading of the industry in question. Yet, the struggles of rural e-commerce entrepreneurs to move beyond shanzhai suggest this optimism is unfounded.

BRANDING, SELF-BRANDING, AND THE NEW FACES OF INNOVATION

The Question of Innovation

In the post-2008 regime of entrepreneurial labor, pressure is mounting on entrepreneurs to innovate—to transcend the imitation of the shanzhai model. Amid growing anxiety over lack of product innovation, a handful of resident e-commerce entrepreneurs stepped up to become the face of innovation in W Village. When politicians, journalists, scholars, or other notables come to visit the famous village, they are introduced to these innovative entrepreneurs. Not coincidentally, all of them are males in their thirties.

Wei, the early-bird village entrepreneur introduced in chapter 4, is one of them. I was introduced to him by An, the village's Communist Youth League Secretary, who described Wei as "the most innovative e-commerce entrepreneur in the village." Wei and I first met in his home office in a house near the eastern edge of W Village that he rented for his business. I told Wei that I was interested in handicraft innovation, what constituted innovation and why some entrepreneurs were "better" at creating new products in W. In the middle of our interview, he led me to the storeroom where he kept samples of all the products he had ever sold online. "This is an example of a shanzhai product," he said, pointing to a bulrush futon in the corner of the room. "Can you tell the difference between it and the traditional-style bulrush futons produced here?" he asked. I looked closer and noticed that there was an extra handle on one side of the shanzhai futon, making it more convenient to pick up and carry. Wei explained that this was an example of "shanzhai logic": existing designs were modified to add some small variation in response to consumer demand, or in hopes of generating demand. Then, he showed me another shanzhai design: a traditional futon with patterned cloth stitched around the edge to set it apart from similar products.

"I don't think these shanzhai designs are innovations," Wei explained. "Real innovation happens when the innovator invents a new line of products that has never existed in W Village." As we were talking, he pointed at a coffee table set in the middle of the showroom. He said he came up with the original design of the set, and now its many different variations constitute one of the most popular product lines in the village. When I asked what inspired him to make this product, he credited Ikea's online catalogue with giving him the idea:

One day, I came across a table set that I really liked. The table and its matching seats were made of wood and the shape of the table was slightly different. The moment I saw it, I started to imagine in my mind what it would be like if I covered it with a layer of banana leaves. I wanted the set to look more casual and comfortable, so I decided to make the edge of the table and seats rounder. I first made a sketch of my design and worked with the village carpenter to create a wooden mold. Then I took the mold and my sketch to one of the most experienced and dexterous weavers that I knew in the village and explained my concept. She followed my sketch and added a layer of braided banana leaves. She was so good that she delivered the sample product in three days! When I received the sample, I thought that the seats still looked cheap (*lianjia*, 廉价). So I decided to stain the whole thing dark brown. Then I took a picture of the set in my photo studio and created a new product page on Taobao.

The next day, I received more than twenty inquiries and ten orders. I really didn't expect it to sell so well.

Wei's delineation between real innovation and shanzhai logic, as well as his firsthand account of "inventing" a new product line, raised more questions than it answered. Although "innovation" is fetishized and valued over "copying" within W's handicraft e-commerce industry, the boundaries separating them remain fuzzy and fluid. From Wei's perspective, the source of inspiration (i.e., an Ikea catalogue vs. existing village products), the extent to which a new design departs from its source, and the resources and effort invested in creating the new product all determined whether it is "real innovation." This judgment is subjective and can vary from case to case, which is to say that distinctions between innovation and copying in W are socially constructed and highly contingent.

Crucially, Wei's story about working with a skilled village weaver to quickly prototype the new product demonstrated how their collective and open production network could be conducive to "innovation." More important, it also revealed the constructed and mystifying nature of innovation in W Village. Wei came up with the idea by browsing an Ikea catalogue and collaborated with a villager weaver to develop it. This begs the question: Can a design be truly "original" if cultural production is always collective? Laikwan Pang has argued that our individualistic notions of authorship and commodification under the current global IPR system have abducted "individual" ideas from "the chain of creativity." The fetishization of individualized intellectual property works to mystify the true nature of innovation as a social process that is inevitably collective and memetic.[21]

As the public face of handicraft innovation in W Village—and an example of rural e-commerce's potential to foster innovation nationwide— Wei had, consciously or unconsciously, adopted an individualistic notion of creative agency to position himself as the sole "author" of the baokuan table set. But his account of the actual process of innovation, involving as it did an established network of village handicrafters who prototyped and mass produced his new design, betrays the collective (and gendered) manual labor behind his "innovation." Under the entrepreneurial labor regime, digital and mental labor are valorized at the expense of manual labor. As individualized conceptions of "creativity" and "innovation" are exalted, the social and collective nature of innovation in the handicraft e-commerce industry is rendered invisible. The resulting entrepreneurial regime not only constitutes a new system of differentiation, breeding new inequalities, but it also threatens the sustainability of e-commerce production in W Village.

Branding and Self-Branding

Branding is another element of successful e-commerce businesses in W. A good brand can help a store raise the value of its products, build a loyal customer base, and stand out among the many e-commerce shops selling similar products. For small, family-owned e-commerce businesses, commercial branding is intertwined with the practice of self-branding, what Alice Marwick has termed "the strategic creation of an identity to be promoted and sold to others."[22] Branding is as much about culture as it is about economics, and is intimately linked to identity formation in late capitalism, argues Sarah Banet-Weiser.[23] As W Village entrepreneurs seek to "upgrade" their businesses and transcend shanzhai logic, branding and self-branding have become additional sources of tension between individualization and persistent collective (including family) relations and identities.

Learning to brand a business is an individualizing process. Entrepreneurs must locate and articulate their niche and market positioning to better distinguish their businesses and themselves from competitors. Critics of neoliberal market subjectivities often link contemporary branding and self-branding practices to the formation of individualized identities.[24] However, for the rural e-commerce entrepreneurs I encountered during my fieldwork, branding and self-branding were typically informed by residual, geographically specific community identities. These were mutually constitutive with the emerging collective politics of platform-based rural development, as well as the "buy-rural" consumer citizenship common among urban middle-class Chinese. The persistent relevance of collective identities and politics and their subjugation to the logic of capital in Chinese branding resonate with Banet-Weiser's analysis of American commodity activism and Lilly Irani's study of the branding of handicrafts in rural India.[25]

Irani showed how product branding lessons given by middle-class designers to Indian rural handicraft makers were framed as an "invitation" for peasants "to tweak symbolic forms and material cultures while remaining within elite understandings of community, culture, and authentic group difference."[26] This is the paradox between individualizing calls for peasants to be entrepreneurial, to find their niche and "manifest their own aspirations," and the demands of communitarian national politics and the lingering significance of age-old collective identities in authenticating rural handicrafts for urban middle-class consumer tastes.[27] Even more so in China, rural entrepreneurs must balance tensions between individualization and community in their branding and self-branding practices.

For peasant e-commerce entrepreneurs, successful branding and self-branding requires a certain level of cultural, linguistic, and technological literacy (digital photography, graphic processing, and web design skills). Equally important, it demands a cosmopolitan sensibility aligned with the tastes of urban middle-class consumers, the corporate agendas of platforms, and the state's political imperatives. In China, these high requirements have produced a new regime of differentiation and governmentality that disciplines rural entrepreneurs as they reinvent themselves and their product lines.

Xiao and Ling's e-commerce business was widely seen as having one of the strongest brands in W Village. Both were college-educated and had spent years in white-collar jobs in a nearby city. This made them more attuned to urban consumer tastes than villagers who had always lived in the countryside or migrants who had worked in cities as manual laborers. The couple's sociable, expressive personalities also helped them adapt to the new economy's demands for personal expression, interactivity, and networking. Xiao, an articulate man in his mid-thirties, was a natural politician. During my stay in W, I noticed that he closely followed national news and enjoyed sharing his insights into village and county politics. The couple's prior entrepreneurial endeavors also made them more business-savvy than most of their fellow villagers. After returning to W in 2008, they registered the first village trademark for their e-commerce business in 2009, and in 2011 they were the first to upgrade from Taobao to Alibaba's more advanced platform, Tmall.[28]

I first met Xiao and Ling on a tour of the village led by the head of B County. These tours are a continuation of socialist mass line politics.

During mass mobilization campaigns, exemplary rural villages and urban work units are thrust into the national limelight by the party-state's powerful propaganda machine. The rest of the country is expected to emulate these "model villages" or "model danwei." At the national level, these models help propagate the central state's policy ideas. Locally, they showcase the local cadres' political achievements (*zhengji*, 政绩), and become political pilgrimage sites for leadership teams from other work units or villages.[29] Upon entering Xiao and Ling's workshop on W's main street, I was greeted by an exhibition wall covered with certificates and plaques awarded by various government units, and photos taken with important journalists, politicians, and representatives from e-commerce companies, near the huge Jack Ma poster emblazoned with the quote "Never Give Up!" (figure 5.2).

We have seen how Alibaba helped reinvent China's centralized minimalist governance regime by allying with local governments to construct and promote the Taobao village initiative. The company's integration with, and appropriation of socialist mass mobilization campaign

FIGURE 5.2 Inside Xiao and Ling's home e-commerce workshop. Photo by author.

tactics to energize digital entrepreneurialism shaped the branding strategy of many of the best rural e-commerce entrepreneurs I met during my fieldwork. Their brands and self-brands were crafted in accordance with commercial logic and the political demands of the corporate-state nexus.

Few were more successful at this than Xiao and Ling. Their brand, Mu Xin, reflected Xiao's self-branding as a socially responsible young entrepreneur returned from the city to help his home village "modernize" and digitalize its traditional handicraft industry. Xiao's rise to fame started in mid-2013, when a journalist from the agricultural channel on Shandong's provincial TV station came to W to report on the development of e-commerce in the area. Not long after Xiao and Ling's first media profile, W became one of China's first Taobao villages. Boosted by the village's commercial and political success, Xiao's career as a model e-commerce entrepreneur took off.

In almost no time, his daily schedule filled with tasks like hosting visiting politicians, speaking with journalists, and flying around the country to attend award ceremonies, e-commerce workshops, and publicity events. His public image got an important endorsement when Shandong's governor visited the couple's workshop on a political tour of the village. Soon after this inspection tour, Xiao was awarded the prestigious title of "National Young Leader in Rural Development" by the Communist Youth League and the Ministry of Agriculture. In 2014, Xiao was one of eight individuals invited by Alibaba to ring the bell at the company's NYSE IPO, though he was unable to attend.[30] In April 2017, he realized his dream of meeting Jack Ma in person when he was selected by Alibaba to participate in "E-Commerce Week" at the United Nations annual Conference on Trade and Development in Geneva.

The couple's "About Us" page on their e-commerce shop gives us an idea of how their branding efforts link to China's broader political and economic context. Any shopper who opens the page immediately sees their brand's logo: the company's name juxtaposed with a close-up of two worn female hands weaving a futon. According to the page, the company's business goals are to "rejuvenate the rural handicraft industry, help absorb rural surplus labor, and promote rural economic development." Shoppers scrolling down the page learn about the history of Hubin's handicraft industry and the steps involved in turning wild bulrushes into a Mu Xin futon. Glossy stories form the backdrop to the public recognition garnered over the years by Xiao and Ling's entrepreneurial efforts to digitalize this age-old village industry. The middle of the page presents shoppers with photos and narratives of the couple hosting government officials, being interviewed by journalists from China Central Television and Russian state TV, and attending national political and commercial events.

As a whole, the webpage tells a coherent story about the Mu Xin brand and the peasant entrepreneurial couple who started it. Ling and Xiao's personal identities as model peasant e-commerce entrepreneurs are thoroughly intertwined with Mu Xin's brand image, endowing the latter with social and cultural meaning. The authenticity of their story instills trust and respect in consumers searching for reliable sellers in a depersonalized virtual shopping mall. By purchasing handicrafts from Mu Xin, urban middle-class shoppers can derive virtuous satisfaction from supporting rural rejuvenation that benefits their "peasant brothers and sisters" (*nongmin xiongdi jiemei*, 农民兄弟姐妹). As for Alibaba, Mu Xin's brand story, like many similar narratives of grassroots entrepreneurs found on the company's platforms, bolsters its corporate image as a champion of grassroots empowerment. In turn, this corporate brand image aligns with China's latest nation-building efforts to promote rural economic and social restructuring through micro-entrepreneurship.

Like Xiao and Ling's personal brands, Mu Xin's brand image was built around the collective politics of corporate- and state-backed digitalization. But the couple still must carefully navigate tensions between their individual achievements and their public role as the face of a collective movement. Xiao's personal fame as a nationally recognized model entrepreneur has connected him to elite political and commercial networks outside of the village, but it has also made him a target of envy within the village. Some villagers I interviewed questioned the authenticity of Mu Xin's brand image and the couple's motives in promoting village e-commerce. In the words of one resident: "I know it's a tough job being a representative of your village, not to mention being a national symbol for peasant entrepreneurship. They should get paid for the hard work they do. But it's problematic when you use your public image as a community representative for personal enrichment. What you do does not really benefit the community in any real sense. You are just a mouth-piece for the politicians and CEOs."

Later, I learned that this respondent was engaged in a price war with Xiao over a new line of handicrafts on Taobao. He suspected that Xiao received preferential treatment from the platform's algorithms so "He [Xiao] could live up to his role as a model entrepreneur." These suspicions were echoed by several other village entrepreneurs I interviewed. Although such allegations may have been groundless speculation motivated by jealousy or personal grudges, they speak to the escalation of interpersonal tensions within the community. Other villagers questioned the logic of the new economy altogether. They felt it was unfair for companies and the government to promote a few individuals as model entrepreneurs, hyping their atypical experiences to boost interest in e-commerce. "I don't feel represented at all by the media propaganda," one villager told me. "All those stories about e-commerce villages did was to drive more people into an already overcompetitive market. My e-commerce business is suffering now because of competition and no one wants to hear my story."

Therein lies one of the key contradictions of entrepreneurial labor in rural China. While it appropriates the village-based regime of handi-craft production and the collective politics of mass line mobilization by rendering rural development and peasant labor "entrepreneurial," the government has essentially aligned itself with digital platform monopo-lies in offloading its responsibilities to peasants and the countryside onto the individuals themselves.[31] Essentially, the state's attitude is that if some villagers can succeed in the digital marketplace, everyone can.

Meanwhile, although media narratives surrounding rural e-commerce tap into and reference the village handicraft tradition and its community-based division of labor, they primarily celebrate personal empowerment and digital entrepreneurship and romanticize the hard physical labor of weaving. The entrepreneurial labor of branding in rural e-commerce necessarily involves appropriating rural identities and community-based traditions, which are repackaged to sell a niche prod-uct or an "authentic" self in a competitive market. In doing so, it privi-leges "the individual, rather than the social, as a site for political action (or inaction) and cultural change (or merely exchange)."[32] The new econ-omy rewards those who are more adaptive to its logic of accumulation.

It has opened opportunities for villagers who are more outgoing, expressive, better educated, and who can better perform "urban" and "middle-class" identities, while reinforcing existing regimes of inequality according to gender, age, education, wealth, and migration experience. This constitutes a new regime of subjectification and differentiation among peasant identities.

Within Xiao's own family, his personal brand as a young male entrepreneur overshadowed the contributions of other family members to his success. Xiao was the sole recipient of most of the political awards the family business has garnered. Yet. while he was attending public events and socializing with political and corporate elites as one of W Village's "model entrepreneurs," Ling and his parents actually ran the business and cared for the couple's three young children. Xiao's family dynamics reflect the broader inequalities in the rural entrepreneurial labor regime. At the Taobao Village Summit in 2013, I noticed that all of the rural e-commerce entrepreneurs who received awards were males in their twenties or thirties. Gender and generational inequalities remain prevalent in Taobao villages like W.

Also obscured by the euphoric coverage of digital empowerment and entrepreneurial success in China's countryside is the impending shortage of women weavers. The declining value of physical labor and the challenges villagers face in organizing collectively against increasingly extractive digital platforms have made weaving less appealing. Weavers' hidden stories are key to understanding the tensions between the personal and collective amid the entrepreneurial reinvention of China's countryside. IT entrepreneurialization has not been able to resolve the systematic problems at the core of contemporary Chinese capitalism: persistent inequality, structural labor shortages, and the unchecked power of political-economic elites.

THE CHALLENGES AND FAILURES OF ENTREPRENEURIAL REINVENTION

The Depreciation of Gendered Handicraft Labor

E-commerce was championed by the state-corporate nexus as a way to reinvigorate traditional handicraft making. In practice, however, the rapid growth of e-commerce has contributed to the devaluation of hand-icraft labor and decline in the relative socioeconomic standing of female weavers, most of whom are older. This depreciation of gendered handi-craft labor has deepened interclass and intergenerational inequalities among women in W Village. Younger women may have been empowered by entrepreneurial reinvention, but the gendered division of labor within the family production system underpinning rural e-commerce perpetu-ates patriarchal and androcentric norms and gender inequalities.

In contrast to the expanding army of e-commerce entrepreneurs and the celebration of internet entrepreneurship, the number of handicraft makers in W has dwindled over the past decade. The shrinking and aging population of women weavers has tightened the supply of available prod-ucts and compromised the quality of local handicrafts.

The traditional gendered division of labor in W and its neighboring villages along the Hubin Strip ensured the intergenerational transmis-sion of weaving skills among female villagers. The industrialization of handicraft making, especially in the reform-era, export-oriented handi-craft TVEs, solidified this labor structure. Since the late 2000s, new alter-native labor opportunities for the region's younger women have led to a weaving labor shortage, power shifts in inter-generational relations, and rising intravillage economic inequalities. At their core, all these changes are driven by evolving perceptions of what constitutes "good work" for women. The valorization of "mental labor" (*naoli laodong*, 脑力劳动), including digital entrepreneurship or jobs in the urban services indus-try, diminished the value of home-based manual labor like weaving, not only financially, but also culturally.[33] While it has become easier for better-educated young women to reinvent themselves as internet entre-preneurs or service workers, older women have been left behind because of their age, family responsibilities, and lack of education.

During my first trip to W in 2013, the majority of weavers were women in their late forties or older. Their average age has advanced with the passing years: when I last visited in the summer of 2019, most of the women weavers I met were in their mid-fifties or older. Many had never worked away from the village and quite a few were illiterate. Their deci-sion to stay at home and weave was primarily motivated by childcare and eldercare responsibilities. The majority of women in their forties and younger opted to work in the B County seat or in nearby counties, often in the service sector or in factories.

My conversations with Hua, the owner of a handicraft export business and a weaver in her late forties, delineated the challenges older women face in keeping up with the new economy and the rapidly changing labor regime. Born in the early 1970s, Hua picked up weaving from her mother at an early age. Despite her good grades, she was unable to attend junior high school due to the sudden death of her father when she was fifteen. To support her family, she wove at home and was apprenticed with a local tailor. "Hubin women of my mother's and my generations were very proud of our weaving skills," Hua told me. "The booming handicraft export industry in the 1980s improved our earning power and also our status inside the family."

Hua's sense of pride was echoed by many older women in the villages. They generally agreed that Hubin women weavers' greater contributions to their families' earnings allowed them to be more assertive, independent, and stronger-minded than their female counterparts who did not participate in the handicraft industry. Hua married into W Village in her mid-twenties. A few years after giving birth to her first son, she moved up the handicraft industrial value chain and became a product collector, an intermediary between village women weavers and local export companies. In 2004, at the height of the handicraft export boom, Hua had accumulated enough capital to set up her own handicraft-making workshop employing several local weavers (figure 5.3). A versatile, creative artisan trained in tailoring and fashion design, Hua excelled at inventing and executing new handicraft designs based on the demands of export companies. As Hua's business expanded in subsequent years, she became one of the village's few successful female handicraft export entrepreneurs, a group otherwise dominated by men.

However, her business cratered in 2008 with the sudden contraction of the export market. Although export demand gradually recovered, e-commerce further destabilized Hua's business. In the early days of rural e-commerce, it was relatively easy to make quick money on Taobao, and several weavers at Hua's workshop—women in their early to mid-forties— left to open their own e-commerce shops. By the mid-2010s, however, the e-commerce industry was increasingly professionalized, and none of

FIGURE 5.3 Hua sewing handicraft products at her home workshop. Photo by author.

the weavers who had left Hua's shop made enough money online to support their families.

Nevertheless, only two returned to work for Hua, both of them reluctantly. The others sought service industry jobs in B County as supermarket cashiers or restaurant servers. Hua was sympathetic: "I don't blame them. Weaving is hard work. No one wants to get stuck as a manual laborer forever." She herself had joined the e-commerce gold rush, setting up a Taobao shop with the help of her teenage son. "My e-commerce shop has very little traffic," Hua informed me. "I just couldn't keep up with the rapid development of the platform. There was some new digital tool or new rule that you had to learn every day. I couldn't even type fast enough to keep the customers happy."

"Either you are a tech-savvy and hard-working young college graduate, or you pay out tons of money to hire e-commerce professionals," Hua concluded. "If you are an old person working alone like me, don't waste your time."

Very few Hubin women in their thirties or younger were willing to join the home-based weaving force. Most of the young women I talked with expressed contempt for weaving as a profession. Born after China's one-child policy came into effect in 1980, members of this group were usually only children or one of two siblings.[34] Growing up in better material circumstances than their elders, they were generally better educated than their mothers. Many had graduated from junior high school or high school and were exposed to urban middle-class lifestyles from a young age through TV and other media. Some studied outside of B County, and a few had gone to college or spent time working as migrant laborers in urban centers before returning home. They were uninterested in following in their mothers' or grandmothers' footsteps, spending the rest of their lives engaged in home-based manual labor. Weaving was considered only as a last resort when other options were unattainable.

The story of Xiaolan, a thirty-one-year-old shop assistant in B County, offers insight into the intergenerational shifts in women's labor underway in rural and semi-urban China. I met Xiaolan at an independent clothing shop on B County's "Fashion Street" where she worked as a shop assistant.[35] She also managed an e-commerce business on the messaging platform WeChat, helping the store owner sell clothes online and marketing village-made handicrafts. Born and raised in W, Xiaolan lived in the village with her husband, her four-year-old daughter, and her in-laws. She commuted to work in the township every day on her electric scooter. Xiaolan's mother and mother-in-law were both home-based weavers in their mid-fifties. After Xiaolan started working in B County, her mother-in-law cared for the couple's child and cooked for the whole family, in addition to her weaving work.

During my stay in W, I was a regular customer of the shop where Xiaolan worked. As we got to know each other better, we often talked about the experiences of different generations of village women. Xiaolan confided in me that she felt guilty about leaving her daughter in her mother-in-law's care, but she was unwilling to become a home weaver herself. Her primary reason was financial: the shop owner paid her a base monthly salary of 2,500 yuan (about US$353), in return for which Xiaolan was expected to work nine hours a day, six days a week. She also received a monthly bonus ranging from 500 to 2,000 yuan. Handicraft making, in comparison, was poorly paid. An adroit weaver in her forties or early fifties would have to work from dusk to dawn seven days a week just to earn Xiaolan's base salary. Older weavers, who worked slower on less sophisticated products, earn even less. As the number of women weavers dwindled in recent years, handicraft piece rates have gradually risen, but not enough to make weaving competitive with new alternative employment or self-employment opportunities.

Financial considerations aside, younger women in Hubin no longer identify with the lifestyles of home-based weavers like their mothers and grandmothers. Xiaocai, Xiaolan's eighteen-year-old cousin who worked as an e-commerce customer service assistant at her brother's online shop, told me she preferred the service sector and willingly undertook the constant personal reinvention necessary to keep up with the tech industry's latest developments. A recent high school graduate, Xiaocai earned a monthly salary of 2,000 yuan. She considered the job an "internship": a way to garner experience before applying for work at one of the county's more established e-commerce enterprises—where salaries could be as high as 3,000 yuan a month—or starting her own e-commerce business. She told me that girls her age rarely considered becoming weavers: "No one wants to work in a dark, humid, and dirty room with grass like their mothers and grandmas. You can stay in air-conditioned rooms and meet new people if you work in a mall or supermarket. E-commerce is much better. It's the job of the future. It's better to get into a new media industry earlier than later." For her, the difference between weaving and e-commerce customer service is not just about pay, but also about lifestyle. As she told me: "the younger generation of village women lead a very different lifestyle."

According to younger village women like Xiaolan and Xiaocai, jobs in the urban service sector or e-commerce industry offer greater opportunities to meet and communicate with new people, whether face-to-face or through the internet. They also promise greater mobility: the former require commuting to the city, while the latter allow women to work any-where. The homes of the female e-commerce workers that I visited were usually clean and well decorated. Many were frequent online shoppers themselves, buying clothes, cosmetics, and home decor on sale—a practice which female entrepreneurs saw as a perk of working in the e-commerce industry. In contrast, home-based weavers were confined to the domestic sphere. They had few opportunities to expand their social circles or enjoy the trappings of modern urban life. Their houses and backyards were also difficult to keep clean and tidy, as these spaces were used to process and store bulrush or other weaving materials.

In additional to its financial, cultural, and lifestyle disadvantages, weaving fell out of favor because it's monotonous and physically strenu-ous. Weavers spend all day hunched over a stool, repeating the same hand motions again and again. As the demand for woven products grew and the number of weavers shrank, weavers came under increasing pressure to produce more goods faster. To speed up production, most weavers spe-cialize in making a few types of handicrafts. Thus, female weavers work more like human looms than the romanticized image of rural artisans constructed by entrepreneurs for their online branding material. All of the women weavers I met suffered from chronic back pain and arthritis after a lifetime spent weaving. Auntie Fang, a fifty-six-year-old weaver who specialized in weaving futons, made a point of showing me her deformed hand joints, adding,

almost all women weavers of my age have rheumatoid arthritis. It's really painful, especially in the morning when my knuckles are all swollen. But what else can I do? I was one of six siblings in my fam-ily. We were so poor that my older sisters and I had to take up weav-ing when we were about eleven or twelve. We were only able to stay at the village school for a few years before we had to drop out and work to support our family. This is why I worked hard to sup-port my daughter to go to college. I don't want her to be stuck in the same life.

Over the course of my fieldwork in W, I only came across one female weaver in her twenties. I first met the twenty-eight-year-old Xiaodou in her mother's village convenience store. There, Xiaodou, her mother, and her grandmother spent their days weaving and attending to occasional customers. Xiaodou's father had passed away when she was very young, forcing her to drop out of junior high to help run the family convenient store and support her grandparents and an older brother with an intellectual disability. Dressed in a pair of old blue jeans and an old-fashioned jacket, Xiaodou appeared more introverted than the other young village women I spoke with. During our interview, she was initially quite reserved and reluctant to give her opinion as to why weaving had lost its appeal for young village women. As our conversation went on, I came to understand that her silence had to do with the sense of shame and inferiority she felt as a young female weaver. As she put it: "You will lose face if you tell people your age that you weave at home to make a living. People will think that you are lazy and incapable (*you lan you meibenshi*, 又懒又没本事). I weave at home because I have to take care of my two-year-old baby daughter and our family store. Some young mothers like me, their husbands are rich, and they don't even have to work. They just stay at home and do nothing! But this is my lot in life" (*shou shenghuo suopo*, 受生活所迫).

The intergenerational power dynamics and intragender class inequalities in Hubin reflect broader trends in reform-era rural China. "Girl power" benefited from the Maoist collectivization of agricultural production and socialist egalitarian gender politics when younger women were freed from the Confucian patriarchal family structure and empowered to participate in collective production and village affairs. Although dismantling the socialist collective system made it harder for women to participate in rural public spaces, the rise of TVEs in the 1980s, the proliferation of urban employment opportunities since the early 1990s, and the shortage of marriage-age women combined to mitigate the effects of this shift on younger women.[36] Older peasants, however, especially older women whose labor is less desirable in the urban employment market and who shoulder childrearing and/or eldercare responsibilities, have been left behind as victims of the hollowing out of rural public resources (figures 5.4 and 5.5).[37]

To an extent, the post-2008 popularization of e-commerce in the Chinese countryside opened further spaces for young rural women to reinvent themselves.[38] Young Hubin women's embrace of constant self-reinvention to meet the demands of the new economy resonates with

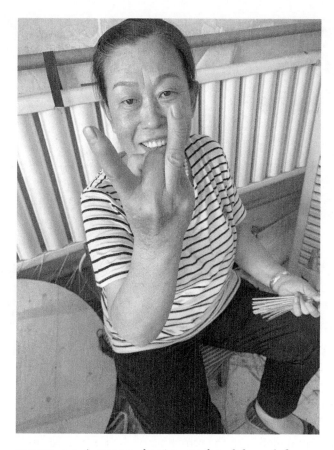

FIGURE 5.4 A weaver showing me her deformed fingers. Photo by author.

working-class experiences in other parts of the world. Opportunities offered by service and cultural sector jobs, and attendant imperatives to maintain an "attractive" and "well-groomed body," constitute a "feel-good" factor for young women in an increasingly individualized, consumerist society.[39]

Since the 1990s, increased targeting of female consumers by the cosmetics and fashion industries has gone hand in hand with the rising number of pink-collar service jobs in China.[40] Since the late 2000s, e-commerce has also featured this proliferation of gendered consumption and service labor. The pressures and desires underlying women's constant self-reinvention as entrepreneurial laborers and consumers form

FIGURE 5.5 Women weavers at home. Photo by author.

a common thread connecting the experiences of rural, urban, and trans-national Chinese women, as the formation of new labor subjectivities becomes entangled with the remaking of their gendered rural and cosmopolitan selves.

However, compared to the transnationally mobile middle- and upper middle-class urban women discussed in the next chapter, the self-reinvention of rural female e-commerce entrepreneurs is disadvantaged and constrained by their rural and local identities.[41] The empowering potential of e-commerce in rural women's lives is further compromised by persistent intergenerational inequalities, as in Xiaolan and Fang's stories, and intraclass unevenness, as in Xiaodou's experiences. Nevertheless, most villagers whom I talked with recognized e-commerce's positive contributions to the region, arguing that even Hubin's older and poorer residents were better off than those in neighboring villages without a strong local industry. "As long as I can still move my fingers, I can support myself into my old age without being a financial burden to my only daughter," said Auntie Fang.

Still, the devaluation of gendered handicraft labor threatens the sustainability and long-term development of the region's e-commerce industry.

The Challenges of Collective Organizing

Like many other platform-based Web 2.0 businesses, Taobao strategically deployed a "free model" in its early days to attract users and consumers.[42] Financed by venture capital, Taobao operated at a net loss from 2003 to 2007. During that time, the platform charged no fees for opening shops or listing products—which helped it outcompete eBay in 2006 while building brand awareness and raising market share. My informants in W remember the period between 2006 and 2013 as Taobao's golden age. Platform-based e-commerce entrepreneurship seemed an alluring alternative to the grim urban job market, and it was easy for peasant entrepreneurs to make money on the site, "as long as you knew how to type, upload photos, and send packages."

These early advantages gradually faded after Taobao secured its monopoly. Beginning in 2008, Taobao began to monetize its platform by setting up a search ranking bidding system and offering online payment services. The most effective strategy involved splitting the platform in two: a basic version offering the free model and a premium version with a service fee. In June 2011, Taobao's premium service, Tmall.com, launched as an independent website. In a strategic move to monetize Alibaba's platforms before its IPO, the company significantly raised entry fees for setting up shop on Tmall, then adjusted its algorithms to redirect search traffic away from Taobao and toward its more profitable cousin.[43] The fees were beyond the means of most rural entrepreneurs in W. In 2016, only ten out of W's hundreds of e-commerce family businesses could afford a Tmall shop.

The boom-and-bust dot-com business cycle, especially the IPO-driven "growth-before-profit" models of digital platforms, has rendered platform-based e-commerce entrepreneurship increasing competitive and precarious.[44] Despite Alibaba's sustained marketing efforts, most of my informants believed that the best days for grassroots rural entrepreneurs were in the past. They identified 2013 as a turning point when, except for a few big sellers, most of W's existing Taobao businesses began to fall into decline. Ironically, this was also the year when—hyped by media publicity, political endorsements, and promotional events like the Taobao Village Summit—Taobao villages became a national craze.

The increasingly exploitive and competitive behavior of platforms aggravated village entrepreneurs' anxieties over existing industry problems and their desire to transcend shanzhai logic. In the process of reinventing themselves as digital entrepreneurs, villagers realized that the decentralized, atomized nature of family e-commerce sales had rendered them especially vulnerable to the vagaries of a market dominated by monopolies like Alibaba. Two new industry associations emerged in 2015, a time when W villagers hoped that collective organizing could help them overcome the limitations of atomized micro-entrepreneurship. However, neither association succeeded in mobilizing village entrepreneurs to work together. Most villagers I talked with saw the associations as "empty shells" set up by successful entrepreneurs and local elites to serve their own interests, or to help officials showcase their political achievements.

The challenges rural e-commerce entrepreneurs faced in self-organizing should be understood in the context of the changing regime of governance in rural China after agricultural taxes were abolished in the 2000s. Starting in the late 1970s, dismantling the socialist collective system created a vacuum of governance in the Chinese countryside. With the decisive shift toward urban reform in the early 1990s, this void was quickly filled by private capital. China's export-oriented developmentalist policy brought together urban capital, local bureaucrats, and business elites, both rural and urban, who were enriched by the new commercial opportunities opened up by the reforms. Bureaucrats relied on their connections with capital to advance their personal interests and political careers, both of which were heavily reliant on boosting GDP and employment. As interests of the political and economic elite intertwined, it became increasingly common for rural businessmen to be elected as village leaders.[45]

In the mid-2000s, the Hu-Wen leadership rolled out new policy initiatives aimed at redressing the rural/urban gap by easing peasants' tax burdens, improving basic social security provisions for rural residents, and building rural infrastructure. Yet, these policies were less effective in reconciling conflicts between community interests and rural elites' drive for personal enrichment. The mounting inequalities within Chinese villages deepened rural differentiation and "elite capture," or the interception and appropriation of state subsidies and preferential policies by the local bureaucrat-entrepreneur nexus.[46]

This was the context for the e-commerce expansion into rural China. The digitalization of labor and other industries created new sites for economic growth and new opportunities for (self-)employment. However, despite the new economy's rhetoric of grassroots empowerment and the rejuvenation of the countryside, the entrepreneurial reinvention of W did not reconcile existing tensions between the individual and the collective, nor did it narrow the chasm between rural elites and ordinary peasant families. Instead, the industry further disarticulated the village's social structure, minting new elites while leaving most residents dependent on monopolistic digital platforms. New e-commerce elites soon formed alliances with existing village elites to curry favor with officials and platforms, deepening inequalities.

The village's two e-commerce associations show the limits of techno-entrepreneurialism in redressing structural inequalities and strengthening rural communities. The first cooperative, the "B County E-commerce Industry Association" was initiated by An, secretary of W Village's Communist Youth League, and Boss Lang, manager of a local supermarket chain. An army veteran turned handicraft business owner, An is a typical village-level bureaucrat-entrepreneur in his mid-forties. Occupying the "third sphere" between state and market, he serves as a bridge between the county government, local business elites, and the village community.[47] Although An's handicraft wholesale business stagnated after the rise of e-commerce, his role as secretary of the village's CYL chapter allowed him to liaise between village e-commerce entrepreneurs and the outside world, including government officials, media representatives, and e-commerce associations. After W became a nationally known e-commerce village, An spent more time on his political and publicist roles, while his family business verged on bankruptcy. He hoped that becoming secretary of a village e-commerce industry association would help him monetize his political work and legitimize his role as an e-commerce bureaucrat-entrepreneur.

Boss Lang likewise wore two hats. In addition to managing a local supermarket chain, he served on the Standing Committee of B County's People's Political Consultative Conference. Anxious about the threat to his supermarket business posed by e-commerce, Boss Lang attempted to secure a slice of the e-commerce cake for himself. In 2014, he launched an e-commerce company that offered "entrepreneurship services," including start-up training and lessons in operating and marketing e-commerce shops, to small businesses in B County.

Boss Lang and An had gone to high school together, but a shared ambition to expand their influence over the local e-commerce industry formed the basis of their partnership. An's ties to W Village e-commerce entrepreneurs and the constellation of media, corporations, scholars, and politicians orbiting the village, combined with Lang's financial capital and connections to local bureaucrats, convinced the friends that they could launch a successful e-commerce association for the entire county. In June 2015, with 30,000 yuan in start-up capital from Boss Lang, the two men launched the "B County E-commerce Industry Association." They spent six months obtaining official permissions and informal endorsements from several county-level government departments. Those departments—the Bureau of Small and Medium Enterprises (*zhongxiao qiye ju*, 中小企业局), the Bureau of Commerce (*shangwu ju*, 商务局), and the Propaganda Department *(xuanchuan bu,* 宣传部)—had all been vying with each other for administrative control over this lucrative new industry. Boss Lang, as head of the association, and An, as general secretary, leveraged their political connections to collect the necessary official stamps.

In December 2015, An told me that the association had more than a hundred members. The W entrepreneurs that I talked to, however, expressed skepticism as to whether the association could bring real positive change to the industry. One entrepreneur said he had joined the association "just to see what's going on," since he "doesn't have to pay anything." Another said she joined the association's social media chat group after receiving an invitation from an organizer, but she had only participated in one event. "I felt like I was just a stage prop in a show put on for the officials in attendance," she told me. "Most of the time was spent listening to a county cadre talk about how the government would better 'serve' us. You know what? The best service they could give us would be to leave us alone!"

Another villager felt disappointed after initial interactions with the association's organizers and soon quit its chat group. As one of the most successful sellers in W, this person had been approached by a platform administrator from Alibaba who offered to organize an online sales event (*cuxiao huodong*, 促销活动) featuring W handicraft products. Alibaba regularly hosts such events to promote popular products on its platforms and to stimulate consumer demand. Although shop owners often have to lower their profit margins to participate in these events, increased consumer traffic can be a boon to the long-term development of small sellers on Alibaba's overcompetitive platform. Sensing that this offer would be a great opportunity to collectively raise the profile of W Village handicrafts on Taobao, the entrepreneur reached out to the association for support, hoping it could negotiate a better deal with Alibaba on behalf of village sellers. To his surprise, the association organizers turned down the offer. "That's when I realized that they don't really care about the collective interest of fellow e-commerce entrepreneurs in the village, let alone representing us in negotiations with Alibaba," he told me. "From then on, I decided that I wouldn't have anything to do with this association."

Instead of facilitating the self-organization of village e-commerce entrepreneurs to canvass for policy and financial support from the government, or to negotiate with e-commerce platforms on behalf of the village, the association primarily focused on organizing events in response to state policy initiatives and obtaining subsidies. Responding to the central state's call for "mass entrepreneurship and innovation," the association set up e-commerce training workshops for beginners interested in joining the already oversaturated industry. In August 2015, the association signed a contract with a local vocational college to establish an "entrepreneur incubation base" (*chuangye fuhua jidi*, 创业孵化基地). As part of the state's rural poverty-alleviation project, An and a couple village handicraft makers took trips to economically less developed villages in western and northeastern China to teach weaving skills and share W's experiences as a model digital entrepreneurship village, which served the state's developmental and redistributive projects in rural China. In return, the B County E-commerce Industry Association became recipient of state subsidy in 2019.

The other e-commerce association in W Village, the "Bulrush and Wicker Handicraft Industry Association," was founded in October 2015 by four e-commerce entrepreneurs and a local real estate developer. The five founders pooled roughly 100,000 yuan in cash and electronic equipment to use as start-up capital. One of its cofounders was Xiao. In a 2015 interview, he tried to distinguish the new association from the one founded by An and Boss Lang, telling me that he and his cofounders intended it to be an association established by village entrepreneurs for village entrepreneurs. Their main goal was to represent the village in negotiations with both e-commerce platforms and government agencies. Hua, another cofounder, hoped that the association would better coordinate handicraft production process in the village to finally overcome the problems of shanzhai, price wars, and other forms of vicious competition. Hua's once-successful handicraft export subcontracting business had been hard-hit by shrinking demand and competition from rising e-commerce firms. She had experienced firsthand the negative impacts of e-commerce on the traditional handicraft industry in Hubin and hoped that the association could help preserve traditional practices while improving the income of female weavers.

All this was easier said than done. In follow-up interviews with three of the cofounders in 2017, I found that the association was struggling to stay afloat after its initial funding had run out. To keep going, the founders began to seek government subsidies, like the B County E-commerce Association, and also got involved in training new e-commerce entrepreneurs. To curry favor with the county government and help local officials burnish their political resumes, they collaborated with the B County Association for the Handicapped to run an e-commerce internship program for disabled county residents, which lasted until the funding ran out. Disagreements broke out among the cofounders regarding the distribution of funds and equipment. One cofounder was not reimbursed after paying out of pocket for a business trip. Another "volunteered" the third floor of his new family home to serve as the association's photo studio in a bid to use the association's start-up funds to spruce up his personal property.

As infighting broke out, the real estate developer decided to exit the association. His initial investment had been an attempt to win a contract from the provincial government to build "Taobao City"—a "Handicraft Culture Innovation Park" that would double as a way to improve the area's e-commerce infrastructure (figures 5.6 and 5.7). He had hoped that being a founding member of an e-commerce association would improve

FIGURE 5.6 The newly constructed "Taobao City" in W Village. Photo by author.

FIGURE 5.7 Display board inside the "Taobao City" stadium showcasing the local CCP chapter's promotion campaign for e-commerce. Photo by author.

his chances of winning the contract and recruiting tenants from the associations' ranks. After he lost the bid to another developer—one rumored to have closer connections with local officials—he decided the association was no longer a worthwhile investment. Unable to secure regular government subsidies, the Bulrush and Wicker Handicraft Association faded away. When I talked to its founders in the summer of 2019, they were trying to transfer control to the county government to avoid paying the 2020 association fee.

Rural family-based digital entrepreneurialism emerged as an appealing solution to structural rural problems. Platform-based family production, according to proponents of rural e-commerce, would lower the threshold for starting a business and directly connect small handicraft producers to national markets. This model of digital entrepreneurial labor was eulogized as a market-driven, "bottom-up" way of organizing family-based small peasant production—more effective and democratic than existing "top-down" models led by local governmental institutions or so-called dragon head companies.

However, the actual existing labor of entrepreneurial reinvention in W Village problematizes the techno-entrepreneurial optimism surrounding platform-based "bottom-up" capitalism. The fact that state subsidies meant to support rural e-commerce development were easily captured by B County's local business and political elites reflects the larger national problem of elite capture in the countryside.[48] Channeling government investment and local collective land resources into building a "Taobao City"—widely perceived by villagers as a political "face project" serving the interests of local cadres and real estate developers—exacerbated issues like rural land seizure and local governments' overreliance on debt-financed real estate development to drive GDP growth.[49]

The failure of the two local e-commerce associations to effectively organize family-based e-commerce production and address entrepreneurs' problems suggest that platform technologies and digital entrepreneurship, on their own, cannot overcome rural China's structural inequalities as long as collective and public interests remain subordinate to the powerful alliance of political and economic elites.[50] If anything, monopolistic firms like Alibaba, while perhaps empowering and enriching some entrepreneurs in the early days of its expansion, have perpetuated elite capture and differentiation in Chinese villages as they consolidate their market monopoly.[51]

Like the other stories told in this chapter about innovation, branding, and gendered weaving labor, the challenges that W Village's e-commerce entrepreneurs encountered in self-organizing speak to the paradoxes inherent in the labor of entrepreneurial reinvention. Instead of an elegant solution to the structural contradictions in China's countryside, digital entrepreneurialism's reinvention of existing regimes of production and valuation has intensified tensions between the individual and collective, innovation and copying, and manual and mental labor immanent in digital capitalism and in the new entrepreneurial labor regime. This is particularly true in rural areas, where the recent disruption of China's strong collectivist tradition has been poignantly felt, where the distinction between innovation and copying is contested, and where manual and mental labor uneasily coexist in close proximity. While the digital economy has minted new winners, it has also brought together a confluence of new and preexisting systems of differentiation and inequalities. The varied experiences of W villagers in the new economy remind us of the culturally specific ways in which transformations in labor regimes are experienced by differently positioned subjects.

PART THREE

Transnational Encounters

CHAPTER SIX

Between Individualization and Retraditionalization

Reinventing Self and Work Through Platform-Based Daigou

When I met her, Vicky was a twenty-four-year-old Chinese student study-ing design and planning in Italy. Like many young middle-class women, she loved fashion and shopping. Unlike most of her peers, however, she regularly shopped at Italy's high-end luxury boutiques. Twice a week, Vicky took a train to the nearby malls. There she browsed the shops of brands popular with Chinese consumers, snapped selfies wearing the newest items, and chatted up sales associates with whom she'd made friends. Around lunch, she posted the pictures to her social media accounts, grabbed a bite to eat, checked her phone, and returned to the boutiques to purchase the items her customers had picked out. After a typical shopping trip, she might return home with a carry-on suitcase full of Prada handbags, Tiffany necklaces, and La Mer skincare products for her Chinese clients.

In China, entrepreneurs engaged in Vicky's line of work are known as daigou (代购). Generally young women who live abroad or travel regularly, they earn money reselling Western luxury goods and brands to middle-class Chinese consumers through social media and e-commerce platforms.[1] The daigou market first emerged in the mid-2000s in response to middle-class consumers' growing brand awareness and spending power, a concurrent increase in Chinese transnational mobility, and significant price disparities between luxury goods sold in China and abroad. Chinese consumers accounted for one-third of global luxury sales in 2016; just one-fifth of those sales took place in China.[2] The daigou industry took off in the aftermath of the 2008 global financial crisis as the country's quick economic rebound helped transform China into the world's largest luxury market.[3] A search of two of the most popular platforms for resellers, Sina Weibo and Taobao, returned more than 33,000 shops specializing in reselling foreign luxury goods and almost 20 million items for sale. According to Bloomberg News, at the industry's peak in 2014, four out of every ten luxury goods purchased by Chinese consumers were bought through daigou. In 2016, Bain & Company estimated the daigou industry to be worth 43 billion yuan annually.[4]

This massive informal sector represents a significant drain on government tax revenues. In an effort to bring the daigou trade under control, the state has tightened customs inspections, cut taxes on imported luxury products, and even prosecuted a few resellers.[5] Established businesses have also reacted to daigou's popularity. In addition to new import-oriented offerings from e-commerce platforms like Tmall, JD .com and Amazon China, decentralized social-commerce platforms like Xiaohongshu and Ymatou have sought to formalize the industry and incorporate its microentrepreneurs into their ecosystems to capitalize on the lucrative and growing sector of "cross-border e-commerce" (*kuajing dianshang*, 跨境电商).[6] According to a report issued by the China e-Business Research Center in 2018, e-commerce platforms sold 26.7 percent more imported goods than the previous year for a total of 1.9 trillion yuan.[7]

The feminized, transnational, middle-class nature of daigou entrepreneurial labor offers a perspective on China's post-2008 transformations distinct from those of ZGC IT entrepreneurs and peasant e-commerce sellers. Unlike those sites of entrepreneurial reinvention—both of which, as we have seen, enjoy strong state support—platform-based daigou have operated in a legal gray area from the very beginning. The practice runs counter to the state's protectionist trade policies and economic and political imperatives to encourage consumption of domestic brands. Global luxury brands also have a love-hate relationship with daigou agents. Some have sought to crack down on daigou resellers, while others have used daigou to expand their reach into the Chinese market.

Straddling the public and private, personal and commercial, individual and collective, these women's productive labor is inextricable from their reproductive labor at home or the emotional labor involved in self-branding and building communities and client networks. They're not just selling Western luxury goods, but also a gendered "self" constructed through their entrepreneurial practices in a process intimately related to China's collective refashioning after 2008.[8] "The question of what women should do and be was a constant topic of public debate during China's transformation," feminist historian Gail Hershatter has argued.[9] In this third and last case study in this book, I examine the gendered dreams, yearnings, and aspirations of a constantly debated group of women navigating China's entrepreneurial reinvention. I want to question how their transnational experiences reflect China's changing position in the international division of labor and the contentious post-2008 global capitalist transformation.

Globally, women's work experiences under capitalism are rife with paradoxes. Entrenched divides between home and workplace, private and public spheres, and reproductive and productive labor all subject women to a double burden while simultaneously devaluing women's work or rendering it invisible. More recently, the global digital economy has encouraged the feminization of labor, even as it imposes new demands on women workers: namely, that they be versatile, flexible, mobile, and affectively invested in their work.[10] Scholars who study the intersection of gender and digital and cultural labor have grappled with the implications of these transformations for feminist politics, asking whether and how digital platforms have empowered women, or if they merely perpetuate the contradictions women experience under capitalism.

The valorization of "feminine" skills such as communication, affective and emotional labor, aesthetic judgment, and the ability to sustain networks and social relations, together with the blurring boundaries between labor and consumption, work and life, and production and reproduction, have generated unprecedented opportunities for women to experiment with new career tracks and lifestyles as they reinvent the dominant scripts of femininity. The liberating potential of the new paradigm has been tempered, however, by the normalization of precarity and flexibility and the celebration of a form of consumer citizenship articulated to postfeminist retraditionalization and the retrenchment of feminist politics.[11]

The contradictory experiences of women in the new economy epitomize the contradictions of entrepreneurial labor explored throughout this book, and feminist scholars have brought unique insights to the debate over digital labor and entrepreneurialism. Many have identified, in women's digital labor and entrepreneurship, the coexistence of pleasure and exploitation—including self-exploitation. They highlight women's historical labor experiences under capitalism and the new economy's feminization and digitalization of labor as potential sites for transformative politics, albeit in ways that are immanent to capitalism.[12]

The entrepreneurial experiences of transnationally mobile Chinese middle-class women examined in this chapter complicate these arguments. As I have argued, the persistent, evolving significance of Confucian family tradition in China, the nation's historical experience of socialism, and its changing, post-Mao regime of state governance have shaped the lived experiences of all contemporary Chinese. Sitting at the intersection of class and gender, the entrepreneurial labor and life experiences of women daigou entrepreneurs are both constrained and enabled by what media scholars Bingchun Meng and Yanning Huang call "patriarchal capitalism with Chinese characteristics": a combination of consumer capitalism, patriarchal ideology, and state-led nationalism and developmentalism.[13]

In this context, the entrepreneurial labor of daigou emerged as a gendered response to the crisis of China's mixed economy, what Nancy Fraser described as the crisis of care (childbirth and rearing, caring for friends and family members, maintaining households and communities).[14] Far from being an expression of radical redistributive feminist politics, the daigou industry is reinventing traditional familism and working within the confines of state-championed patriarchal capitalism to energize women's participation in digital and transnational entrepreneurialism.

The rise of daigou showcases the transformative potential and inherent limitations of China's entrepreneurialized response to the crisis in its mixed economy from the perspective of middle-class Chinese women. I wanted to know how the logic of transnational digital capital is reinventing traditional gender norms and state governance, thereby shaping emergent feminine entrepreneurial subjectivities and labor practices. This process appears in the gendered strategies, resources, and networks women have deployed since the late 2000s to navigate between competing gender regimes and participate in the national and global project of entrepreneurial reinvention. Their experiences say much about entrepreneurialism's opportunities and limits.

Situating the labor experiences of female daigou entrepreneurs in the history of women's work in China shows how platform-based reselling emerged after 2008 as a solution to conflicts between individualization and retraditionalization. The women resellers I interview tell this story as they describe their motivations for engaging in entrepreneurship, the emotional labor involved in online self-branding and customer service, and the risks, stigmas, and precarity inherent in entrepreneurial labor.

Problematizing boundaries between work and consumption, public and personal, virtual and physical, many transnationally mobile middle-class Chinese women have turned to digital entrepreneurship to reconcile the competing demands of different gender regimes in post-2008 China. Like the experiences of the ZGC and W Village entrepreneurs, this gendered response to tensions inherent in China's post-Mao transformation has allowed some women more choice, autonomy, flexibility, and mobility. Through the strategic performance of gender identities and utilization of feminine networks, female daigou entrepreneurs have reinvented and redefined what constitutes work in the new economy. However, as a tactical individual solution to these structural problems, their entrepreneurial reinvention is limited by the biopolitical power of digital capitalism and developmentalism in the patriarchal Chinese state. Like women workers in e-commerce villages, the transnational daigou community is characterized by gendered labor at the confluence of consumerism and entrepreneurialism, and under persisting patriarchal power.

STATE, FAMILY, AND WOMEN'S WORK IN CHINA

This historically informed perspective on women's work in China serves as a backdrop for examining the labor of women daigou entrepreneurs and the subjectivities their labor produces. The articulation of evolving structural forces—the changing faces of Confucian patriarchy, state socialism and nationalism, and capitalist development—provides space for women to construct feminine identities via labor and consumption, even as it constrains those identities.

Before the early twentieth century, Chinese women existed within a Confucian moral universe.[15] Confucian women were defined by their allegiance to father, husband, and son, and ideal womanhood was associated with chastity, loyalty, moral uprightness, and self-sacrifice.[16] Like the Victorian "cult of domesticity" and the Western separation of domestic and public spheres, the home was considered to be women's "proper place" in traditional Chinese society, while men monopolized the public sphere.[17] However, underneath Confucian norms, boundaries demarcating public and private spheres were negotiable. Women's lived experiences were diverse and dependent on era, age, class, and geographic region.[18] The diversity and fluidity of women's experiences under Confucianism have important implications for our analysis of contemporary women daigou entrepreneurs.[19]

The modern Chinese feminist movement emerged with the simultaneous demise of imperial power and the rise of China's modern nation-state. Influenced by the era of its birth, it was defined by a confluence of women's issues and national questions—chiefly, how to secure China's sovereignty.[20] Often championed by male modernists, the initial introduction of modern feminist ideas into the Republic of China had dual effects on Chinese women.[21] The modernist promotion of feminism—albeit to rescue the Chinese race and strengthen the Chinese nation-state—freed women, to some extent, from their domestic confines. As full-fledged citizens, women gained access to the public sphere through education and participation in capitalist production.[22]

However, interpretations of modern science, especially Darwin's evolutionary paradigm and Smith's dichotomy between "productive labor" and "unproductive labor," perpetuated female inferiority by scapegoating women as the cause of China's subordination.[23] By emphasizing women's domestic role as agents of reproduction without critiquing the gendered division of labor, women were objectified and codified as national symbols: "Republican mothers" or "good wives and wise mothers" only indirectly linked to national and public spheres.[24]

The Chinese socialist revolution and its Communist regime, founded in 1949, were partially legitimized by promises to liberate women from patriarchal domination.[25] Yet, as in the Republican period, the socialist state's project of women's liberation was soon subsumed under broader objectives of class leveling and industrialization.[26] In most respects, the socialist state liberated women from Confucian patriarchal bonds and the confines of family and empowered them to participate in the public sphere as citizens with equal rights. At that time, women's subjectivities were mainly defined by what their labor contributed to state-led socialist, revolutionary and modernizing causes—not by consumption.[27]

Because it did not acknowledge gender differences, the socialist feminist project could not challenge the gendered division of labor. In the private sphere, women were still responsible for the bulk of housework. Like their sisters in Western capitalist economies, they were burdened by a second shift of domestic and reproductive labor.[28] Blurred distinctions between the public sphere (state-governed collective society) and private sphere (individual small households embedded within the collective) in socialist China partially eased women's domestic burdens via programs like collective childcare, public canteens, and state-led distribution of daily necessities.[29] Yet, labor responsibilities continued to be defined by gendered divisions of labor. Women were still assigned to service roles and auxiliary work and were expected to prioritize their husbands' career development.[30] Despite leveling class differences and reducing relative poverty, gender inequalities persisted in socialist China, and intersected in various ways with the country's rural-urban, ethnic, generational, and geographical disparities (figure 6.1).[31]

Following the advent of reform and opening-up in the late 1970s, the Chinese government shifted away from its socialist commitment to egalitarianism and its efforts to empower women. China's abandonment of class politics paralleled the rise of capitalism in emphasizing essentialized gender differences suppressed by Maoist feminism. This new emphasis not only fueled consumerism, but it also encouraged women to attend to traditional gender roles within the family as caregivers and agents of reproduction at the expense of their productive labor responsibilities.[32] Some women saw China's new feminized labor and consumption choices as liberating after decades of state-enforced asceticism and erased sexuality. They sought out and constructed new feminized subjectivities and individualized cultural expressions.[33] On the other hand, feminist empowerment was tempered by growing inequality, generational gaps, and the

FIGURE 6.1 Poster depicting ideal femininity during the Maoist era that reads "Time Is Different, Women and Men Are Equal." Source: ICity, https://art.icity.ly/events/ui9ngsg.

rural-urban divide and compromised by revitalized patriarchal norms, which the market-state nexus used to justify rising gender disparities and discrimination in privatized workplaces.

Though China continued to have one of the highest female employment rates in the world, female labor participation dropped significantly in the post-Mao years.[34] The state urged women to "return home" (*huijia*, 回家) and sacrifice their careers and economic freedom to ease China's childcare crisis and the state's unemployment burden.[35] In the backlash against socialist politics in the 1980s, proponents of liberal market principles criticized women's high employment under socialism as one of the many ills of Maoist egalitarianism. Dismantling the socialist work unit privatized the infrastructure of the collectives: this included the kindergartens, canteens, and public bathing houses that made women's high rate of economic participation possible. These transformations have contributed to retraditionalizing gender roles in post-Mao China as the family has once again become the basic economic unit of society and housewifery a preferred economic strategy for households.[36]

Following Deng's 1992 Southern Tour, state embrace of export-oriented, labor-intensive manufacturing and expanded urban consumer markets further facilitated the resurgence of gendered labor divisions and intra-gender class differentiation. Marketization and state promoted consumerism spawned a booming consumer sector targeting middle-class women, including high-end shopping malls, beauty salons, and cosmetic surgery clinics (figure 6.2).[37] These trends paralleled the rise of feminized labor across the economic spectrum. Feminized labor subjects ranged from middle-class "white-collar beauties" (*bailing liren*, 白领丽人) to

FIGURE 6.2 Photos from popular calendar books of the 1980s showing the ideal female images of the era. Source: BJ News, http://www.bjnews.com.cn/feature/2019/12/30/668258.html.

"working sisters" (*dagong mei*, 打工妹) and pink-collar service workers, whose class position is more ambiguous.

Given the systemic discrimination women faced in the workplace, entrepreneurship became popular among women wanting to achieve social mobility and greater economic autonomy. This partially explains the dramatic increase in the number of women entrepreneurs in China since the early 2000s.[38] Yet, closer examination of the statistical profiles and experiences of Chinese women entrepreneurs during that period reveals that this quantitative increase in female entrepreneurship did not translate into qualitative improvements in gender equality. A 2004 study found that, although 16 percent of Chinese women engaged in entrepreneurship, only a quarter of them embraced it as an opportunity, as opposed to being driven to it by lack of alternatives.[39]

These findings are echoed in my own research into the history of IT entrepreneurship in ZGC. There were few women among the first generation of red scientists and engineers turned IT entrepreneurs in the 1980s and early 1990s. Although more women took part in the dot-com boom in ZGC,[40] including well-known figures like InfoHighWay founder Jasmine Zhang (Zhang Shuxin, 张树新), few women entrepreneurs were as successful, visible, and politically connected as their male counterparts.[41] The vast majority of women entrepreneurs in China engaged in necessity-based entrepreneurship driven by the inability to meet basic economic needs through other means.[42] These statistics are consistent with studies showing that women are overrepresented in China's informal economy. Thus, women's work and entrepreneurship highlight the ambivalent politics and heterogeneity of female entrepreneurship in post-Mao China. The rise of female daigou entrepreneurs in the post-2008 period represents both a continuation of, and a break from earlier forms of women's labor and entrepreneurship.

THE REINVENTION OF THE FEMALE DAIGOU ENTREPRENEUR

The Younger Generation's Dilemma

Over the past decade or so, transnationally mobile, social media-based female resellers have come to exemplify a new generation of middle-class women who carve out entrepreneurial spaces for themselves amid trends toward market-driven individualization and retraditionalization. The younger generation's experiences differ from their foremothers in an added emphasis on women's agency in constructing their own lives and identities in the context of the state-market promotion of consumption, entrepreneurship, and traditional gender roles. The discourse of markets and technology-enabled empowerment has rendered intra-gender class disparities increasingly invisible, but it does little to address women's lack of access to supposedly universal consumerist and entrepreneurial opportunities. Taken together, these themes present gender-specific manifestations of the larger contradictions in China's post-2008 entrepreneurial reinvention.

The overwhelming majority of women engaged in online luxury reselling are college-educated, transnationally mobile middle- or upper-middle-class young women in their twenties and thirties. Members of the urban post-'80s (*balinghou*, 八零后), post-'90s (*jiulinghou*, 九零后), and now post-2000s (*linglinghou*, 零零后) generations, they were all born after the advent of reform and opening-up in the late 1970s. They benefit from opportunities created by the post-Mao one-child policy and China's rapid economic expansion, which made it possible and necessary for families to send their daughters to school.[43] They also benefit from socialist state feminism, including gender-neutral educational opportunities and many other by-products of socialist egalitarianism.

Yet, few identify with collective-oriented, gender-neutral socialist femininity. Growing up in the 1990s or 2000s immersed them in commodities, images, and ideas from the West and other Asian countries. As they came of age, China's entry into the WTO in 2001 empowered them to become cosmopolitan, enterprising, transnationally mobile consumers attuned to trends in global pop culture. Part of what Fengshui Liu called the technology-savvy "net generation," they are accustomed to using the internet and other digital tools to access information, communicate, and spend their leisure time, and they identify more with an individualistic, interactive communication style.[44] Upon graduating from college, many of these women, like their older sisters, chose to work in white-collar jobs in major cities. Heavily subsidized by their parents, a growing number obtained Western degrees or migrated abroad as professionals or middle-class wives. Their skills, experiences, education credentials, and "can-do" attitudes made them as, or even more competitive than men in the new knowledge economy.

An important way this group constructs individuality is through consumption. Armed with purchasing power, consumer confidence, and a global outlook, young Chinese women have turned to international luxury brands as markers of cosmopolitan identity and class distinction. Well-groomed, youthful, and luxury brand-clad female bodies have become the ideal "empowered" female subjects, capable of exercising their consumer agency and financial clout to express their unique identities via commodity ownership. This gendered "consumer citizenship" has been encouraged by the post-Mao state/market nexus, which enjoins women to seek self-worth through consumption rather than political participation or citizen rights. The proliferation of transnational e-commerce and global travel has facilitated this trend.

Indeed, it is unclear how much the gains in education and consumption achieved by young, urban middle-class women have translated into political empowerment. Many women found their pursuit of personal realization and individual achievement curtailed by the bleak reality of persisting gender inequalities, growing workplace discrimination, and the revitalization of traditional patriarchal ideologies. Between 2006 and 2018, the proportion of female professional and technical workers increased by 23.5 percent, but the gender income gap only widened. Persistent barriers to managerial opportunities left women heavily concentrated at the base of the job market "pyramid."[45] Meanwhile, the growing competitiveness of Chinese businesses in global markets has been driven in part by increased worker exploitation, resulting in mounting alienation and work-related stress. Professional women who juggle roles as workers, wives, and mothers are particularly vulnerable to conflicts between successful careers and their marital and childcare duties.[46]

These conflicts have been exacerbated by the privatization of childcare and education, the growth of an urban middle-class desirous of maintaining its social status and advantages, and the state-backed human capital regime that aims to cultivate fully rounded talents competitive in the neoliberal, global capitalist market. All of these pressures have contributed to the new culture of "intensive mothering." Intensive mothering places greater demands on mothers to ensure their children do not "fall behind at the starting line."[47] Conflicts among women's multiple gender roles have been heightened by state efforts to reverse China's demographic decline by promoting two-child families since 2015, and three-child families since 2021.[48]

These transformations have renewed the importance of family in Chinese society, rekindled traditional Confucian norms of separate gendered spheres, and pushed and pulled women to "return home" and become housewives.[49] Compared to previous efforts encouraging women to return home in post-Mao China, post-2008 retraditionalization is not only endorsed by top political leaders but also embraced as an active, rational choice by urban middle-class women themselves.[50] As part of his effort to promote the CCP's new "core socialist values"—another reinvented form of Confucianism meant to secure party hegemony—President Xi Jinping gave a 2013 talk to a key body within the All-China Women's Federation in which he emphasized that "special attention should be paid to women's unique role in propagating Chinese family virtues and setting up a good family tradition."[51]

Two years earlier, Zhang Xiaomei, the director of a national women's fashion magazine and a member of the Chinese People's Political Consultative Conference, proposed "encouraging some women to return home." Zhang argued that many middle-class women were willing to reduce their double burden of "career-plus-family" by focusing on traditional tasks, such as "housework, caring for the elderly, nursing, educating children, and creating a happy and harmonious family life."[52] This was the first time in PRC history that a female political figure, not a male scholar or politician, had publicly called on other women to become housewives. A survey taken in 2009 suggests that Zhang's ideas did represent the preferences of many middle-class women: 70 percent of working women surveyed said they had "experienced a conflict between their family and career," while women willing to be full-time housewives increased from 3 percent in 2007 to 8.4 percent in 2009.[53] As sociologist Song Shaopeng observed, "when employment comes to stand not for liberation, but rather for alienation, fatigue, and burnout, family life may come to seem like the only retreat, and marriage the only way out."[54]

Ironically, this state- and market-championed retraditionalization and revival of Confucian patriarchal gender ideals is often framed through the cosmopolitan discourse of "work-life balance" as a means of expanding women's choice and freedom. Searching for "authentic" feminine identities, women have drifted away from both the socialist archetype of the androgynous "iron girl" and its capitalist counterpart, the career-minded professional woman, who came to be associated in popular imagination with selfishness and a lack of balance.[55] According to the new gender ideals, the smartest women not only "succeed in the job market" (*gande hao*, 干得好), but also "win in the marriage market" (*jiade hao*, 嫁得好).[56] This shift has led a growing number of professional women to give up their careers and become full-time housewives or to tone down their career ambitions after marriage. Becoming a "full-time wife" is no longer associated with "laziness," as it was under socialism. Increasingly, it is a privileged choice made by a well-off, middle-class woman who has "the ability and experience of working but chooses to be at home to take care of her family."[57] This valorization of domesticity is especially prevalent among immigrant housewives on dependent visas in developed countries like the United States: a category that includes many female daigou entrepreneurs.[58]

Solutions of E-commerce Entrepreneurialism

Championed by the state as a new engine driving China's post-2008 economic growth and restructuring, e-commerce quickly integrated women from various backgrounds into its regime of accumulation. Envisioning women as consumers and entrepreneurs in the "she economy" (*ta jingji*, 她经济), e-commerce promised to resolve tensions between individualizing and retraditionalizing impulses by offering women new career paths and a better work-life balance while channeling their consumer and entrepreneurial labor toward the state-capitalist project of entrepreneurial reinvention.

One glimpses the construction of this ideal female economic subject in AliResearch's 2016 "Report on Research About Women in Alibaba's Ecosystem."[59] The opening slide, titled "The Ali Ecosystem: Women Are Very Happy," shows a diagram in which female consumers and sellers alike enjoy the benefits of Alibaba's sophisticated e-commerce infrastructure. The next slide, titled "Women Are Important," reports that more than 200 million women live the "Consume, Consume, Consume!" lifestyle on Alibaba's e-commerce sites. Another slide, "Women Are Quite Capable Workers," claims that almost six million women entrepreneurs are selling in the Alibaba ecosystem. The rest of the report follows a similar vein, focusing on how Alibaba has empowered women through e-commerce consumption and entrepreneurship.

AliResearch also worked with China Women's University, a public university affiliated with the All-China Women's Federation, and the Development Research Center of the State Council to document and promote Alibaba's contributions to expanding female IT entrepreneurship in China.[60] This state/market collaboration took place as part of a larger governmental campaign to more effectively mobilize women under the "mass entrepreneurship and innovation" banner.[61] A symbolic moment in this alliance came on November 11, 2015, the day of the "Double Eleven Shopping Festival"—largely the creation of Alibaba marketers. That day, the State Council met to discuss the importance of the "new consumption," including e-commerce, to the nation's economic restructuring. Premier Li Keqiang made a personal call to Alibaba's board, congratulating the company on its "pioneering" achievements in boosting consumerism by establishing the massive shopping holiday.[62]

But media reports and official pronouncements euphorically celebrating digital and market empowerment either evade or downplay the differences in class status and social positioning of female consumers and entrepreneurs and the specificities of women's digital entrepreneurial labor. Their universalist discourses of digital consumption and entrepreneurism conceal not only the mixed effects of feminized and informal labor on women's livelihoods, but also how different the digital and entrepreneurial experiences of variously positioned women have been.

Founding an IT start-up is a very different endeavor from opening an e-commerce shop on Taobao. My ethnographic interviews with female IT entrepreneurs in ZGC showed me that China's IT start-up scene remains essentially segregated. Women entrepreneurs face more barriers in the male-dominated start-up world, and they largely concentrate in "feminized" fields like e-commerce, health, and corporate services. Coworking and entrepreneurial spaces like the Garage Café remain boys' clubs where women are underrepresented and marginalized. Lack of female representation among IT company founders and in management is well documented. According to the "30 Chinese Women Entrepreneurs 2019" report, issued by the tech research firm EqualOcean, female entrepreneurship in China was still more necessity-based (26 percent) than opportunity-based (9.3 percent). Most of the thirty female IT entrepreneurs profiled in the report specialized in health and medical services (32 percent), corporate services (29 percent), and e-commerce (23 percent).[63] As we have seen, female e-commerce entrepreneurs in rural China are even more constrained than their urban sisters by patriarchal norms, rural identities, geography, and age.

Female daigou constitute a group of transnationally mobile middle-class Chinese e-commerce entrepreneurs. Between traditional gender norms and individualization, they carve out space for self-fashioning and entrepreneurial reinvention in spite of structural constraints. They are not passive consumers of Western luxury goods, but savvy shoppers who use "feminine" consumer skills and knowledge to locate the best deals. Importantly, their technological know-how and cosmopolitan worldliness help them convert their "feminine" knowledge and gendered networks into capital for innovative businesses and self-actuating careers. Their entrepreneurial selves often manifest in their self-conscious, highly skilled, and publicized constructions of personal brands based on class and gender identities, experiences, networks, and bodies.[64] This technology-empowered form of gendered entrepreneurship seems to resolve tensions between individualization and retraditionalization, between living for oneself and living for one's family, and between labor participation and domestic work. It also links women's gendered consumerism and entrepreneurial self-reinvention to the state's nation-building project. Although these young women might still be structurally disadvantaged, their entrepreneurial practices are a coveted alternative or supplement to a white-collar career, academia, or housewifery.

The celebration of entrepreneurial labor encourages women to quit traditional nine-to-five employment and become their own boss. In theory, this helps them balance the labor demanded by their multiple gender roles. However, this entrepreneurial solution to structural problems risks making legitimate, and even desirable, the flexible and gendered segregation of labor, the atrophying of public welfare and social provisions, the retrenchment of gender inequalities, and the return of private patriarchy. Far from being equalizing, this emergent regime of value generates new forms of exclusion while privileging certain versions of "femininity" and making others less valuable, visible, or desirable. Moreover, the gendered practices of daigou walk a fine line between what the state considers legitimate and illegitimate, which renders the entrepreneurial labor of women daigou highly precarious.

TRANSNATIONAL QUESTS OF SELF-REINVENTION

There are two primary types of female daigou: those who treat reselling as a day job and those who moonlight on a part-time basis, usually to supplement formal employment or educational pursuits. The former consists mainly of housewives with young children and professionalized resellers. Only five out of the forty-two women I interviewed described themselves as professional resellers. All five said they got into reselling as "a means to an end," that is, to "make it out of China." Conversely, the majority of women I interviewed "accidentally stumbled upon" luxury reselling while living, studying, or traveling abroad. Of my forty-two interviewees, sixteen were stay-at-home housewives. The others either worked full-time or were university students. They often started out by purchasing and sending or carrying products back to China for their relatives or friends. The realization that one could actually make money and build networks by shopping came as a pleasant surprise. Later on, they began charging a service fee as they gradually expanded their circle of customers. For part-timers, reselling is more like an extension of leisure activities than a real job: they share sales information or new purchases via social media, go shopping after work or school, and follow the latest fashions in blogs and magazines.

Yet, distinctions between full-time and part-time work are often blurred. Women take on different roles as they become wives or mothers, switch tracks professionally, or move between academic and professional worlds. The main reason for the popularity and resilience of luxury reselling as a gendered occupation is its flexibility. Women can easily fit it into their various social roles and pursuits. Reselling grants women a certain degree of financial and psychological independence, supplements a not-so-satisfactory full-time job or subsidizes their education. For immigrant wives and mothers, and others unable to work a full-time day job because of their responsibilities, reselling can take on the dimensions of a career. In these cases, transnational luxury reselling helps women resolve tensions between their desire to "live for themselves" (e.g., enjoy the freedom of geographic mobility; pursue educational, professional, and consumer goals; and secure financial independence) and "living for others" (e.g., being a mother, wife, or girlfriend who prioritizes the needs of family members or romantic partners).

In 2013, Amanda quit her job as a secretary in a private Chinese company to become a full-time luxury reseller in Dubai. "I know a few Chinese women who are in the same business here," she told me. "They are very much like me, former white-collar office ladies who felt stuck in their old professions, have a good fashion sense, and want to explore the world." After two years of hard work bouncing between high-end shopping venues, social media platforms, and post offices, Amanda had built a six-person team comprising one online customer service representative in China and five buyers scattered across Europe and the United States.

Similarly, Sally left her job in 2013, a year before our interview, because of what she called a "passport epiphany": "This woman in my office who was in her early thirties always wore a smile on her face at work, unlike everyone else. She never worked overtime like us, and she just didn't seem to care as much as we did about work. I was bewildered until she told me that she holds a Canadian passport and bought a house in Vancouver a few years ago. I said to myself: 'You need to get one of these [passports].'"

Daigou is one of the few ways women can accrue the capital needed to emigrate. By 2015, Sally was operating a luxury reselling business through her Sina Weibo account while she completed her MBA in Los Angeles. "Hopefully, I will find a way to stay permanently in the United States," she said. Western developed nations signify cosmopolitanism. They represent a sought-after alternative to what many of my interviewees thought of as an overpopulated, environmentally compromised China. In the same way, luxury reselling offers a seemingly more desirable working life than the hyperexploitative Chinese workplace.[65] The emblematic superiority attached to Western citizenship, luxury commodities, and lifestyles is alluring to young middle-class Chinese women like Sally and Amanda, while the perks that come with the job—VIP memberships with luxury brands, pampered shopping experiences, and staying current on global fashion trends—only reinforce their sense of mobility and empowerment, whether real or imagined.

The feeling of empowerment associated with Western consumer culture resonates even with daigou based in China. Their frequent overseas "shopping trips" serve multiple purposes, allowing them to mix the commercial and personal, business and tourism. In 2013, Mina left her research job at a cosmetics company in northeastern China to start an e-commerce shop specializing in reselling international cosmetics. Alternating with her business partner, a full-time white-collar worker in a Beijing-based German-owned company, they made shopping expeditions every other week to duty-free shops in Seoul. Like most of my China-based interviewees, international travel was a major attraction for Mina, along with the profession's cosmopolitan cachet and the sense of mobility it afforded.

Consider also the comments made by Ellen, a full-time daigou agent just returned to Beijing from graduate school in the United States. Ellen compared her current job to the alternative put forward by her parents: "I just couldn't take that job [at a state-owned petroleum corporation]. I know it's going to be much more secure and much less stressful and risky, but it's simply too boring and stable. I can't bear doing the same tasks, in the same office, all day, every day. I like traveling, getting to know different cultures, and going shopping too much to trade my soul for security!" For Ellen, the job at the state-owned corporation meant security and boredom, whereas the life of a daigou entrepreneur was none of that.

As China unmoors itself from socialism, more and more young middle-class Chinese women have come to prefer entrepreneurial values to the tired socialist promise of an "iron rice bowl." Even for women who choose not to work in the state-owned sector, a part-time gig as a daigou can "enrich" their lives, both socially and financially. This is the case with Xiaowen, a reseller who works as a civil servant in Jinan, in northern China. When I met her in 2019, she had been working for three years with a high school classmate based in Australia to sell cosmetics and baby formula. Compared to her female friends in nongovernmental jobs, Xiaowen's workday was less stressful, and she seldom had to work overtime. But she also earned less. To make up for the excitement and money missing from her current job, Xiaowen multitasked at work and spent much of her spare time talking to customers and mailing packages. "I really enjoy this part-time job since I can earn some extra cash to buy cosmetics and clothes from abroad for myself," Xiaowen told me. "This year, I've saved enough for a trip to Europe with my husband during the Spring Festival holiday."

Ella, Mina, and Xiaowen are not alone in their longing for the exotic, cosmopolitan cultural experiences that come with overseas tourism and luxury consumption. Recently, China's fast-growing middle class has fueled a boom in transnational air travel and consumption. In 2012, China surpassed the United States as the world's leading outbound tourism market. Six years later, Chinese tourists spent twice as much overseas as tourists from the United States, the next largest global market.[66] Since the late 2010s, the Chinese government has gradually cut tariffs on imported luxury goods and set up domestic free trade zones (FTZs) in a bid to redirect overseas spending back to China. Luxury daigou were already well established by the time these policies were unveiled, however. It is hard to say how successful the measures will be in achieving their goals.

The gendered entrepreneurial labor of luxury resale aligns economic rationality and pragmatism with the romanticized cosmopolitan sensibility of overseas tourism to constitute a new kind of feminine subject in post-2008 China.[67] Gail Hershatter documented the feelings of empowerment—"the sense of adventure, excitement, and sometimes trepidation"—that Chinese women experienced during the socialist years as they "took to the rails and the roads to see Chairman Mao or emulated the CCP's Long March in treks across China."[68] As gendered memories and practices of the Maoist years faded, cultural tourism, especially transnational luxury-hunting trips laden with cosmopolitan symbolism, have replaced Mao-era hunts for political symbolism as part of young Chinese urban women's search for a "truly free self."[69] Broadly speaking, the Maoist, class-based spatial yearning to "go to the countryside"— with its associated class politics and self-transformation through farm labor and living among peasants—has been replaced by the contemporary call of "going global" by embracing global capital, entrepreneurship, and consumerism. If women's political activism and labor participation in socialist years liberated them, to a certain extent, from family constraints and parental control and expectations, women daigou entrepreneurs' engagement in transnational digital entrepreneurship reflects the current generation's continued reliance on family support amid the search for independence and autonomy.

For young unmarried women fresh out of college, becoming a daigou entrepreneur can mean freedom from their parents. A novel, informal form of employment, a career in daigou often appears illegitimate from the perspective of an older generation who spent their adult lives working in the same work unit. Middle-class parents expect their daughters to get good grades in school before entering a stable and "reputable" profession, such as teaching or working for the government or a big corporation. As one of my informants put it, her parents expected her to "get a stable job, marry well, and enjoy a 'balanced life.'" Several women shared stories of being misunderstood or facing parental disapproval when they first started their businesses. Dada, an e-commerce entrepreneur who ran a daigou business on WeChat, said, "I was so afraid of her disapproval that I didn't tell my mom about my business, not until I started to make a solid profit. She was still quite mad at me because I was making a good salary at the newspaper. [To her,] being a journalist sounds right for a girl like me." Echoing Dada's rebellion against her parent's expectations before negotiating for their approval, Mina recalled her parents' mild but sarcastic reaction to her quitting her job as a chemist to become a daigou entrepreneur:

> I remember when I first started my online shop on Taobao and sold only a couple of things in the first month, my parents teased me about giving up a well-paid job to become "unemployed." One day they saw this female contestant on [the popular Chinese dating show] *If You Are the One*. She was an e-commerce shop owner and quite a character. Being more outspoken and bolder than the other female participants, she was teased by the anchor and her potential dates all the time for being out of place. My parents made a big joke out of it and kept referring to me as her throughout the whole season.

Daigou is a particularly desirable and legitimate "job" for women with small children, be they young immigrant housewives or new moms based in China. Their entrepreneurship, if pursued moderately, helps them navigate tensions between career and family, and between financial independence and the domestic responsibilities of child-rearing and household chores. As an important source of supplementary family income, daigou labor produces a much-needed sense of achievement as well as a feeling of autonomy from housework, unemployment, or underemployment. In the words of Xiaomei, a full-time mom whose husband works as a scientist at a lab in Chicago: "I just want to show my baby boy that his mom is working hard, not just for the family, but also to keep a dynamic life and stay pretty for herself. I don't want him to think that I am sacrificing myself for him." Xiaomei told me that she usually did her grocery shopping during her weekly shopping trips to luxury outlets and interacted with her customers on her smartphone while cooking or walking the family dog.

Ran, a woman in her mid-thirties who immigrated to Poland with her husband and young son two years before our 2014 interview, also said she juggled housework and her duties as a luxury daigou. As her business expanded, her retired factory-worker mother and younger sister joined her team. Ran's mother helped her transfer the bulk products that she sent from Europe to her clients in China, while her sister, an accountant, assisted with bookkeeping and customer service. This transnational familial division of labor, in which female family members work together to build up family businesses, was typical of the transnational daigou enterprises I encountered.

Like most other immigrant wives I interviewed for the study, both Xiaomei and Ran were working professionals in China before their migration. Xiaomei was a sales associate at a car dealership in her home city of Chongqing, and Ran was a successful banker in Hangzhou. Both had to give up their careers after emigrating due to restrictive visa policies, lack of affordable childcare in their destination countries, and personal choices to focus on childrearing and domestic work. This strategy of "refeminization" is typical of immigrant Chinese wives living in Western developed countries as they "take on more conservative roles in the domain of reproduction for motherhood and homemaking after migration."[70] According to Yalan Huang, immigrant wives adopt refeminization partially "as resistance to hegemonic Chinese gender norms that devalue domesticity."[71] This stance was echoed by Ran, who said she identified more with the family-oriented lifestyle of the middle-class women she met in Poland, which propelled her to reject her previous "workaholic self" in China. "I worked my ass off so that I could better provide for my children, but I neglected their real need: parental companionship," Ran told me.

Similar trends toward refeminization and reinventing the family-based gendered division of labor in service of digital entrepreneurship are also present among women entrepreneurs based in China. Factors like the decline of public support for domestic work and child-rearing, gender discrimination in the workplace, and the revitalization of patriarchal norms all played a role in this trend. The story of Wanwan is typical of many China-based full-time moms that I met. A young woman in her early thirties, Wanwan commuted frequently between China and South Korea, where her Korea-educated husband worked at an overseas branch of a Chinese firm. When I first met her in 2015, she was living with her parents in Jinan and working three days a week. To supplement her income and take better advantage of her commute at least once a month between Seoul and China, she began selling Korean beauty products using her private WeChat account. Like Ran's family, Wanwan's mother, a retired middle-school teacher, contributed to the business by helping her daughter package and mail items to customers. The last time I met Wanwan, in 2019, she had quit her day job to take care of her first child and was devoting more time and energy to her daigou business. Wanwan told me that she was part of a WeChat group made up of other female daigou entrepreneurs in Jinan who were also young mothers with small children. This group reached WeChat's maximum capacity of five hundred members the day it was set up.

Over the past decade, young mothers in China are increasingly becoming full-time housewives. According to a 2019 survey of childrearing practices in China, 58.6 percent of surveyed mothers with children less than a year old said they were full-time moms. This ratio was significantly higher among younger women born after 1995 (82 percent).[72] The normalization and expansion of flexible entrepreneurial self-employment practices like daigou have contributed to and been reinforced by the popularity of full-time motherhood. Platform-based entrepreneurship merges the private with public, and the domestic with commercial, thereby helping reconcile the contradictions between women's traditional gender roles and their individual pursuit of business success as they craft their feminine selves. For this reason, the appeal of gendered entrepreneurial labor should be understood in the context of the broad euphoria surrounding the national project of technology-enabled collective reinvention.

Yet, simply equating women's luxury daigou with leisure or feminist empowerment risks romanticizing this form of gendered entrepreneurial labor. As we saw with ZGC-based and rural e-commerce entrepreneurs, women's sense of empowerment is often compromised and always constrained. The situation is also complicated by the emotional labor these women assume in managing their business personae and maintaining their online networks, as well as in the larger structural and gendered challenges they face in their everyday lives.

THE EMOTIONAL LABOR OF TRANSNATIONAL SELF-BRANDING AND ONLINE SERVICE WORK

In the competitive market of service-oriented social media sales, gendered affective relationships between sellers and customers can be key to business success. The social media–based marketplace of daigou is also a transnational space where cultural identities are formed, cultural values clash, and human interactions take place. "What is produced and reproduced" in and through these new entrepreneurial labor practices, are not merely products and transactions but also the "material embodiment" of gendered roles and identities.[73] This mutual constituency of culture and commodity and the shifting of "cultural labor into capitalist business practices" are defining features of the internet-based entrepreneurial labor regime.[74] The breaking down of boundaries between public and private, work and leisure, consumption and production, and global and local, challenges the "long held dichotomy between instrumental and affective action" rooted in "Western European cosmology."[75]

While women's experiences of capitalism have long been characterized by hybridity, the fact that gendered practices and subjectivities have become directly monetizable and are increasingly crucial to capitalist production distinguishes the present moment from the past.[76] The valorization of women's hybrid labor practices and subjectivities also generates contradictions, however, and women entrepreneurs must reconcile the multiple tensions they experience on a daily basis. My informants strategically engaged in new media practices like online branding and livestreaming as both "authentic" expressions of their cosmopolitan feminine selves and as a less intrusive means of product promotion. Platform-based networks and interactions facilitate transnational communication and solidify emotional ties and cross-cultural solidarities, but in excess, they also become emotional and physical burdens.

In particular, fashioning an "authentic" self-brand—one that successfully annexes an individual's unique personality and life experiences to commercial products through visual and discursive narratives—is necessary for attracting customers, enhancing "stickiness" and customer retention, and increasing profit margins.[77] Given the fierce competition in this sector, women must be skilled at communicating their personal and affective appropriation of and engagement with Western luxury brands. In turn, the brands and their cultural meanings become resources women use to articulate "authentic" gendered identities, which are, in fact, heavily coded with class markers, patriarchal feminine codes, and cosmopolitan distinctions. Successful female daigou creatively highlight a product's aura of authenticity while conveying personalized messages to their target customers. One glimpses this creativity in the names these women give to their online businesses and in the multiple ways they describe their personal brands:

> *My European Home (欧洲的家)*: I came up with this name to make customers feel at home doing business with me. . . . Of course, adding "European" gives me cachet—everyone knows that Europe is high-end luxury heaven.
>
> *Global Spendthrift (全球败家娘)*: My shop's name contains an element of self-mockery. But it's who I am: I like shopping, especially global brands. I believe that most of my customers do as well. Oh, I know the word "global" makes me sound too ambitious. (Laughter)
>
> *Kevin's Mom @ USA(凯文妈妈 @ 美国)*: Kevin is my two-year-old's name. I named my shop after him partly because I set up this business to give him a better life. I realized after a while that my customers trust me more because of my identity as a mother. Many of them are young mothers, too, so in a way we are not just doing business but are helping each other out to make life better.

In addition to strategically naming and presenting their businesses, many of the women I followed engaged in social media "lifecasting."[78] They juxtapose selfies taken inside fitting rooms with photos of their children, family pets, houses, meals, or daily activities. Products are curated by entrepreneurs based on personal engagement with an item or as part of a "customer show" (*maijia xiu,* 买家秀) that presents client-generated visual and discursive testimonies of the products and services provided. Quite a few of the resellers I interviewed had been customers of daigou before following in the footsteps of their trusted agents and starting their own businesses.

Here, the gendered authenticity of women's personal brands as transnationally mobile middle-class housewives, mothers of young children, and luxury aficionados becomes entangled with the commercial authenticity of the global luxury brands they market. This reflects and shapes a distinct structure of feeling for contemporary middle-class Chinese. Many consumers prefer to purchase Western luxury goods from daigou rather than from domestic boutiques, not only owing to lower prices but also because they have greater faith in the authenticity of products purchased from abroad and appreciate the extra emotional labor that daigou entrepreneurs invest into "authenticating" their consumers' experiences.[79] The Chinese middle-class obsession with branded "authenticity" both encourages and is motivated by the abundance of "fake" branded products in China. This is made all the more ironic by the fact that many of the luxury products highly sought after in China are manufactured cheaply by ethnic Chinese workers either inside or outside of the country. The obsession with Western luxury brands reveals not only an internalized inferiority complex, which endows Western luxury products with the "aura" of authenticity and associates China-made products with inferior quality or deception, but also the anxiety and eagerness of the rapidly expanding middle class and nouveau riche to distinguish themselves through conspicuous consumption.[80] In reifying branded "authenticity," women entrepreneurs' labor of reinvention perpetuates these structural inequalities and social anxieties (figure 6.3).

Intimately familiar with their customers' material and psychological needs, some of my informants livestream their shopping trips, taking orders via their smartphones. In their view, this is smart promotional strategy that authenticates their products and offers their clients vicarious pleasure. These bits and pieces constitute a coherent, gendered self-brand related to women's various social roles as businesswomen, mothers, daughters, wives, girlfriends, or students. However, these feminine images are never value-free, but always encoded with middle- or upper-class

FIGURE 6.3 Photos shared by daigou entrepreneurs via their social media apps. Source: WeChat Moments.

cosmopolitanism via branded material or other status symbols. A quick scan of the "leisure photos" my interviewees posted—which were not explicitly related to their daigou activities—reveals a showcase of conspicuous consumption and leisure at well-known global landmarks, such as a romantic dinner for two at a Michelin-starred restaurant in Beverly Hills, an evening at a fashion show in downtown Dubai, a facial at an upscale beauty salon in Hong Kong, or a relaxing Sunday morning spent with girlfriends at an art gallery in Warsaw.

This annexation of affect by economic rationality works to reconcile contradictions among global capital's individualist, consumerist, and enterprising femininities demands and the respectable, family-oriented, and altruistic womanhood anchored in traditional Confucian gender norms. Women entrepreneurs deploy traditional female "virtues" and family-oriented gender roles to mitigate excessive commercialism on their personal brands. The resulting imbrication of traditional and neoliberal gender scripts shapes their labor of entrepreneurial reinvention.

One identity that embodies the gendered labor of reinvention is the family-oriented but also self-loving and caring middle-class "yummy mommy" (*lama*, 辣妈). Well-educated, cosmopolitan, and technology-savvy, these women actively use new technologies to enhance their "scientific" mothering techniques and produce globally competitive children.[81] They take pleasure in domestic chores such as cooking, baking, decorating, and cleaning, and pride themselves on maintaining a well-kept middle-class home.[82] At the same time, they consciously distinguish themselves from traditional self-sacrificial femininity and socialist gender-neutral laboring women by asserting their agency and independence and pampering their individual desires.[83] The female daigou entrepreneur exemplifies the yummy mommy archetype because the business supports individualistic pursuits of self-expression, consumption, and looking good. It also links with networks of like-minded women and lets them fulfill their domestic roles.

Ellen, the entrepreneur in her early thirties who was introduced earlier in this chapter, frequently deployed the "yummy mommies" brand on her livestreams and in her promotional posts on WeChat. I first interviewed her in 2014, after she had finished graduate school in the United States and returned to Beijing. In 2015, she began posting pictures and narratives of her pregnancy and child-rearing experiences, interspersed with ads for products she was selling. Ellen had resold Western luxury products when she lived abroad. Upon returning to China, she expanded her business to include her own brand of traditional Chinese nutritional supplements that promised to keep buyers looking youthful and beautiful. Soon, she began posting pictures and videos of her daily routine. Cooking videos were shot in the spacious American-style kitchen of her luxury Beijing villa, and clips of her exercising with a private coach were shot in a high-end gym. Her products were seamlessly integrated into these pictures and videos. Two months after giving birth to her first daughter, Ellen posted pictures of her best-selling products next to photos of her youthful, well-kept postpartum body (figure 6.4). In an accompanying line of text, she wrote: "I want to tell my yummy mommy sisters (*lama jiemeimen*, 辣妈姐妹们) that, based on my experience, you can have it all: a fulfilling career and a happy family, all while staying young and beautiful."

FIGURE 6.4 Advertisement with before-and-after-pregnancy images of a young "yummy mommy" entrepreneurs. Source: Lamaying, https://www.lamaying.com/qinzi/yunqi/65773.html.

Stories of entrepreneurial reinvention like Ellen's might sound empowering for aspiring yummy mommies who want to "have it all," but they constitute a new code of femininity that sets extremely high standards for women to live up to, whether through excessive exercise, luxury consumption, or other forms of personal care, but celebrates commodity-coded cosmopolitan middle- and upper-class gendered identities while marginalizing working-class and rural women. Most Chinese women, even some Ellen's middle-class clients, cannot afford a luxury villa in Beijing or a private gym coach, nor can they hire helpers to assist with childcare and housework. These implicit cultural expectations function as a form of biopolitical power to discipline women's bodies. Only certain identities and stories are brandable. Maintaining one's brand in the online luxury goods market requires constant self-improvement and the willingness to reshape one's feminine self in compliance with, rather than as a challenge to, the gendered scripts of mainstream consumer culture.

For example, Xiaolan, who sells high-end bags from brands like Hermès and Chanel, told me that she had hired a "personal nail technician" who visited her home twice a week to keep her nails looking good for photo shoots. Lily, who sells designer items online, gave birth six months before our interview. She confided that she felt extreme pressure to "slim down fast" and "tighten up her muscles" so she could feel confident about posing in promotional photos. Staying photogenic requires intense self-surveillance. It involves a form of "aesthetic labor" that subsumes everyday leisure activities in "the productive domain" to create a "look" for work.[84] The physical labor female daigou entrepreneurs invest in self-branding and customer interactions debunks the myth that platform-based "immaterial labor" is "laborers without bodies."[85]

Based on my interviews with female daigou entrepreneurs, their experiences are more ambiguous than their social media postings would suggest, though the extent to which the need to be "always online" feels like "labor" varies according to each woman's degree of involvement in her business. Among established agents, self-exploitation and overwork were common. These daigou resellers often managed a large base of regular customers with little outside help. As their businesses expanded and customer networks grew, many interviewees started to feel overwhelmed by their clients' expectations of constantly availability, even though personal attention might not lead to a deal.

Operating across different time zones exacerbated the problem. Consider this comment from Sally, a full-time daigou in Los Angeles: "I was on the verge of a breakdown when my client network ballooned during the last holiday sales season, between Thanksgiving and New Year's Day. I became obsessed with my laptop and smartphone for fear of losing a client. I couldn't go to bed till 3:00 or 4:00 in the morning, since people kept bugging me after midnight. My boyfriend and friends were pissed because I was always distracted." Her frustration was echoed by another full-time daigou, Xiao Ou: "Sometimes I feel so sick and tired of my cell phones. The nonstop message alerts drive me crazy, especially after I've gone to bed. It looks like an easy job, just chatting with people, but I tell you, talking to people, tending to their needs, and persuading them to buy something is not easy! Not to mention dealing with after-sale queries, returns, and refunds. I have very little control over my time."

The daigou business model can also jeopardize women's personal relationships. A few of my informants told me that they had been "unfriended" by old acquaintances on WeChat or Sina Weibo or received complaints from friends asking them to "stop bombarding them with ads for things they cannot afford." The full-time entrepreneurs I talked to often found it hard to maintain an autonomous self, independent of their business personae, due to the collapse of personal and business identities inherent to online self-branding and the tight links between their work and personal lives. Quite a few full-time entrepreneurs reported feeling guilty about spending less time enjoying leisure activities with family and friends after becoming a daigou. The tensions they felt between "work" and "life" are particularly ironic, since many of them went into the business hoping it would help them better balance work and family life.

For more laid-back participants in the daigou industry, shopping for family or a small circle of loyal customer-friends, can be pleasant. In moderation, the interactive emotional labor helps these women maintain workplace or friendship ties across national borders while expanding their social networks. In my interviews, these virtual interpersonal ties were especially beneficial to the emotional well-being of stay-at-home moms like Xiumei: "It used to be just me and my baby. My husband is super busy during the day and tired at night after work. It is hard for me to make friends in the suburban neighborhood where we live. Now I feel much happier waking up every morning knowing that there are people waiting for me online who find my advice useful and who appreciate my taste and hard work. I guess this is what motivates me." Because most of Xiumei's customers are also mothers, they often exchange tips about child rearing. She told me this helps her "make better sense of the cultural differences in family pedagogy between China and the United States," where she now lives.

For entrepreneurs like Xiumei, who face barriers to building offline careers and social networks, the daigou business stands out as a desirable entrepreneurial alternative. Xiumei's experience of building a virtual network through transnational reselling to escape social isolation and improve her emotional well-being was not an isolated case. Her sense of empowerment echoes with recently published research about transnational daigou practices among Chinese international students in Australia, female dependent visa holders in Japan, and social media-based communities for immigrant housewives in the United States.[86]

Blurring private and public, leisure and labor, and personal and commercial in platform-based transnational daigou entrepreneurship has a way of marrying the empowerment and social recognition of gendered networks with self-exploitation and overwork. This further blurs distinctions between the social logic of mutual sharing and female solidarity with the profit imperative of commercial utilitarianism. Transnational daigou work helps ease some women's frustrations and provides ways to cope with tensions resulting from retraditionalized women's roles. However, the gendered entrepreneurial subjectivities it creates are thoroughly immersed in consumerist doctrines and essentialized beauty ideals. The industry urges women to take pleasure and pride in consumer pursuits while maintaining well-groomed, attractive bodies, values that align seamlessly with entrepreneurialist demands that women trade job security for the autonomous, flexible technological cachet and glamour of informal work.

Because daigou work is exclusive to transnationally mobile middle-class women, the entrepreneurship it represents is at best an individualized solution to gendered structural problems, even as it reinforces the post-Mao myth of capitalist modernity as a "classless wonderland."[87] Gendered transnational forms of microentrepreneurship, like daigou, are of limited utility in countering the power of the state's patriarchal capitalist norms. Nor can they challenge the unequal international division of labor and the immigration systems that sustain these inequalities.

THE LIMITS OF TRANSNATIONAL GENDERED ENTREPRENEURIAL CITIZENSHIP

In September 2012, a news story sent shockwaves through the daigou community. A twenty-six-year-old former flight attendant, Li Xiaohang, was detained at Beijing Capital International Airport. Convicted of smuggling goods from South Korea, she was sentenced to eleven years in prison, plus a hefty fine. The young woman had set up an e-commerce shop on Taobao three years prior to her arrest, not long after she was fired from her flight attendant job for having a chronic disease. Alluding to her former professional identity, Li named her online daigou store the "Flight Attendant's Small Shop," and her business reselling branded cosmetics bought in Korean duty-free shops was reasonably successful. Between 2010 and 2011, Li Xiaohang and her boyfriend made twenty-nine shopping trips between Beijing and Seoul and evaded customs duties worth more than 1 million yuan. They were first caught passing through customs at Shenyang Taoxian International Airport in April 2011. Four months later, they were arrested again, this time carrying six bags of cosmetics with an estimated value of 100,000 yuan.[88]

Two years later, Chinese language media in New York described the frustrating experiences of two Chinese women reselling Western luxury brands. Zheng, a luxury reseller in Los Angeles, said she was a frequent customer of Louis Vuitton's American website. Repetitive purchases eventually set off alarms within the company, and it blacklisted her credit card. To maintain her business, Zheng kept applying for new cards and changing her shipping address, sometimes using her husband's and friends' names for orders. This didn't work for long. Louis Vuitton eventually placed a permanent ban on her name.[89] The other story concerned an unnamed Chinese woman who visited the Coach boutique in Manhattan twice, buying forty bags worth thousands of dollars. When she paid for her purchases, the shop assistant offered her free home delivery. To her surprise, the woman found out that Coach not only canceled her order but blacklisted her from ever purchasing their products again.[90]

The incidents, taking place within two years of each other in different parts of the world, reveal the dark side of the daigou industry. Beneath the veneer of glamor, female daigou entrepreneurs in China and abroad must navigate the varied risks and uncertainties inherent in the legal gray area surrounding their industry. These include, but are not limited to changing immigration, tax, and customs laws; luxury-brand hostility toward reselling practices; unreliable clients; fake merchandise; and transnational shipping and banking policies.

The humiliating experiences of these three daigou agents stand in sharp contrast to the Chinese state's enthusiastic promotion of e-commerce, digital entrepreneurship, and domestic consumption, and global luxury brands' eager embrace of Chinese consumers after 2008. The daigou entrepreneurs' fraught relationships with state and capital, in China and abroad, reveal contradictions inherent to gendered, racialized global digital capitalism, and the paradoxical role of female entrepreneurial laborers as both the embodiment and the solution of these problems. Ultimately, they demonstrate the limits of gendered entrepreneurial citizenship as a fix to the structural problems of global capitalism.

Li Xiaohang's lengthy sentence triggered a backlash on Chinese social media. An examination of discussion threads on Sina Weibo shows that the majority of public comments were sympathetic to Li and opposed her harsh sentence. Some argued that the government deliberately made an example of Li in order to intimidate other daigou and limit tax revenue lost to such business. Others believed that Li suffered because she lacked state connections. As one commenter put it: "This is how the Chinese legal system works. If you don't have any connection in the government, you might be imprisoned for a decade for stepping on an ant. This is power. You will only feel its suppression when you are the victim yourself!" A few pointed out that Li was a scapegoat for a common workaround to China's protectionist taxation system:

We should look beyond the prevalence of daigou to seek the root of the problem in the Chinese taxation system. Tariffs, consumption taxes, and value-added taxes can double the cost, insurance, and freight [expenses associated with imports]. Not to mention all the fees charged by the customs and shopping malls. Most Chinese citizens today find many of the imported products sold in domestic shopping malls unaffordable. Our imperial court (*tianchao*, 天朝, a euphemism for the Chinese government) would rather let Chinese consumers spend trillions of dollars during trips abroad than cut taxes at home. So, who should we blame?

Beijing's municipal court eventually reduced Li Xiaohang's sentence from eleven to three years. For all the public debate surrounding her case, the discussion never touched on underlying issues like corporate refusal to take responsibility for sick employees or state complicity in making the feminized labor of flight attendants—a typical "rice bowl of youth" profession—even more precarious. Instead, the entrepreneurial labor of daigou was presented as a technological, market-based fix to gendered precarity that women had a right to access—even though it was beset by the same precarity it was supposed to fix.

The initial success and subsequent downfall of Li's daigou business makes plain the shifting boundaries between what the state considers legitimate, and illegitimate consumption and entrepreneurship. Li Xiaohang was not the first high-profile woman entrepreneur prosecuted for smuggling. In 1991, Jin Yanjing faced a similar fate. As founder of one of the most successful early ZGC IT companies, and the only female IT founder of her generation, Jin won numerous awards and was widely recognized for her achievements during the 1980s. However, she was detained and imprisoned in 1991 for smuggling PCs, printers, and ultrasound machines from Hong Kong to resell on the mainland. This was common practice among early ZGC IT companies during the transition from a centralized command economy to a market-driven economy. Yet, Jin became the only IT company manager and one of the few people in ZGC's history to be prosecuted for smuggling.[91]

It's not a coincidence that both Li and Jin were women entrepreneurs. Many scholars have documented the victimization of women in modern Chinese history. Dorothy Ko, for example, described how women came to be a "symbol of the Chinese nation:" backward, dependent subjects who, "like China itself, desperately needed to catch up with the West."[92] In a paper on the recent antifeminist backlash in China, Angela Xiao Wu and Yige Dong argued that, because "class inequality is systematically rendered unrecognizable in popular representation," entrepreneurial women are considered transgressors against patriarchal norms and become targets for displaced and suppressed class antagonism.[93]

Similar to Jin Yanjing's prosecution in the early 1990s, Li Xiaohang was made an unfortunate scapegoat for a widely committed economic crime at a time of technological and economic reinvention. A few years after Jin's downfall, trade in imported electronics became legal and was encouraged as a part of China's reform and opening-up campaign. History repeated itself in the years following Li's prosecution: the informal gendered economy of daigou was formalized, rebranded, and encouraged by the Chinese state as "cross-border e-commerce."

Since the mid-2010s, Chinese and foreign e-commerce giants have been locked in fierce competition to set up new platforms to grab a share of the lucrative daigou market. Some new platforms, such as JD Global and TMall Luxury Pavilion, bypass microentrepreneurs to connect domestic Chinese customers directly with Western luxury companies like Prada, Valentino, Burberry, and Delvaux. Others, like Taobao Global and Ymatou, recruit transnational buyers and monetize via commissions. The most unique model belongs to the social e-commerce app Xiaohongshu, which pioneered a new path to transnational IT entrepreneurship for aspiring middle-class young women by allowing them to focus exclusively on social media marketing (disguised as user-generated shopping diaries) rather than selling products. By formalizing daigou as cross-border e-commerce, these platforms not only help the Chinese state collect tariffs and other fees, but they also push microentrepreneurs to take a more active self-branding role to cultivate consumers. Daigou agents who fail to adapt are squeezed out of the market or see their profit margins significantly reduced.

State endorsement of corporate cross-border e-commerce initiatives and promotion of "legitimate" female IT entrepreneurship stands in sharp contrast to its draconian control of the "illegitimate" e-commerce entrepreneurship of daigou. Starting in 2010, the state began to tax mailed commodities passing through customs, including those for personal use.[94] It also tightened custom inspections and put brakes on capital flight by restricting outward cash flows.[95] In 2018, a new e-commerce law required online resellers to register with Chinese tax authorities so as to "squeeze, or even eliminate, their profit margins."[96] This is in addition to clamping down on daigou and overseas spending by Chinese tourists amid efforts to boost domestic consumption.[97] These changes have significantly reduced the number of daigou entrepreneurs and transformed the experiences of those with no better alternatives into something more like platformized labor than entrepreneurship.

The Chinese state's responses to the gendered entrepreneurial labor of daigou parallel the contradictory approaches of foreign luxury companies and governments to Chinese resellers. Deeply rooted in historic Western ambivalence toward gendered and racialized Asian (immigrant) labor, these contradictions are also informed by China's changing position in global capitalism—its rising luxury consumption, technological prowess, and foreign investment.

Despite their relatively elite status, the feminized labor practices of women daigou entrepreneurs are part of a long tradition of Asian immigrant women conducting home-based subcontracting work in peripheral regions of global capitalism, outside the watchful eyes of immigration and law enforcement agencies in their new homes. It was the "nimble fingers" and "disciplined personalities" of Asian women and girls that made them ideal workers in the global fashion industry or for Silicon Valley's global tech companies.[98] Compared to exploited working-class female workers, women daigou entrepreneurs are agentive, autonomous middle-class entrepreneurs. However, despite their class privilege, they must still negotiate their gendered and racialized identities and bodies in transnational encounters. Such negotiations are made trickier by Western anxieties over growing reliance on Chinese labor, investment, and purchasing power, and exacerbated by surging anti-Chinese racism and fears of a perceived "China threat."[99]

Yet since 2018, the global luxury industry has grown increasingly reliant on the Chinese market. According to the consulting firm, McKinsey & Company, more than half of the global growth in luxury spending between 2012 and 2018 came from China. In 2018, Chinese consumer spending on luxury goods at home and abroad constituted a third of the global total.[100]

At times, female daigou entrepreneurs have benefited from the eagerness of luxury brands and sellers to expand into the vast Chinese market (figure 6.5). Quite a few of the women I interviewed had formed cordial relations with shop assistants at local luxury boutiques. In return for helping boost sales, they were given VIP access to new and limited-edition products, exclusive information about upcoming sales events, and even small gifts. Niche brands, like the Australian cosmetics brand Jurlique, strategically market to daigou entrepreneurs as low-cost intermediaries to China's huge domestic market.[101] In a sign of how important daigou was to the global luxury market, the stock prices of Western luxury brands like LVMH, Burberry, Gucci, Coach, and Tiffany and Japanese and Korean cosmetic companies like Kao, Kose, and Amorepacific dropped in 2018 in the wake of China's e-commerce law targeting daigou.[102]

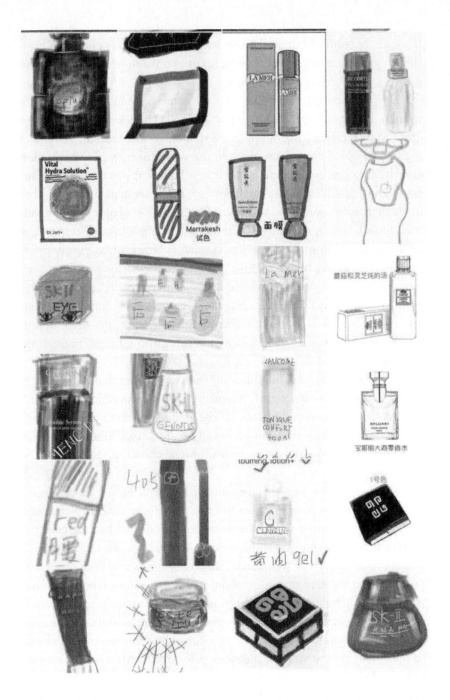

FIGURE 6.5 Product pictures hand-painted by daigou entrepreneurs to elude social media platform's picture detection AI. Source: Sohu, https://www.sohu.com/a/286101511_255783.

Still, a lot of ambivalence surrounds daigou abroad. Mounting fears of China's economic and political clout have triggered racist and nationalist critiques of China's conspicuous consumption. Immigrant communities to which daigou belong have become victims of various forms of racialized targeting, ranging from immigration constraints and mild local discontent with the Chinese presence to active discrimination and xenophobia.[103] Targeting is sometimes carried out by brands themselves. The two stories leading this section were substantiated by several of my interviewees, who reported that luxury brands screened Asian and Chinese customers online and offline in order to project brand exclusivity and ensure the profitability of their overseas branches. The Paris department store Galeries Lafayette actually segregates busloads of Chinese tourist-consumers from local customers by diverting them to a separate store catering exclusively to Chinese tour groups.[104] Relations between daigou entrepreneurs and annoyed locals are especially tense in Hong Kong, where many local residents feel that their daily lives are disrupted and their access to resources squeezed by rich mainlanders.[105]

The nationality and racialist challenges daigou entrepreneurs face are particularly ironic, since many of the luxury products they buy are made by working-class Chinese factory girls who will likely never be able to afford the goods they produce.[106] In the words of Asian studies scholar Minh-Ha Pham, the two groups are locked "in a strange circuit of production in which one group's free, highly visible, and rewarding labor . . . depends on another group's free or severely underpaid, invisible, and largely alienating labor."[107]

Most of the women I talked to were aware that their work fostered the widening of social inequalities, encouraged stereotypes of Chinese consumerists, and promoted commodity fetishism. Many felt "alienated" by consumption after the initial joy in their work had worn off. One told me that, at first, she was very excited about "shopping with someone else's money." Later, she started to develop "aesthetic fatigue" after "buying similar products and going to the same boutiques over and over again." As countermeasures, some women tried establishing clear work-life boundaries. Common strategies included separating personal social media accounts from those devoted exclusively to "work" and turning off electronic devices at certain times of day to preserve time for family and friends.

Some informants saw luxury reselling as a supplementary job to their main role as mothers and wives. Others saw it as a temporary side gig affording transnational mobility and skills, experiences, and resources that could be useful in finding more stable and lasting work. Quite a few of the women I talked to considered transnational daigou work as a way to build up their online networks and enrich their multimedia portfolios as entrepreneurial workers. Dada, for example, owned a multiplatform e-commerce business that sold Western luxuries and quick fashion products imported from Korea, but she earned most of her money modeling for other e-commerce businesses. She used her social media accounts and blog to advertise the businesses she modeled for—part of her strategy for not remaining dependent on the "rice bowl of youth." In our 2014 interview, she explained: "I know that I get paid well for modeling because I am young and pretty. But my youth won't last. That's why I am building up my own platform not only selling products but also advertising for others. So as time goes by, the value will be transferred to my website and business—not just my face and body."

The conscious move to reinvent the self by externalizing and transferring value from the feminine body to something external, such as a website, network, or more stable business enterprise, was echoed by several of my interviewees. For example, in 2015, Mina told me that she and a former college professor were setting up a new cosmetics line and credited her reselling business with helping her understand the marketing and sales side of the industry. Others desired to cope with the uncertainties of the daigou industry by opening a brick-and-mortar shop or accumulating enough capital to invest in real estate or art.

Although the appetite of Chinese middle- and upper-middle-class consumers for foreign luxury products continues to grow, so have the available purchasing channels. Chinese citizens increasingly travel abroad. Foreign luxury companies are growing their presence in China to cut the price of their products in the domestic market, and Chinese government policies reducing import tariffs and promoting cross-border e-commerce have all made the daigou industry more competitive and less lucrative.

Quite a few of the women entrepreneurs I interviewed have left the industry, but most of them stayed on an entrepreneurial path. Dada partnered with an investor in 2017 to set up her own internet celebrity (*wanghong*, 网红) incubator. Mina cofounded a cosmetics brand manufacturing and marketing China-made cosmetics products.

The feminized entrepreneurial labor of daigou emerged in the late 2000s as a specific techno-economic "fix" to the crisis of global financialized capitalism. In China's mixed and increasingly global economy, young and transnational middle-class Chinese women experienced this crisis through the lens of competing gender regimes in culturally specific ways. While Chinese women were largely confined to the domestic/ inner sphere (nei, 內), according to Confucian tradition, boundaries separating the inner and outer (wai, 外) spheres have always been fluid and negotiable, especially for urban and elite women. For the younger generation of daigou entrepreneurs, their boundary-crossing entrepreneurial experiences reflect the individualizing desire to shift away from socialist class politics and embrace cosmopolitan consumerism and entrepreneurship, the rise of neofamilism under patriarchal state capitalism, and China's changing position in the uneven global labor division. This inherent flexibility helps global-trotting women find a balance—albeit a delicate and precarious one—between fulfilling traditional gender roles and living individual, independent, enterprising lives "set free" by global capital.

However, daigou labor can hardly be said to challenge global capital's profit-maximizing logic, the uneven global division of labor, or the inequalities built into immigration systems. It also begs the question of whether the gendered entrepreneurial labor of reinvention has been a real counterweight to revitalized patriarchal norms that disadvantage women in the workplace and in the domestic sphere. Caught between the contradictory politics of the Chinese state and the ambivalence of global luxury capital, these middle-class women entrepreneurs, despite their transnational mobility, cannot entirely escape draconian state policies and everyday racism and nationalism. Their specific gendered and racialized experiences, along with the widening social inequality in China, are constant reminders of the limits of global "entrepreneurial citizenship."

Women entrepreneurs derive real pleasure from monetizing female "reproductive labor"—transnational travel, luxury brand consumption, novel identities, and online connections. Yet, they also incur real pain from the imperatives of online self-branding and interactivity, the constant juggling of professional and domestic responsibilities, and always being emotionally responsive and invested in customer service, all while being subjected to government policing, racial discrimination, and xenophobia.

Still, we miss the bigger picture if we see these women as mere passive victims. Their ingenuity in piecing together different cultural and social resources—at times exploiting and at other times resisting or outwitting various regimes of subjugation—reinvents and redefines what constitutes work. Caught in between the market, the state, and resurgent traditional norms, the struggles of these women embody China's contradictions in the second decade of the twenty-first century as the country seeks to transcend its historical position in the hierarchical international division of labor in an increasingly hostile geopolitical climate.

Epilogue

Toward a China Paradigm

I had no idea when I visited my cousin ten years ago that it would send me on an investigative odyssey and produce this book. The inspiration first came to me in 2010 when I took a bus to visit my uncle's family in Shandong Province. Anyone who has traveled in and around the Chinese countryside is familiar with the endless parade of ads and government slogans painted along the roadside. These have a way of tipping visitors off to the most pressing political and commercial trends of the moment. I vividly remember learning to read as a child in the early 1990s, practicing by reciting the contents of the "one child policy" posters plastered around my hometown. Later, in the 2000s, I was often amused by the rural cultural references and in-jokes that savvy advertisers were using to convert peasants into consumers.

Yet, that fateful summer, riding through the countryside on an intercity bus, I saw something unexpected—multiple advertisements for the e-commerce platform Taobao, all targeting peasants. Two of the ads stood out in particular: "Tired of life as a migrant worker? Why not come home and work on Taobao?" and "A cup of coffee and an internet cable— stay at home, become an e-commerce entrepreneur, and your millionaire dream will come true." Well, I thought to myself, who wouldn't want a job like that?

My cousin, a former migrant factory worker in his early thirties, had apparently reached the same conclusion. Not long after arriving, I learned that he had recently reinvented himself as an e-commerce entrepreneur (figure E.1). Over dinner, he explained that he had decided not to return to his old factory after that year's Spring Festival holiday. After more than a decade spent floating in the city, the birth of his second daughter the previous year had finally convinced him that it was time to start anew, closer to home. At a middle school reunion party, he had learned from a former classmate about a new business opportunity selling small, hand-braided furniture items and home decorations online. After making a trip to W Village—the same village featured in the Taobao ads I passed on the bus—some online research, and a long conversation with his family, he tapped into their savings and set up a Taobao store.

My cousin's experiences as an entrepreneur, however, suggested that the billboards' promises, if not false, were at least greatly exaggerated. Though his life was more comfortable than it had been on the factory line, he was far from becoming a millionaire. It took him four months to

FIGURE E.1 Wall advertisement in B County promoting e-commerce: "a cup of coffee and an internet cable—stay at home, become an e-commerce entrepreneur, and your millionaire dream will come true." Photo by author.

recover his start-up costs, and six months into his entrepreneurial adventure, his monthly revenues were barely topping his wages as a factory worker. It turns out that a successful e-commerce venture requires more than just an internet cable and a cup of coffee. He had to learn how to set up, design, and brand his online shop, not to mention more complicated tasks like product sourcing, storage, packaging, mailing, and dealing with the intermediaries who dealt with local home-based weavers on his behalf.

During my stay, I found that his time was packed with chores like taking product pictures, talking to buyers on the internet or over the phone, and analyzing his sales statistics. His workday stretched well into the evening as he watched online tutorials taught by e-commerce gurus and took classes to hone his design skills. Nor was this a simple one-man operation. His home had been transformed into an e-commerce workshop, with the bedroom doubling as a makeshift photo studio and the living room cluttered with handicrafts. The whole extended family was involved—my cousin's wife helped with customer service while taking care of their two small kids, my uncle chipped in by packaging and shipping products, and my aunt had taken charge of cooking and other household chores. This was all done on top of tending the family's small wheat plot.

Over the ensuing decade, my cousin's life would take numerous twists and turns. His family e-commerce business boomed between 2011 and 2013, a time that was generally recognized by my informants in W Village as the golden age of rural e-commerce. Starting in early 2014, however, his revenues began to drop as a wave of rural entrepreneurs answered Chinese Premier Li Keqiang's call for "mass entrepreneurship and innovation." When I last visited the family in the summer of 2019, fierce competition had so eaten into their profits that my cousin-in-law had taken a part-time job as a waitress in a nearby town.

As I described in chapter 5, my cousin's experiences were typical of the peasant e-commerce entrepreneurs I met during my fieldwork. The ebbing euphoria for e-commerce entrepreneurship I found in the countryside by 2019 was mirrored by the shifts in attitudes toward high-tech entrepreneurship I observed in Beijing's Zhongguancun neighborhood. After the collapse of the venture capital boom in 2015 and 2016, many of my interviewees in ZGC were less sanguine about the future. Over the preceding decade, a flood of VC investment had helped birth Chinese tech unicorns like Uber rival Didi Chuxing and TikTok-parent Byte-Dance, lesser known but strategically important companies like the semiconductor firm GigaDevice, and a glut of entrepreneurship-adjacent real estate ventures like incubators and coworking spaces. But the recent equity market crash made investors more cautious, and in 2019, what was left of the floor fell out as major Chinese tech companies like Huawei found themselves caught in the crosshairs of the U.S.-China trade war.

Nevertheless, by 2021, over a decade after my cousin's personal reinvention from a factory laborer into a digital entrepreneur, the number of gig workers of all types in China had exploded. That May, at a press conference following China's "Two Sessions" legislative meetings, Li announced that the country was home to some 200 million gig workers (*linggong*, 零工).[1] As the gig workforce expanded, the site of labor struggles shifted from industrial factories to include workers at digital platforms.[2] Even the ostensible winners of this transformation were growing frustrated: April 2019 saw a wave of online petitions and protests against the notorious "996" working culture, in which white-collar workers, primarily at tech firms, are expected to toil from 9:00 a.m. to 9:00 p.m., six days a week. The work regime has its origins in the 2000s, when Chinese tech giants like Baidu, Alibaba, Tencent, and JD were still start-ups battling foreign and domestic rivals for market share. The hustle was still tolerable during the VC boom of the mid-2010s, as my ZGC-based interviewees accepted 996 schedules as a legitimate means to an end: namely, the equity carrots dangling in front of them.

By 2019, however, as workers' entrepreneurial "millionaire dreams" were fading, rank-and-file tech workers and even some disaffected entrepreneurs had come to identify themselves more as "laborers" (*dagong ren*, 打工人) than budding tycoons. Things escalated when an anonymous user posted a protest against 996 on the Github coding repository.[3] Soon, Jack Ma, long an entrepreneurial idol, was knocked off his pedestal when he openly endorsed the 996 labor regime at Alibaba. Online, social media users denounced him as an "evil capitalist" and a "bloodsucking ghost" (*xixuegui*, 吸血鬼).

In place of equity, as the 2010s wore on, justifications for exploitation within China's tech industry increasingly came to be centered on technonationalism, stirred up by the U.S. government's confrontational attitude toward China and amplified by domestic media coverage of the escalating tension. For some ZGC entrepreneurs, the threat of U.S. sanctions and the sense of purpose they derived from being part of China's national drive for technological self-reliance had, by the late 2010s, come to supplement weakening individualistic motives as a rationale for accepting exploitation and self-exploitation at work. As one of my informants who worked at a start-up incubator in Beijing put it: "How can I complain? Everyone here is working hard. I wish I was born in the United States, but I don't really have a choice."

My primary motive in undertaking this study was to better understand what the concept of entrepreneurship meant to Chinese like my cousin, for whom it was not just a new way to make a living but also a means of self-reinvention. We are witnessing an international effort to rebrand "labor" as "entrepreneurialism." IT entrepreneurship, in particular, is often celebrated in corporate, policy, and academic discourses for its potential to drive innovation and generate flexible self-employment opportunities for everyone.

The idea is simple: anyone can be an entrepreneur, but it is incumbent upon individuals to reinvent themselves—that is, to leverage their unique backgrounds and social networks to ride the tidal wave of technological progress. Yet, in touting the universal accessibility of entrepreneurship while ignoring the inherent structural unevenness of contemporary global capitalism, advocates are perpetuating the system's inequalities while offloading the burdens of labor reproduction onto individuals. To aggregate a white middle-class Silicon Valley start-up founder, a Black immigrant Uber driver in London, and a Chinese peasant craftswoman into the category of "tech entrepreneur" is to elide their vastly different class, ethnic, national, racial, and geographic backgrounds and thereby conceal, rather than confront or ameliorate, the structural inequalities that define their disparate access to resources. In idealizing market-based and culturalist solutions, entrepreneurialism seeks in the alliance between developmentalism and culturalism (whether multiculturalism, nationalism, or Confucian familism) solutions to structural problems inherent to global financial capitalism. By calling on individuals, despite their vastly different capacities, to reinvent themselves as entrepreneurs, entrepreneurialism not only legitimizes state and corporate offloading of social responsibilities to "entrepreneurial" individuals (or families) but also seeks to dismiss structural inequalities by resorting to cultural exceptionalism and individual choices.

In this book, I recenter labor in the process of entrepreneurship while also seeking to redefine "labor" in ways that better fit our present context of proliferating entrepreneurialism, mounting inequalities, and global unevenness. My analysis is grounded in the everyday lived experiences of Chinese through an empirical approach that combines ethnography with sociohistorical analysis. This geocolonial- and feminist-informed materialist and substantive theoretical grounding distinguishes my approach from both neoclassical individualistic accounts of capitalism and those based in the subjective theory of value or culturalist approaches.

Instead of endorsing U.S.-centric liberal capitalist universalism (the Washington consensus) or arguing for an alternative premised on Chinese exceptionalism (the so-called China model), my approach was framed by what Arif Dirlik terms the "China paradigm." Rather than search for an established model to be emulated, I sought to identify a set of "procedural principles" by which global forces have been articulated to local conditions and needs while remaining attentive to "the possibilities and limitations of concrete local circumstances as well as location in the world."[4]

In the process, I argue that the proliferation of entrepreneurial labor in post-2008 China is the product of a spatiotemporally and culturally specific process in which global elements were incorporated to reinvent both national and individual selves. China, anxious to tackle challenges like technological dependency, growing social inequalities, and slowing economic growth after 2008, has embraced global trends like financialization, platformization, and entrepreneurialization in a bid to facilitate the restructuring of its economy. However, instead of representing a radical break with the past, these global trends have been articulated in the country's centralized minimalist governance tradition, according to which the Chinese economy is embedded in and made to fit the multipronged national, social, and developmental goals of the Chinese state while also being shaped by the country's decentralized network of local governments and the continued prominence of the family as a unit of both economic production and social reproduction and protection.

To what extent have China's efforts toward collective and individual entrepreneurial reinvention helped resolve the multiple crises that have emerged since the late 2000s? The answer is mixed. In contrast to the euphoria for entrepreneurial progress of the corporate/state nexus, the existing labor of entrepreneurial reinvention has unfolded along zigzag trajectories shot through with contradictions. By adopting a financialized approach to entrepreneurializing technonationalism, social equity, and development, the state has repurposed socialist toolkits to effectively mobilize resources and talents and spearheaded the development of strategic industries, all while maintaining centralized command over the process of financialization. However, tensions between its goals of developmentalism, technological independence, and social redistribution, as well as conflicts of interest between central and local authorities, have spawned new forms of financialized risks, rent seeking, and precarity.

In a similar vein, the reinvention of family production through platformization and entrepreneurialization since 2008 has helped energize China's new digital economy, attenuating the negative effects of the global financial crisis on economic growth and employment and providing marginalized social groups—peasants and peasant workers, disadvantaged urban youth, and women—with new economic opportunities and choices. However, the continued failure to address the crisis of care has intensified contradictions between the valorization of the individualized entrepreneur and the reality that productive and reproductive labor in rural China remains both highly collective and family-based. This has deepened inequalities along gender, class, and geographic lines, as well as between mental and manual laborers.

In following China's own historical trajectory, the stories in this book can be read as a supplement, if not a modest counterweight, to the proliferation of accounts of China in the English-speaking world since the late 2000s, which reflects my own thinking about the politics of producing knowledge about China for English-speaking readers in an atmosphere of escalating U.S.-China tensions. In the years immediately following the 2008 global crisis there was a boom in Sinocentric stories, generally told from the perspective of Western business and tech leaders, that reimagined the country as a new frontier of technological progress and the world's newest economic engine. In unpacking romanticized depictions of Shenzhen by American maker advocates, investors, and corporate suits, Silvia Lindtner smartly noted the ways these narratives were colored by "colonial tropes of adventure, frontierism, and of 'going back in time.'"[5]

Emerging in parallel to these rose-tinted tales was a wave of alarmist accounts of the rising "China threat." These either tapped into anticommunist sentiments to hype up the CCP's ambitions for world domination or adopted orientalist tropes to sell essentialist depictions of the country's economic model. The crest of this wave wasn't a book but a 2020 tweet sent by Republican Senator Marsha Blackburn proclaiming that "China has a 5,000 year [sic] history of cheating and stealing." These hawkish depictions of China were given a boost when the Trump administration launched a trade war against the country in 2018, fueling a bipartisan hardening of attitudes.

Yet the underlying narratives that fuel them are nothing new. In explaining Americans' changing attitudes toward the Cultural Revolution, from that of radical enthusiasm in the 1960s and 1970s to wholesale condemnation since the 1980s, the historians Arif Dirlik and Meisner Maurice highlighted the long history of Euro-American societies freezing non-European cultures in time and refusing "to take history seriously where China is concerned."[6] The result was a kind of "condescending veneration" born of Westerners' admiration of "China for its mystifying antiquity combined with a condescending attitude toward Chinese resistance (or inability) to become more like ourselves."[7]

Such condescension was on vivid display in the recent debate over whether the United States had "failed" in its post-1970s policy of engaging China to make it more like the West. If anything, the latest surge in China bashing in the United States since the late 2010s, like the previous shifts documented by Dirlik and Maurice, is less a specific response to China and more about uniting the United States against a common enemy to paper over domestic divisions, thereby "making America great again."

As I have shown throughout this book, China has in fact changed significantly since rejoining the capitalist world system in the 1970s. And in many respects, including pursuing financialization, building scientific infrastructure, and promoting IT entrepreneurship, China has closely followed in America's footsteps. China's post-2008 reinvention, though it may have had the effect of destabilizing American global hegemony, has mainly been propelled by a desire, if not an anxiety, to overcome its own structural problems and contradictions in the wake of its integration into this same American-led global capitalist system, including technological dependency, overproduction, uneven development, and crises of ecology and care. Yet it is also true that it has maintained a distinct trajectory, one influenced by its imperial, revolutionary, and socialist traditions and conditioned by the country's geographical limitations and ever-shifting position in the global capitalist world order. By framing the continuities and ruptures that characterize China's post-2008 labor of entrepreneurial reinvention as the results of an ongoing experiment to articulate global forces to local conditions, this book takes a different approach from narratives of China told from the perspective of the current American-led world order.

This brings me to my second point: the importance of recognizing the spatiotemporally and culturally specific nature of the China paradigm. Being attentive to the specificities of the China paradigm helps us better situate China's experiences relative to those of other countries at different historical conjunctures without losing sight of the heterogeneity, inequalities, and unevenness that exist within China. By telling three distinct stories of China's post-2008 reinvention, from urban, rural, and transnational angles, respectively, I have shown how the country's economic restructuring has produced both winners and losers and demonstrated how national and collective efforts toward reinvention have been experienced differently by variously situated individuals.

I have also sought to highlight the specific ways in which China's economy is embedded in central-local state politics and family institutions. In doing so, I challenge the state/market antithesis and neoclassical assumptions about the autonomous individual as a rational economic subject. This emphasis on specific Chinese experiences should not be interpreted as an argument for Chinese exceptionalism, nor should it be confounded with efforts, often championed by the Chinese government, to construct an idealized "China model" that can be emulated by other countries. The strong roles played by the state and family in the Chinese economy are *not* unchanging or culturally essential. Rather, they are products of China's distinct historical and cultural trajectories and institutional evolution.

With regard to state/market relations, the active role played by the Chinese state in industrial policy hardly makes it an outlier. When now-developed economies such as Britain and the United States were at an early stage in their industrialization, their respective states played a central role in creating and regulating markets—when they weren't intervening in market activity outright.[8] The United States and other major industrialized economies all leaned heavily on active industrial policies between the 1930s and 1960s, under which the state invested in infrastructure and key industries. For the first few decades after World War II, most industrializing countries, including those in East Asia and Latin America, adopted a similar state-led development model to achieve relatively high and stable growth rates.[9]

Nor is China alone in its reliance on the family as a provider of welfare and an agent in socioeconomic and political reproduction. Similar patterns can be found in other industrialized and industrializing nations in Asia, southern Europe, and Latin America.[10] According to sociologists Theodoros Papadopoulos and Antonio Roumpakis, the continued prominence of family-based labor in these regions should not be seen as symptoms of domestic "rudimentary development" but rather as "outcomes of the ways in which these national political economies were integrated into regional and global economies as (semi-)peripheries."[11]

The neoliberal shift beginning in the 1970s, characterized by the global hegemony of the Washington consensus and the post–Cold War international expansion of financialized capitalism, led to the ascendancy of neoliberal market fundamentalism worldwide. Yet, although it formed a partial alliance with global neoliberal forces, China's state-led gradual reintegration into the global capitalist system and its entrenched rural/urban dual economic system not only set it apart from developed nations at the center of the neoliberal world order but also set it on a distinct path relative to many other emerging economies undergoing neoliberalization.[12]

The years following the 2008 global financial crisis represented a watershed moment not only for China but for the entire neoliberal world order, one marked by the rise of entrepreneurialism and the concurrent resurgence, in many national economies, of state power and the "familization" of social risks in the face of proliferating insecurity, instability, and precarity.[13] Decades of financialized global capitalism have wreaked havoc on national economies around the world, and the resulting mix of weak labor protections, high inequality, and debt-financed economic bubbles created the conditions for entrepreneurialism's rise. In this sense, China's post-2008 entrepreneurial reinvention, though built on the country's centralized minimalist tradition and a continuation of its distinct developmental trajectory over the previous decades, is a spatially specific manifestation of a global shift, in which national economies, to overcome global risks and economic instability, have reembedded themselves in state and family institutions. Unfortunately, as historian Jake Warner has observed, anxiety and insecurity at both the popular and elite levels in both countries have made it convenient to blame structural problems of the global system on individual countries, and I would add, on individual groups and persons, in the case of surging racism and exophoria.

As I was putting the finishing touches on this book, the world found itself mired in yet another major crisis, this time triggered by the global Covid-19 pandemic. For months after the new coronavirus was first identified in the central Chinese city of Wuhan, international borders were blocked, embassies closed, and international flights canceled as people retreated into their homes and relied on their families for support. This abrupt disruption of our global interconnectedness has forced countries around the world to reprioritize safety, protection, and security over market-based freedoms and to rethink once again an already beleaguered neoliberal policy regime.

Under the dual pressure of the "zero-covid" policy and U.S. sanctions, China rolled out a new developmental strategy known as "dual circulation" in May 2020. The announcement was a response to not just the ongoing pandemic but also escalating geopolitical tensions with the United States as the Trump administration pursued a strategy of economic and political "decoupling." China's plan puts greater emphasis on "common prosperity" and the "internal circuit" of the domestic market—which it hopes to stimulate through rural rejuvenation, poverty reduction, investments in "green" technologies, and reregulation of monopolistic digital platforms and overheated industries such as real estate and after-school education—over the increasingly unstable and unpredictable "external circuit" of export and international trade. In this, the dual circulation strategy represents a continuation of the country's post-2008 entrepreneurial reinvention, which has consistently attached great importance to boosting indigenous innovation and domestic consumption.[14] However, it also further ramps up state intervention in all aspects of social life beyond the economy in the name of national security and social control and protection. Many commentators outside of China have come to view this new political and economic shift as "China's Red New Deal," ushering in the nation's own progressive check on decades of runaway "capitalism with Chinese characteristics."[15]

Not coincidentally, the Biden administration, despite resistance and blockages from both the GOP and within the Democratic Party, has been pushing forward the "Build Back Better" bill that vows to improve middle-class welfare, combat urgent challenges of climate change, and grow the U.S. economy "from the bottom up and the middle out."[16] The Senate's "Innovation and Competition Act" and the House's updated version of "America COMPETES Act," which strategically target "China" as a foil to America's technological competitiveness, quickly garnered bipartisan support.[17]

What this suggests is that despite escalating geopolitical conflicts based on ideological differences, the world's two biggest economies are in many ways converging as they both seek to bolster the state's role in economic planning while reemphasizing domestic redistribution and economic security over neoliberal principles like market freedom. As the world moves past the neoliberal "era of small government and unlimited globalization,"[18] China's post-2008 experiences offer valuable insight into the potential benefits and pitfalls of state-led financialization and technology-driven entrepreneurialization of labor as strategies for dealing with shared problems like technological inter-dependency, slowing growth, and unbalanced and uneven development. The question that will likely haunt us in the years to come is whether the United States and China—the world's biggest economies—can find a way to coexist peacefully in their respective, converging paths of reinvention.

Notes

PREFACE

1. Between January 8 and February 21, 1992, China's then-paramount leader, Deng Xiaoping, embarked on a tour of cities in southern and southeastern China, where he gave speeches endorsing their pro-reform and opening-up policies. The tour jump-started China's postsocialist economic reforms after a short period of conservative retrenchment in response to the Tiananmen Square protests in 1989.

2. Christian Fuchs, "Labor in Informational Capitalism and on the Internet," *The Information Society* 26, no. 3 (April 30, 2010): 179–96, https://doi.org/10.1080/01972241003712215.

3. Mark Banks, *The Politics of Cultural Work* (Basingstoke, UK: Palgrave Macmillan, 2007); Sarah Banet-Weiser, *AuthenticTM: The Politics of Ambivalence in a Brand Culture* (New York: New York University Press, 2012); Richard Barbrook and Andy Cameron, "The Californian Ideology," *Science as Culture* 6, no. 1 (January 1, 1996): 44–72, https://doi.org/10.1080/09505439609526455; E. Gabriella Coleman and Alex Golub, "Hacker Practice: Moral Genres and the Cultural Articulation of Liberalism," *Anthropological Theory*, September 1, 2008, https://doi.org/10.1177/1463499608093814; Melissa Gregg, *Work's Intimacy* (Cambridge: Polity Press, 2011); Michael Hardt, "Affective Labor," *Boundary 2* 26, no. 2 (1999): 89–100; Henry Jenkins, *Spreadable Media: Creating Value and Meaning in a Networked Culture* (New York: NYU Press, 2018); Alice E. Marwick, *Status Update: Celebrity, Publicity, and Branding in*

the Social Media Age (New Haven, CT: Yale University Press, 2015); Angela McRobbie, *Be Creative: Making a Living in the New Culture Industries* (Cambridge: Polity Press, 2016); Gina Neff, *Venture Labor: Work and the Burden of Risk in Innovative Industries* (Cambridge, MA: MIT Press, 2012); Andrew Ross, *No-Collar: The Hidden Cost of the Humane Workplace* (New York: Basic Books, 2002); Trebor Scholz, ed., *Digital Labor: The Internet as Playground and Factory* (New York: Routledge, 2012).

4. Ana Alacovska and Rosalind Gill, "De-Westernizing Creative Labour Studies: The Informality of Creative Work from an Ex-Centric Perspective," *International Journal of Cultural Studies* 22, no. 2 (March 1, 2019): 195–212, https://doi.org/10.1177/1367877918821231.

5. Antonio A. Casilli, "Global Digital Culture: Digital Labor Studies Go Global: Toward a Digital Decolonial Turn," *International Journal of Communication* 11 (September 29, 2017): 3946; Rebecca E. Karl, *The Magic of Concepts: History and the Economic in Twentieth-Century China* (Durham, NC: Duke University Press, 2017).

6. Alacovska and Gill, "De-Westernizing Creative Labour Studies," 3.

7. Bingchun Meng, "China Media Colloquium| Moving Beyond Democratization: A Thought Piece on China Internet Research Agenda," *International Journal of Communication* 4 (May 3, 2010): 8.

8. Scholz, *Digital Labor*.

9. Philip C. C. Huang, *The Peasant Economy and Social Change in North China* (Stanford, CA: Stanford University Press, 1988); Hill Gates, *China's Motor: A Thousand Years of Petty Capitalism* (Ithaca, NY: Cornell University Press, 1997); Yu Hong, *Networking China: The Digital Transformation of the Chinese Economy* (Champaign: University of Illinois Press, 2017); Chingkwan Lee, *Against the Law* (Berkeley: University of California Press, 2007); Jack Linchuan Qiu, *Goodbye ISlave: A Manifesto for Digital Abolition* (Champaign: University of Illinois Press, 2017); Cara Wallis, *Technomobility in China: Young Migrant Women and Mobile Phones* (New York: NYU Press, 2015); Hairong Yan, *New Masters, New Servants: Migration, Development, and Women Workers in China* (Durham, NC: Duke University Press, 2008); Guobin Yang, *The Power of the Internet in China: Citizen Activism Online* (New York: Columbia University Press, 2011).

10. Some examples include Bingchun Meng, *The Politics of Chinese Media: Consensus and Contestation* (New York: Palgrave Macmillan, 2018); Lin Chun, *China and Global Capitalism: Reflections on Marxism, History, and Contemporary Politics* (New York: Springer, 2013); Adrian Băzăvan, "Chinese Government's Shifting Role in the National Innovation System," *Technological Forecasting*

and *Social Change* 148 (November 1, 2019): 119738, https://doi.org/10.1016/j
.techfore.2019.119738; Hong, *Networking China*; Yuezhi Zhao, *Communication
in China: Political Economy, Power, and Conflict* (Lanham, MD: Rowman & Littlefield, 2008); Philip C. C. Huang, "Rethinking 'the Third Sphere': The Dualistic Unity of State and Society in China, Past and Present," *Modern China* 45,
no. 4 (July 1, 2019): 355–91, https://doi.org/10.1177/0097700419844962; Tiejun
Wen, *Baci Weiji: Zhongguo de Zhenshi Jingyan 1949–2009* (Eight Crises: Lessons from China, 1949–2009) (Beijing: Dongfang Press, 2013).

11. Casilli, "Global Digital Culture: Digital Labor Studies Go Global;" Julie Yujie
Chen, "Thrown Under the Bus and Outrunning It! The Logic of Didi and Taxi
Drivers' Labour and Activism in the On-Demand Economy," *New Media & Soci-
ety* 20, no. 8 (August 1, 2018): 2691–711, https://doi.org/10.1177/1461444817729149;
Lilly Irani, *Chasing Innovation: Making Entrepreneurial Citizens in Modern
India* (Princeton, NJ: Princeton University Press, 2019); Avle Seyram et al.,
"Additional Labors of the Entrepreneurial Self," *Proceedings of the ACM on
Human-Computer Interaction*, November 7, 2019, https://dl.acm.org/doi/abs/10
.1145/3359320; Minh-Ha T. Pham, *Asians Wear Clothes on the Internet: Race,
Gender, and the Work of Personal Style Blogging* (Durham, NC: Duke Univer-
sity Press, 2015); Winnie Wong, *Van Gogh on Demand: China and the Ready-
made* (Chicago: University of Chicago Press, 2014); Gabriella Lukács, *Invisibil-
ity by Design: Women and Labor in Japan's Digital Economy* (Durham, NC: Duke
University Press, 2020); Marc Steinberg, *The Platform Economy: How Japan
Transformed the Consumer Internet* (Minneapolis: University of Minnesota
Press, 2019); Silvia M. Lindtner, *Prototype Nation: China and the Contested
Promise of Innovation* (Princeton, NJ: Princeton University Press, 2020).

12. "Mike Pompeo China Speech Transcript July 23 at Nixon Library," *Rev* (blog),
accessed January 31, 2021, https://www.rev.com/blog/transcripts/mike-pompeo
-china-speech-transcript-july-23-at-nixon-library.

13. Arif Dirlik, "The Idea of a 'Chinese Model': A Critical Discussion," *China Information* 26, no. 3 (2012): 280.

14. Kuan-Hsing Chen, *Asia as Method: Toward Deimperialization* (Durham, NC:
Duke University Press, 2010). Chen decenters Marxian historical materialism,
shifting away from the Eurocentric question of "why a Chinese mode of production cannot develop into a real (i.e., European) capitalist mode of production" (the same question that Marx posed when he conceptualized the concept
of the "Asiatic mode of production") and toward a geocolonial historical materialist framing. That is, "Within the imminent historical-geographical formation, how does a geographical space historically generate its own mode of
production?"

15. Nancy Fraser, "Contradictions of Capital and Care," *New Left Review* 100, no. 99 (2016): 117; Nancy Fraser, "Why Two Karls Are Better Than One: Integrating Polanyi and Marx in a Critical Theory of the Current Crisis," 2017, https://www.semanticscholar.org/paper/Nancy-Fraser-Why-two-Karls-are-Better-than-One-%3A-in-Fraser/ca001162d4478e474915ff02ac2b58af9e7cb1de. Fraser expounds an "expanded understanding of capitalism," locating the contemporary crises of financial capitalism at the intersection of its "intra-economic contradictions" (i.e., financial crises) and "inter-realm contradictions" (i.e., crises of care, politics, and nature, just to name a few).

16. In explaining what she means by an "inter-realm contradiction of capitalism," Nancy Fraser gives three examples: "First, that capitalism separates commodity production, based on wage work, from social reproduction, based largely on the unpaid labor especially of women; in making the former depend on the latter, whose value it nevertheless disavows, capitalism periodically destabilize s social reproduction and potentially jeopardizes economic production." "Second, that capitalism separates 'the economic' from 'the political,' even as it also makes the free ride on the latter; thus, in periodically hollowing out the public powers that secure the possibility of the private appropriation of surplus value, it potentially disrupts such appropriation." Third, "that capitalism's institutionalized imperative to limitless accumulation combines with its construction of 'nature' as 'humanity's other' to ensure the latter's instrumentalization and cannibalization, in ways that could eventually redound to imperil the former." She concluded by saying that "capitalism harbors at least three inter-realm contradictions, which correspond to crisis tendencies: the social-reproductive, the political, and the ecological." See N. Fraser, "Why Two Karls Are Better Than One," 5.

17. Jamie Peck, "For Polanyian Economic Geographies-," *Environment and Planning A*, January 1, 2013, https://doi.org/10.1068/a45236; Jamie Peck and Jun Zhang, "A Variety of Capitalism with Chinese Characteristics?," *Journal of Economic Geography* 13, no. 3 (May 1, 2013): 357–96, https://doi.org/10.1093/jeg/lbs058.

18. Aihwa Ong and Stephen J. Collier, eds., *Global Assemblages: Technology, Politics, and Ethics as Anthropological Problems* (Malden, MA: Wiley-Blackwell, 2004).

19. Ong and Collier, *Global Assemblages.*

20. Huang, "Rethinking 'the Third Sphere.'"

21. Ong and Collier, *Global Assemblages.*

22. Lawrence Grossberg, *Cultural Studies in the Future Tense* (Durham, NC: Duke University Press, 2010), 101.

1. THE LABOR OF ENTREPRENEURIAL REINVENTION

1. Angela McRobbie, *Be Creative: Making a Living in the New Culture Industries* (Cambridge: Polity Press, 2016).

2. Sarah Banet-Weiser, *Authentic™: The Politics of Ambivalence in a Brand Culture* (New York: New York University Press, 2012), 21.

3. Lilly Irani, *Chasing Innovation: Making Entrepreneurial Citizens in Modern India* (Princeton, NJ: Princeton University Press, 2019), 2, 12.

4. Carla Freeman, *Entrepreneurial Selves: Neoliberal Respectability and the Making of a Caribbean Middle Class* (Durham, NC: Duke University Press, 2014), 29.

5. Mark Casson et al., "Introduction," *The Oxford Handbook of Entrepreneurship* (New York: Oxford University Press, 2008); Freeman, *Entrepreneurial Selves*.

6. Casson et al., "Introduction," 10.

7. Nick Srnicek, *Platform Capitalism* (Cambridge, UK: Polity Press, 2016), 30.

8. Ulrich Bröckling, *The Entrepreneurial Self: Fabricating a New Type of Subject* (Thousand Oaks, CA: Sage Publications, 2015); Michel Foucault, *The Birth of Biopolitics: Lectures at the Collège de France, 1978–1979* (New York: Picador, 2010).

9. It was not until the 1970s, first in Latin America and later in the United States and Western Europe, that the doctrines of neoliberalism came to exert a dominant influence on political rhetoric and policies. The "stagflation" of Western capitalist countries in the 1970s, argues Steven Vogel, "created the space for a radical turn toward a market liberal agenda of tax cuts, privatization, deregulation, and containment of the welfare state." See Steven K. Vogel, "Neoliberal Ideology and the Myth of the Self-Made Entrepreneur," Social Science Research Network (SSRN) Scholarly Paper, August 13, 2020, 2, https://doi.org/10.2139/ssrn.3698179.

10. George Yúdice, *The Expediency of Culture: Uses of Culture in the Global Era* (Durham, NC: Duke University Press, 2004).

11. Philip C. C. Huang, "China's Neglected Informal Economy: Reality and Theory," *Modern China* 35, no. 4 (July 1, 2009): 405–38, https://doi.org/10.1177/0097700409333158.

12. Andrew Smith and Miriam Kaminishi, "Confucian Entrepreneurship: Towards a Genealogy of a Conceptual Tool," *Journal of Management Studies* 57, no. 1 (January 2020): 25–56, https://doi.org/10.1111/joms.12439; Jing Su, Qinghua Zhai, and Hans Landström, "Entrepreneurship Research in China: Internationalization or Contextualization?," *Entrepreneurship & Regional Development* 27, nos. 1–2 (January 1, 2015): 50–79, https://doi.org/10.1080/08985626.2014.999718.

13. Yasheng Huang, *Capitalism with Chinese Characteristics: Entrepreneurship and the State* (New York: Cambridge University Press, 2008).
14. Jamie Peck and Jun Zhang, "A Variety of Capitalism with Chinese Characteristics?," *Journal of Economic Geography* 13, no. 3 (May 2013): 288, https://doi.org /10.1093/jeg/lbs058; 388; Su, Zhai, and Landström, "Entrepreneurship Research in China," 20.
15. Citing cultural-cognitive factors such as "cultural perceptions of entrepreneurs," religion, and morality to explain cross-cultural/regional variations in entrepreneurship, culturalist accounts attribute the recent economic success of "Confucian Chinese" communities to the entrepreneurial reinvention of quasi-religious moral values, such as family harmony and "benevolent paternalism." See Hung-chao Tai, *Confucianism and Economic Development: An Oriental Alternative?* (Washington, DC: Washington Institute Press, 1989); Gordon Redding, *The Spirit of Chinese Capitalism* (Berlin: De Gruyter, 1995).
16. Rebecca E. Karl, *The Magic of Concepts: History and the Economic in Twentieth-Century China* (Durham, NC: Duke University Press, 2017), 108.
17. Nancy Fraser, "Why Two Karls Are Better Than One: Integrating Polanyi and Marx in a Critical Theory of the Current Crisis," 2017, https://www.semantic scholar.org/paper/Nancy-Fraser-Why-two-Karls-are-Better-than-One-%3A -in-Fraser/ca001162d4478e474915ff02ac2b58af9e7cb1de.
18. Alice E. Marwick, *Status Update: Celebrity, Publicity, and Branding in the Social Media Age* (New Haven, CT: Yale University Press, 2015).
19. Alex Rosenblat, *Uberland: How Algorithms Are Rewriting the Rules of Work* (Berkeley: University of California Press, 2018).
20. Writing in 2012 for *Forbes*, tech commentator Venkatesh Rao compared hacker hostels and coworking/maker spaces to college dorms, "highly-standardized angel-legible pipelines" at "lean start-ups" to vocational schools, and acqui-hiring to the graduation ceremony for entrepreneurial labor. See Venkatesh Rao, "Entrepreneurs Are the New Labor: Part I," *Forbes*, September 3, 2012, https://www.forbes.com/sites/venkateshrao/2012/09/03/entrepreneurs-are -the-new-labor-part-i/?sh=6a008b884eab; Michael Hiltzik et al., "How the Uberization of Work Is Rooted in the Cult of 'Shareholder Value,'" *Los Angeles Times*, January 5, 2016.
21. Ho-fung Hung, *The China Boom: Why China Will Not Rule the World* (New York: Columbia University Press, 2017); Philip C. C. Huang, *The Peasant Economy and Social Change in North China* (Stanford, CA: Stanford University Press, 1988).
22. Hill Gates, *China's Motor: A Thousand Years of Petty Capitalism* (Ithaca, NY: Cornell University Press, 1997).

23. The evidence was persistent imperialism, an underdeveloped capitalist entrepreneur class, a declining state, and a huge pool of poor and surplus rural labor that resulted in the semi-proletarianization of peasant laborers.

24. Maurice Meisner, *Mao's China and After: A History of the People's Republic*, 3rd ed. (New York: Free Press, 1999).

25. Chun Lin, *The Transformation of Chinese Socialism* (Durham, NC: Duke University Press Books, 2006), 64. Lin Chun's social/national/developmental triad provides a cogent framework for understanding the aims of the Chinese socialist state-building program: "Historically, Chinese nationalism was both revolutionary resistance against imperialism and a modern alternative to the Eurocentric assumption about capitalist universality. As such it was also simultaneously socialist—hence the paired formulation of 'Chinese socialism.' Chinese socialism was in turn itself a developmental project that aimed to rise above national backwardness without capitalist distortions, thus the coherence of revolution and modernization. In prescribing and embracing one another, nationalism, socialism, and developmentalism constituted an overriding consensus and legitimating discourse in the PRC. Together they clarified the purpose of a liberated people and their government: nationalism for national greatness, socialism for social justice, development for public welfare."

26. Meisner, *Mao's China and After*; Chun, *The Transformation of Chinese Socialism*.

27. Philip C. C. Huang, "Rethinking 'the Third Sphere': The Dualistic Unity of State and Society in China, Past and Present," *Modern China* 45, no. 4 (July 1, 2019): 357, https://doi.org/10.1177/0097700419844962. According to Huang, "centralized minimalism" is a political system in which "highly concentrated central power combined with a vast small peasant economy . . . [results] in strong tendencies towards minimalist governance both to guard against parcelization of centralized imperial power and to maintain governance at a minimal cost to the state." In Huang's account, this interdependence between centralized imperial power and a mass of loosely governed village communities set the Chinese state system apart from "the divided and yet more extractive and deeply penetrating feudal system of the West."

28. Chingkwan Lee, *Against the Law* (Berkeley: University of California Press, 2007). *Danwei* is a Chinese term for work unit that often stood as a walled compound during the socialist years, with canteens, clinics, bathhouses, and sometimes even nurseries and schools. Work and social life were completely blurred for danwei-based individuals.

29. Shaoguang Wang, "The Great Transformation: The Double Movement in China," *Boundary 2* 35, no. 2 (May 1, 2008): 15–47, https://doi.org/10.1215/01903659-2008-002.

30. Meisner, *Mao's China and After*; Wang, "The Great Transformation."

31. Hung, *The China Boom*, 49.

32. Evan Feigenbaum, *China's Techno-Warriors: National Security and Strategic Competition from the Nuclear to the Information Age* (Stanford, CA: Stanford University Press, 2003), 3.

33. Pun Ngai, *Made in China: Women Factory Workers in a Global Workplace* (Durham, NC: Duke University Press, 2005); Minh-Ha T. Pham, *Asians Wear Clothes on the Internet: Race, Gender, and the Work of Personal Style Blogging* (Durham, NC: Duke University Press, 2015).

34. Jun Zhang, "Marketization Beyond Neoliberalization: A Neo-Polanyian Perspective on China's Transition to a Market Economy," *Environment and Planning A: Economy and Space* 45, no. 7 (July 1, 2013): 1605–24, https://doi.org/10.1068/a45589.

35. David Harvey, *A Brief History of Neoliberalism* (Oxford: Oxford University Press, 2007).

36. Hui Wang, *China's New Order: Society, Politics, and Economy in Transition*, trans. Theodore Huters and Rebecca E. Karl (Cambridge, MA: Harvard University Press, 2003).

37. Wen Tiejun, Dong Xiaodan, Yang Shuai, Qiu Jiansheng, Lau Kin Chi, "China Experience, Comparative Advantage, and the Rural Reconstruction Experiment," in *Global Capitalism and the Future of Agrarian Society*, ed. Arif Dirlik, Alexander Woodside, and Roxann Prazniak (New York: Routledge, 2012), 77–89.

38. Lin, *The Transformation of Chinese Socialism*, 149.

39. Lee, *Against the Law*, 49.

40. The number of outbound rural migrants increased from 25 million in 1988 to 129 million in 2004. See Yu Hong, *Labor, Class Formation, and China's Informationized Policy of Economic Development* (Lanham, MD: Lexington Books, 2011), 117.

41. Huang, "China's Neglected Informal Economy," 406.

42. Huang, "China's Neglected Informal Economy," 406.

43. Huang, "China's Neglected Informal Economy," 406. Many migrant workers leave their parents and children behind in the countryside. Some continue to own the use rights to their household "responsibility land," a vestige of socialist land reform. However, in most cases, these lands are of little value and do not help peasants improve their standard of living. Instead, they become a source of disputes between peasants and local governments eager to repurpose the land for real estate development.

44. These policies ran the gamut from rural fee-tax reform, the abolishment of agricultural taxes, the introduction of comprehensive rural subsidies and medical

systems, and free compulsory rural education. The primary agents of the state's investment into public-serving social and physical infrastructure during this period were SOEs, which were less constrained by the short-term profit maximization imperative and more open to state influence. For more information, see Wang, "The Great Transformation."

45. Thomas Orlik, *China: The Bubble That Never Pops* (New York: Oxford University Press, 2020), 111–13.

46. Tiejun Wen, Junna Zhang, and Jiansheng Qiu, *Juwei siwei: Guojia anquan yu xiangcun zhili* (Be Prepared for Danger in Times of Danger: National Security and Rural Governance) (Beijing: Dongfang Press, 2016).

47. By the end of 2009, the sudden contraction in overseas demand had resulted in the loss of 25 million jobs in export-dependent coastal provinces. In 2008 alone, Guangdong Province witnessed the bankruptcy of about fifteen thousand export firms. For more details on the impact of the 2008 global financial crisis in China, see Orlik, *China*; Tiejun Wen, *Baci Weiji: Zhongguo de Zhenshi Jingyan 1949–2009* (Eight Crises: Lessons from China, 1949–2009) (Beijing: Dongfang Press, 2013).

48. Lawrence Grossberg, *Cultural Studies in the Future Tense* (Durham, NC: Duke University Press, 2010), 290.

2. NAVIGATING THE INVESTOR STATE

1. Hao Chen and Meg Rithmire, "The Rise of the Investor State: State Capital in the Chinese Economy," *Studies in Comparative International Development* 55, no. 3 (September 2020): 257–77, https://doi.org/10.1007/s12116-020-09308-3.

2. Chen and Rithmire, "The Rise of the Investor State."

3. Chris Buckley and Tong Bao, "Bao Tong: Xi Jinping yi Mao fengge zou deng luxian" (Bao Tong: Xi Jinping Took Deng's Line in Mao's Style), *New York Times Chinese*, November 26, 2013, https://cn.nytimes.com/china/20131126/c26bao/.

4. Qifan Huang, *Jiegouxing Gaige: Zhongguo Jingji de Wenti Yu Duice* (Reforming Economic Structure: The Problem with the Chinese Economy and Strategy) (Beijing: CITIC Press, 2020); Jiangyu Wang and Cheng Han Tan, "Mixed Ownership Reform and Corporate Governance in China's State-Owned Enterprises," Social Science Research Network (SSRN) Scholarly Paper, October 27, 2019, https://papers.ssrn.com/abstract=3476155; Sebastian Heilmann and Lea Shih, "The Rise of Industrial Policy in China, 1978–2012," Harvard–Yenching Institute Working Paper Series (2013), 25, https://www.researchgate.net/publication/285003621_The_Rise_of_Industrial_Policy_in_China_1978-2012.

5. Silvia M. Lindtner, *Prototype Nation: China and the Contested Promise of Innovation* (Princeton, NJ: Princeton University Press, 2020).

6. Chun Lin, *The Transformation of Chinese Socialism* (Durham, NC: Duke University Press, 2006); Lin Chun, *China and Global Capitalism: Reflections on Marxism, History, and Contemporary Politics* (New York: Palgrave Macmillan, 2013). According to Chun, the Chinese state's developmentalist mission to "catch up" and overcome the country's backwardness both supports and contradicts its other two main goals: the need to preserve China's national autonomy and sovereignty, and a residual socialist commitment to equality and social justice.

7. Cong Cao, "Zhongguancun and China's High-Tech Parks in Transition: 'Growing Pains' or 'Premature Senility'?," *Asian Survey* 44, no. 5 (October 1, 2004): 647–68, https://doi.org/10.1525/as.2004.44.5.647; Dan Breznitz and Michael Murphree, *Run of the Red Queen: Government, Innovation, Globalization, and Economic Growth in China* (New Haven, CT: Yale University Press, 2012); Adam Segal, *Digital Dragon: High-Technology Enterprises in China* (Ithaca, NY: Cornell University Press, 2010); Yu Zhou, *The Inside Story of China's High-Tech Industry: Making Silicon Valley in Beijing* (Lanham, MD: Rowman & Littlefield, 2007).

8. Lilly Irani, *Chasing Innovation: Making Entrepreneurial Citizens in Modern India* (Princeton, NJ: Princeton University Press, 2019).

9. After the founding of the People's Republic of China (PRC) in 1949, the nascent Chinese socialist state adopted the Soviet model to transform Zhongguancun into its primary science and technology hub. During the 1950s and '60s, the state either set up or relocated top universities and first-class research institutes from elsewhere to ZGC. Prominent among these were Beijing University, Tsinghua University, and the Chinese Academy of Sciences (CAS) and its many specialized institutes. By the mid-1960s, ZGC had become "the largest and most concentrated base for research and education in the Far East," with forty-two research institutes, sixty-seven universities, and at least thirty-five military R&D institutions. Many of the eminent red scientists and engineers who built China into an S&T powerhouse called ZGC home. See Zhou, *The Inside Story of China's High-Tech Industry*, 2007.

10. Zhongguancun-based scientists would later recall having access to a "welfare building" in the residential compound of CAS, complete with a bookstore, activity center, and a restaurant and bakery offering high-quality and Western-style foods. During the great famine of 1958 to 1961, scientists ranked at the associate professor level or higher were given special food ration tickets by the state to spend at the restaurant and bakery. See Hu Yadong, Zheng Minzhe, Yan Luguang, Yang Xiaolin, *Zhongguancun Kexuecheng de Xingqi (1953–1966)* (Hunan Education Publishing House: Hunan, China, 2009) (The Rise of Zhongguancun Science City).

11. During the Cultural Revolution, the majority of ZGC-based scientists and engineers were subjected to intense education, reform, and even violence. For example, at Tsinghua University—the school that historian Joel Andreas called "the cradle of red engineers"—radical experiments were carried out to facilitate the realization of the communist goal of "eradicating the three big disparities": between manual and mental labor, workers and peasants, and city and the countryside. Campus-based factories were set up to encourage hands-on learning alongside rank-and-file workers. Entire departments were dispatched to work with and learn from workers and peasants and to solve "real-world" problems by constructing dams, harvesting crops, and building houses. College entrance exams were canceled and replaced by a danwei recommendation system to encourage more students from worker, peasant, and soldier backgrounds to study at Tsinghua and other top schools. Faculty, administrators, and students were goaded to become "red experts": that is, to give up their individualist and careerist ideologies, humble themselves before the wisdom and ingenuity of the "masses," and unconditionally devote themselves to the grand Communist missions of serving the people and building the nation. See Maurice Meisner, *Mao's China and After: A History of the People's Republic*, 3rd ed. (New York: Free Press, 1999); Joel Andreas, *Rise of the Red Engineers: The Cultural Revolution and the Origins of China's New Class* (Stanford, CA: Stanford University Press, 2009); Guobin Yang, *The Red Guard Generation and Political Activism in China* (New York: Columbia University Press, 2017).

12. A series of major shifts following Mao's death in 1976 facilitated the dive of ZGC scientists and engineers into the "sea of commerce." After a period of intense political struggles within the CCP, Deng secured supreme leadership and assumed the title of general secretary in 1978. At the "Third Plenum" held that year, Deng announced the victory of practice over ideology, officially putting an end to Mao's preference for class politics and permanent revolution. As relations between China and the Western capitalist countries warmed in the 1980s, the latter were portrayed increasingly as examples to be emulated rather than as enemies. Recognizing that the socialist state's primary task was to restore the people's faith in CCP leadership and repair an economy devastated by the Cultural Revolution, Deng launched a suite of reforms that prioritized the development of export-oriented light industries to boost GDP, ease unemployment, and improve the population's standard of living.

The new priority given to light industry, coupled with fiscal reforms that reduced the central government's income, led to sharp budget cuts for the military, education, scientific research, and heavy industry. Instead of limiting their influence to national security and defense, Deng envisioned a new role for scientists and engineers in China's economy. At the 1978 National Science

Conference, Deng officially designated modern S&T as "the most active and decisive factor of the productive forces in the new society." He also elevated the social standing of scientists and engineers by removing the political stigma associated with their class status while encouraging scientists to contribute to the nation's new developmentalist goal of boosting economic growth. However, the technonationalist legacy of the Mao era simultaneously led Deng to reaffirm the importance of science and technology to the defense industry in his ruling ideology of the "Four Modernizations" (industry, agriculture, national defense, and science and technology). In order to maintain political control and safeguard national security, reform and opening up was carried out in a piecemeal and fragmented manner. See Hongzhe Wang, "Machine for a Long Revolution: Computer as the Nexus of Technology and Class Politics in China 1955–1984" (Ph.D. diss., The Chinese University of Hong Kong, 2014), https:// search.proquest.com/docview/1674837503/abstract/615BB139E4D34FB5PQ /1; Breznitz and Murphree, *Run of the Red Queen*.

13. In October 1980, Chen Chunxian, a nuclear physicist at CAS, delivered a talk in ZGC in which he described his experiences visiting Boston and Silicon Valley to an audience of scientists and officials. Leaving China for the first time after decades of isolation, Chen, like many of his ZGC peers who visited the United States in the early 1980s, was mesmerized by American technological achievements and material prosperity. They were particularly fascinated by Silicon Valley's innovation ecosystem and its strong university/industry ties. Determined to overcome China's backwardness by learning from Silicon Valley, Chen announced at the end of his talk the establishment of post-Mao China's first nongovernmental business: Advanced Technology Development and Service (*xianjin jishu fazhan fuwubu*, 先进技术发展服务部). See Zhiijun Ling, *China's New Revolution 1980–2006: From Zhongguancun to Chinese Society* (Wuhan: Hubei Renmin Press, 2008).

14. Ling; Zhou, *The Inside Story of China's High-Tech Industry*.

15. Stone, one of the most successful early ZGC IT companies, built its company culture upon a critique of the centrally planned command economy. Instead of holding on to the outdated culture of the iron rice bowl, Stone employees were given a "clay rice bowl" (*cifanwan*, 瓷饭碗): they were expected to perform hard work in order to prove worthy of their benefits. The company created and upheld the "Four Selves Principle" (*sizi yuanze*, 四自原则): "self-raise funds, free association, self-management, and responsibility for one's own profits and losses" (*zichou zijin* 自筹资金, *ziyou zuhe* 自由组合, *zuzhu jingying* 自主经营, *zifu yingkui* 自负盈亏). Emphasizing the role of market competition and respect for the individual, Stone pioneered a series of management practices in China by implementing annual employee contracts, setting up a graduated salary scale,

encouraging "rapid advancement and mobility among different departments," and fostering "regular dialogue between management and employees." The changing subjectivity of ZGC scientists from the danwei-based socialist to the market-driven "entrepreneur of the self" paralleled the post-Mao dismantling of the danwei system and the decline of public welfare. See Scott Kennedy, "The Stone Group: State Client or Market Pathbreaker?," *The China Quarterly* 152 (December 1997): 746–77, https://doi.org/10.1017/S0305741000047548.

16. Breznitz and Murphree, *Run of the Red Queen*; Segal, *Digital Dragon*.

17. Zhou, *The Inside Story of China's High-Tech Industry*, 2007.

18. Lenovo, the most successful CAS spinoff, was founded in 1984 with 200,000 yuan in start-up funds from the Institute of Computing (IC), its mother danwei, and access to other perks that helped the company keep costs down and weather market risks. For instance, in a break from typical danwei practice, Lenovo was free to hire and fire anyone on its IC staff. After being hired by Lenovo, former IC researchers stayed on the parent work unit's payroll and were allowed to use the IC office and other facilities for free. Most important, Lenovo could commercialize any IC research product without having to pay. This included Lenovo's core technology in the 1980s: the LX-80 Lianxiang Han Card, one of the first Chinese character processing and input systems in the world. The system had been developed by a team of IC engineers working under the state-funded "748 Project" since the Cultural Revolution. In 1985, Lenovo received this technology for free when the project's lead scientist, Ni Guang-nan, joined the company as its chief engineer. See Zhijun Ling, *Lianxiang Fengyun* (The Story of Lenovo) (Wuhan: Hubei Renmin Press, 2008), 61–78.

19. Breznitz and Murphree, *Run of the Red Queen*. Many ZGC companies were spinoffs of central-level state-owned research institutions and universities and used their extensive networks of official contacts to lobby for policy support and protection from the state. This gave them immense advantages over similar companies outside of Beijing and was crucial to their survival and success in the 1980s, when the legitimacy and direction of the reforms were still highly contested.

20. Ling, *China's New Revolution*, 2–56.

21. Zhou, *The Inside Story of China's High-Tech Industry*, 41.

22. Zhou, *The Inside Story of China's High-Tech Industry*.

23. Cao, "Zhongguancun and China's High-Tech Parks in Transition."

24. Zhou, *The Inside Story of China's High-Tech Industry*, 50.

25. Ling, *China's New Revolution*, 182.

26. Zhou, *The Inside Story of China's High-Tech Industry*, 45–62.

27. Ling, *Lianxiang Fengyun*, 267. Lenovo has been celebrated for triumphing over the "foreign invaders" to become the top brand in the Chinese PC market, but

victory came only after a fierce battle against multinational corporations (MNCs) in which it wielded technonationalism in a successful bid for financial and political support from the Chinese government, capitalizing on the lessons it had learned acting as a contractor and sales agent for the MNCs it was competing against.

28. Zhang, for example, utilized his personal connections to obtain seed funding from MIT tech gurus Edward Roberts and Nicholas Negroponte. Their endorsement helped Soho.com secure Series A investment from Intel and IDG in 1998. Sohu was listed offshore on Nasdaq in a way that allowed it to creatively bypass Chinese government restrictions while preserving access to international venture capital, a model that would be followed by many other successful Chinese dot-com businesses in the late 1990s and 2000s. See Luzhou Li, *Zoning China: Online Video, Popular Culture, and the State* (Cambridge, MA: MIT Press, 2019).

29. Zhou, *The Inside Story of China's High-Tech Industry*, 78.

30. Zhou, *The Inside Story of China's High-Tech Industry*, 78.

31. Fang Xingdong and Jiang Shenglan, *Zhongguancun Shiluo* (The Loss of Zhongguancun) (Beijing: China Customs Press, 2004).

32. Chin-fu Hung, "The Internet Entrepreneurs and the Emergence of Civil Society in China: Rhetoric or Reality," paper presented at the 54th Political Studies Annual Conference, Lincoln, UK (April 2004), 26.

33. For example, to maintain control over private internet companies, the state set up a licensing system for internet content providers (ICPs) to enforce government censorship over undesirable content. It also regulated overseas IPOs. Internet entrepreneurs like Charles Zhang, although mostly reliant on foreign venture capitalists for investment, still had to court government regulators in order to succeed in China. Meanwhile, global venture capital funds, worried about the commercial and political risks posed by China's uncertain market environment, preferred investing in ventures modeled after already established businesses in Silicon Valley rather than truly innovative ideas. They also tended to invest in "late-growth stage companies" that had already proven their potential over hardcore technology-driven firms that would take years to turn a profit. See Breznitz and Murphree, *Run of the Red Queen*; Cao, "Zhongguancun and China's High-Tech Parks in Transition."

34. By the mid-2000s, the name Zhongguancun had lost its geographical specificity. Originally associated with a section of Beijing's Haidian District, home to numerous research institutes and universities, it became a general umbrella term for Beijing's technology zones. See Yuhai Liu and Shuxia Yang, "Zhongguancun Ershinian Guimo Guangzhang Yu Quan Beijing Beizhi Quandi" (Zhongguancun Has Expanded to Cover the Whole Beijing City, Accused of

Land Enclosure), *21st Century Business Herald*, July 8, 2013, http://chanye.focus
.cn/news/2013-07-08/3574986.html; Gongzheng Chen, "'Zhongguancun': Cong
Yitiaojie Dao Yipanqi" (Zhongguancun: From a Street to a Game of Chess),
vankeweekly, September 18, 2013, http://www.vankeweekly.com/?p=76068.

35. Fang and Jiang, *Zhongguancun Shiluo*; Cao, "Zhongguancun and China's High-
Tech Parks in Transition."

36. Yu Hong, *Networking China: The Digital Transformation of the Chinese Economy* (Champaign: University of Illinois Press, 2017), 125. Since the early 1990s,
China had played an increasingly important role in the global electronics and
telecom-equipment manufacturing industry. Its importance only grew following the 1997 East Asian Financial Crisis and China's integration into the WTO
in 2001. By 2007, China's IT hardware sector accounted for 95 percent of total
high-tech exports. Unlike the Pearl River Delta and Yangtze River Delta regions,
which focused on electronics manufacturing and assembling, ZGC's position
in this value chain primarily involved retailing and wholesaling consumer electronics products and telecommunications equipment.

37. Ruiqing Lu, *Jiedu Zhongguancun Yihao: IT Maichang de Mimi* (Interpreting
Zhongguancun No.1: The Secret of the Electronics Malls) (Beijing: The Economic Daily Press, 2007).

38. Ling, *Lianxiang Fengyun*; Lu, *Jiedu Zhongguancun Yihao.*

39. Lu, *Jiedu Zhongguancun Yihao.*

40. Rare rags-to-riches stories of successful entrepreneurs from humble backgrounds include JD.com CEO Liu Qiangdong and Aigo CEO Feng Jun. Both
graduates of elite universities in Beijing, they came from ordinary families
before striking it rich as electronics vendors in ZGC.

41. The total floor space of ZGC malls expanded from 60,000 m² to 260,000 m²
between 2004 and 2007. Lu, *Jiedu Zhongguancun Yihao.* The total floor space
of electronic malls in ZGC proper more than quadrupled between 2004 and
2007.

42. Ling, *China's New Revolution*, 394.

43. Vivek Wadhwa, "What We Really Need to Fear About China," *Washington Post*,
September 27, 2011.

44. Xiaowei Ke, *Dangdai Zhongguancun Shihua (Contemporary Zhongguancun
History)* (Beijing: Contemporary China Publishing House, 2012), 175.

45. Ke, *Dangdai Zhongguancun Shihua*, 176.

46. Cui Ge, "Zuo Zhongguancun Da PE: Zhuanfang Zhongguancun Fazhen Jituan
Zongjingli Xuqiang" (Be the Big PE of Zhongguancun: Exclusive Interview with
The Director of ZGC Development Group Xuqiang), March 30, 2012, http://
chanye.focus.cn/news/2012-03-30/1883833.html.

47. Ge, "Zuo Zhongguancun Da PE."

48. The Entity List is a trade restriction list published by the United States of Commerce's Bureau of Industry and Security, constating of certain foreign persons, entities, or governments that are subject to U.S. license requirements for the export of transfer of specific items, especially U.S. technologies. It was first published in 1997 but became weaponized by the Trump administration to sanction Chinese tech firms. The Biden administration lifted sanctions on the Zhongguancun Development Investment Center in June 2021. See more information at https://www.paulweiss.com/practices/litigation/economic-sanctions -aml/publications/president-biden-revamps-communist-chinese-military -companies-ccmc-sanctions-program?id=40293.

49. In addition to the rise of state-owned and profit-driven agents of financialization like the ZGC Group, ZGC also benefited from other state-led efforts to advance IT innovation and entrepreneurship, most notably the deliberately delayed issuance of 3G operational licenses following the 2008 global crisis and the opening of China's Nasdaq-style ChiNext board in Shenzhen in 2009 and the Science and Technology Innovation Board (STAR Market) in Shanghai in 2019. The delayed launch of 3G helped cultivate and protect domestic telecommunications companies, both state-owned enterprises like ZTE and private firms like Huawei and Xiaomi; the new markets provided an alternative to global financial capital, which had little loyalty to the strategic vision of the Chinese state. Both appear to have paid off: the number of Chinese mobile internet users, many of whom had never or only seldom used the internet on PCs, increased by almost sixfold from 117.6 million in 2008 to 695 million in 2016. China accounted for 20 percent of global VC investments in 2017, up from 12 percent in 2009, with the proportion of investments from domestic capital increasing from 42 percent to 81 percent in the same period. See Jun Zhang, "Venture Capital in China," in *China as an Innovation Nation* (New York: Oxford University Press, 2016), chap. 3; Hong, *Networking China*.

50. Thomas Orlik, *China: The Bubble That Never Pops* (New York: Oxford University Press, 2020).

51. Orlik, *China*, 147.

52. Buckley and Bao, "Bao Tong." In an interview with the *New York Times* conducted right after the Third Plenum, Bao Tong, a seasoned Chinese political observer and former political secretary to the late Chinese premier Zhao Ziyang, described the document as characteristic of Xi Jinping's leadership: "You could describe it as Mao Zedong's style applied to following Deng Xiaoping's path.

53. "'Made in China 2025' Unmade?," MacroPolo, https://macropolo.org/analysis /made-in-china-2025-dropped-media-analysis/.

54. Chen and Rithmire, "The Rise of the Investor State," 261.

55. ZGC Group, "Fazhan Jituan Jiji Canyu Zhongguancun Keji Jinrong Pingtai" (Development Group Enthusiastically Participate in the Construction of ZGC Financial Service Platform), November 12, 2013, http://www.zgcgroup.com.cn /zgcadmin/home/content/index.html?id=1097&cate=15.

56. Tu Lan and Lin Zhang, "The New Whole State System: State-Led Financialization, State-Private Fusion, and China's Innovation Policies After 2008," Social Science Research Network (SSRN) Scholarly Paper, April 10, 2021, https://doi .org/10.2139/ssrn.3826658.

57. Orlik, *China*, 152.

58. Orlik, *China*, 152.

59. Edward Tse, "The Rise of Entrepreneurship in China," *Forbes*, April 5, 2016, https://www.forbes.com/sites/tseedward/2016/04/05/the-rise-of-entrepre neurship-in-china/; Yu Hong, "Pivot to Internet Plus: Molding China's Digital Economy for Economic Restructuring?," *International Journal of Communication* 11 (2017): 21.

60. Ziyue Wang, "Li Keqiang: Tuidong Chuangye Chuangzao Rang Gengduoren Fuqilai" (Li Keqiang: Promote Entrepreneurship to Make More People Richer), March 15, 2013, http://www.gov.cn/zhengce/2015-03/15/content_2834239.htm.

61. Jiaosu Zhang, "Zhongguancun Keji Chuangxinzhe de Xinnian Yuanwang" (The New Year Wishes of Zhongguancun Entrepreneurs), January 30, 2017, http:// www.xinhuanet.com/2017-01/30/c_1120394488.htm.

62. Jing Wang, "'Stir-Frying' Internet Finance: Financialization and the Institutional Role of Financial News in China," *International Journal of Communication* 11 (2017): 22.

63. Johannes Petry, "Financialization with Chinese Characteristics? Exchanges, Control and Capital Markets in Authoritarian Capitalism," *Economy and Society* 49, no. 2 (April 2, 2020): 213–38, https://doi.org/10.1080/03085147.2020 .1718913.

64. Neil Gough, "Online Lender Ezubao Took $7.6 Billion in Ponzi Scheme, China Says," *New York Times*, February 1, 2016.

65. Xuehua Zhang, "Wiwen Gongjice Jiegou Gaige: Qianwei Renshi Tan Danqian Jingji Zenmekan Zenmegan" (Seven Questions About Supply-Side Reform: The Authoritative Figure Talks About the Current Economic Restructuring), January 4, 2016, http://www.xinhuanet.com//politics/2016-01/04/c_128592438.htm.

66. Na Yang and Zhengwei Li, "Beijing Zujian 80 Yiyuan Jijin Shengji 'Zhongguancun Dajie'" (Beijing Mobilizes 8 Billion Fund to Upgrade Zhongguancun Street), Sohu.com, April 9, 2016, https://business.sohu.com/20160409/n443751484 .shtml.

67. Xia Yang, "Zhongguancun Xiqu Yetai Tiaozheng Yi Qidong Weilai Buzai Shenpi Xin Dianzi Maichang" (The Transformation of West ZGC Has Started: No

Electronic Malls Will be Approved in the Future), ifeng, September 17, 2019, http://finance.ifeng.com/news/industry/20090917/1247190.shtml.

68. Elizabeth C. Economy, *The Third Revolution: Xi Jinping and the New Chinese State* (New York: Oxford University Press, 2018); Nicholas R. Lardy, *The State Strikes Back: The End of Economic Reform in China?* (Peterson Institute for International Economics, 2019).

69. Yingyao Wang, "The Rise of the 'Shareholding State': Financialization of Economic Management in China," *Socio-Economic Review* 13, no. 3 (July 2015): 603–25, https://doi.org/10.1093/ser/mwv016; Petry, "Financialization with Chinese Characteristics?"

70. Lindtner, *Prototype Nation*, 202.

71. Wang and Tan, "Mixed Ownership Reform and Corporate Governance in China's State-Owned Enterprises."

72. Wang and Tan, "Mixed Ownership Reform and Corporate Governance in China's State-Owned Enterprises"; Chen and Rithmire, "The Rise of the Investor State."

73. Peter Elstrom, "China's Venture Capital Boom Shows Signs of Turning Into a Bust," *Bloomberg*, July 9, 2019, https://www.bloomberg.com/news/articles/2019-07-09/china-s-venture-capital-boom-shows-signs-of-turning-into-a-bust.

74. Wadhwa, "What We Really Need to Fear About China."

75. Yunxiang Yan, "The Chinese Path to Individualization," *British Journal of Sociology* 61, no. 3 (2010): 489–512.

76. Yan, "The Chinese Path to Individualization," 505.

77. Chen and Rithmire, "The Rise of the Investor State," 275.

3. FROM SCIENCE PARK TO COWORKING

1. State Council, "State Council Notice on Promoting Mass Entrepreneurship and Innovation," June 16, 2015, http://www.gov.cn/zhengce/content/2015-06/16/content_9855.htm.

2. Xinhua, "China Tops the World in Incubators, Makerspaces," XinhuaNet, September 19, 2017, http://www.xinhuanet.com//english/2017-09/19/c_136620977.htm; iResearch, "2019 Zhongguo Chanye Changing Fuhuaqi Hangye Baogao" (2019 Chinese Industrial Entrepreneurial Incubation Industry Report), 2019, http://report.iresearch.cn/report/201909/3433.shtml.

3. Joel Andreas, *Rise of the Red Engineers: The Cultural Revolution and the Origins of China's New Class* (Stanford, CA: Stanford University Press, 2009).

4. Di Su, "Cheku Kafei Chuangshiren Sudi: Duiyu Chuangye Kafei, Wode Kanfa" (Garage Cafe Founder Sudi: My View of the Garage Cafe), *36Kr* (blog), August 14, 2013, http://www.36kr.com/p/205115.

5. *Zhongguo Chuangye Fuhua 30 Nian 1987–2017* (Three Decades of Chinese Entrepreneurship and Incubation: 1987–2017) (Beijing: Scientific and Technical Documentation Press, 2019).

6. *Zhongguo Chuangye Fuhua 30 Nian 1987–2017*.

7. Adam Segal, *Digital Dragon: High-Technology Enterprises in China* (Ithaca, NY: Cornell University Press, 2010).

8. Fred L. Block and Matthew R. Keller, *State of Innovation: The U.S. Government's Role in Technology Development* (New York: Routledge, 2015).

9. Block and Keller, *State of Innovation*, 19.

10. Joel Wiggins and David V. Gibson, "Overview of US Incubators and the Case of the Austin Technology Incubator," *International Journal of Entrepreneurship and Innovation Management* 3, nos. 1–2 (2003): 56–66.

11. Colin Barrow, *Incubators: A Realist's Guide to the World's New Business Accelerators* (St. Louis, MO: Wiley, 2001), 15.

12. Wiggins and Gibson, "Overview of US Incubators," 57.

13. Gina Neff, Elizabeth Wissinger, and Sharon Zukin, "Entrepreneurial Labor among Cultural Producers: 'Cool' Jobs in 'Hot' Industries," *Social Semiotics* 15, no. 3 (December 1, 2005): 307–34, https://doi.org/10.1080/10350330500310111; Alice E. Marwick, *Status Update: Celebrity, Publicity, and Branding in the Social Media Age* (New Haven, CT: Yale University Press, 2015); Gina Neff, *Venture Labor: Work and the Burden of Risk in Innovative Industries* (Cambridge, MA: MIT Press, 2012); Fred Turner, *From Counterculture to Cyberculture: Stewart Brand, the Whole Earth Network, and the Rise of Digital Utopianism* (Chicago.: University of Chicago Press, 2008); Richard Barbrook and Andy Cameron, "The Californian Ideology," *Science as Culture* 6, no. 1 (January 1, 1996): 44–72, https://doi.org/10.1080/09505439609526455.

14. Wiggins and Gibson, "Overview of US Incubators," 57.

15. Marwick, *Status Update*; Neff, *Venture Labor*; Andrew Ross, *No-Collar: The Hidden Cost of the Humane Workplace* (New York: Basic Books, 2002).

16. Dan Breznitz and Michael Murphree, *Run of the Red Queen: Government, Innovation, Globalization, and Economic Growth in China* (New Haven, CT: Yale University Press, 2012).

17. Frederic Deng and Youqin Huang, "Uneven Land Reform and Urban Sprawl in China: The Case of Beijing," *Progress in Planning* 61, no. 3 (April 1, 2004): 211–36, https://doi.org/10.1016/j.progress.2003.10.004.

18. Thomas Orlik, *China: The Bubble That Never Pops* (New York: Oxford University Press, 2020), 35.

19. Yu Zhou, *The Inside Story of China's High-Tech Industry: Making Silicon Valley in Beijing* (Lanham, MD: Rowman & Littlefield, 2007).

20. Yuhai Liu and Shuxia Yang, "Zhongguancun Ershinian Guimo Guangzhang Yu Quan Beijing Beizhi Quandi" (Zhongguancun Has Expanded to Cover the Whole of Beijing City, Faces Accusations of Land Enclosure), *21st Century Business Herald*, July 8, 2013, http://chanye.focus.cn/news/2013-07-08/3574986.html.

21. Fang Xingdong and Jiang Shenglan, *Zhongguancun Shiluo* (Zhongguancun Lost) (Beijing: China Customs Press, 2004).

22. Aruna Chandra and Chia-An Chao, "Growth and Evolution of High-Technology Business Incubation in China," *Human Systems Management* 30, nos. 1–2 (January 1, 2011): 55–69, https://doi.org/10.3233/HSM-2011-0739.

23. Breznitz and Murphree, *Run of the Red Queen*; Cong Cao, "Zhongguancun and China's High-Tech Parks in Transition: 'Growing Pains' or 'Premature Senility?,'" *Asian Survey* 44, no. 5 (October 1, 2004): 647–68, https://doi.org/10.1525/as.2004.44.5.647; Zhou, *The Inside Story of China's High-Tech Industry*.

24. Silvia M. Lindtner, *Prototype Nation: China and the Contested Promise of Innovation* (Princeton, NJ: Princeton University Press, 2020).

25. Tu Lan and Lin Zhang, "The New Whole State System: State-Led Financialization, State-Private Fusion, and China's Innovation Policies After 2008," Social Science Research Network (SSRN) Scholarly Paper, April 10, 2021, https://doi.org/10.2139/ssrn.3826658.

26. Dejiang Yu, "Qinghuaxi Ziben Xipai: Xiaoqi Gaigedao Zuqiechang" (A Reshuffling at Tsinghua Capital: The Long and Winding Road of University-Run Reform), *Zhengquan Shibao Wang*, December 5, 2019, http://news.stcn.com/2019/1205/15527448.shtml.

27. Yanping Li and Yang Li, "Zhongmeiying Sanguo Chuangke Kongjian Fazhan de Bijiao Ji Qishi" (The Implications of Comparing Entrepreneurial Spaces in China, the United States, and the United Kingdom), *Guizhou Social Science Journal*, no. 8 (2017): 82–88.

28. Wenyao Li, "Fuhuaqi Cipo Paomo Chuangye Kafeiguan Liangleme?" (The Incubator Bubble Burst, Are Entrepreneurial Cafés Cooling Down?), *Huaxia Shibao*, February 20, 2016, https://tech.huanqiu.com/article/9CaKrnJTYbo.

29. Dongdong Biji, "Paomo Zhong de Fuhuaqi Shichang, Zhizhuan Yaohe Bu Zhuanqian" (The Incubator Industry Bubble: More Noise Than Money), Huxiu.com, December 22, 2017, https://www.huxiu.com/article/226865.html.

30. Shuxia Gu, "Tuoqi Mingtian de Taiyang-Yushi Jujin, Kaituo Chuangxin de Qinghua Xiaoban Chanye" (Lifting Tomorrow's Sun: Tsinghua Enterprises Keeping Abreast with Development and Innovation), *Xinqinghua*, December 18, 2003.

31. Andreas, *Rise of the Red Engineers*, 54.

32. In the heat of the Cultural Revolution (1966–1976), under the banner of "factories lead academic disciplines," Tsinghua went through a restructuring in which

its departments and campus factories were merged. The university, like many others in China, opened its doors to a new class of "worker-peasant-soldier students" recruited through a danwei-based recommendation system. In the transitional years of the 1980s, a growing number of Tsinghua professors and graduates took part in early entrepreneurial ventures. Starting with the founding of the Tsinghua University Technology Service Company in 1980, numerous university spinoff companies were set up in the first decade of the post-Mao reform. One of the most successful was the Tsinghua University Technology Development Company, the predecessor of Tsinghua Unigroup, established in 1988 by a collection of entrepreneurial Tsinghua professors. See Andreas, *Rise of the Red Engineers*, 54.

33. Sunami Atsushi, "Industry-University Cooperation and University-Affiliated Enterprises in China, a Country Aspiring for Growth on Science and Education—Building New System for Technological Innovation," *Keizai Sangyo Journal* (Tokyo: Research Institute of Economy, Trade and Industry, May 2002), https://www.rieti.go.jp/en/papers/research-review/001.html; Weiping Wu and Yu Zhou, "The Third Mission Stalled? Universities in China's Technological Progress," *Journal of Technology Transfer* 37, no. 6 (December 1, 2012): 812–27, https://doi.org/10.1007/s10961-011-9233-8; Zhou, *The Inside Story of China's High-Tech Industry*.

34. Zhou, *The Inside Story of China's High-Tech Industry*.

35. Breznitz and Murphree, *Run of the Red Queen*; Wu and Zhou, "The Third Mission Stalled?"

36. Zhijun Ling, *China's New Revolution 1980–2006: From Zhongguancun to Chinese Society* (Wuhan: Hubei Renmin Press, 2008).

37. Cao, "Zhongguancun and China's High-Tech Parks in Transition"; Breznitz and Murphree, *Run of the Red Queen*.

38. Xiaoxia Zhang, *Mengxiang Wuxian: Qinghua Kejiyuan Chuangjianzhe Jishi* (Unlimited Dreams: A Story of Tuspark's Founder and His Team) (Beijing: Tsinghua University Press, 2014).

39. Hu Haifeng, the son of former Chinese president Hu Jintao (himself an alumnus of Tsinghua) served as the chairman of Nuctech—one of Tsinghua's most successful enterprises—in the late 1990s after graduating from Tsinghua with an MBA. During his term in charge, the company held a monopoly in the Chinese security scanner market. In 2008, Hu was promoted to the party secretary of Tsinghua Holdings. See David Barboza and Sharon LaFraniere, "'Princelings' in China Use Family Ties to Gain Riches," *New York Times*, May 17, 2012.

40. Xinian Tao, "Qidi Gaoxiaoxi Shangshi Gongsi" (Taking a Stock of Publicly Listed University-Affiliated Enterprises), *Shidai Weekly*, March 20, 2014, http://finance.sina.com.cn/stock/s/20140320/085818562006.shtml.

41. Ling, *China's New Revolution 1980–2006*, 171. Beijing's mayor at the time, Chen Xitong, saw the rapid expansion of high-tech zones in Beijing as a way to boost local GDP, raise local government revenues, and attract state investment and preferential treatment. Turning a blind eye to the State Council's 1993 warning against more new zone projects, Chen not only encouraged ZGC's geographic expansion but also allocated land and approved funding for the construction of TusPark and Peking University's Sinobioway biology park. Although Chen was ousted for corruption in 1995, the city remained committed to his GDP-centric logic of boosting development through real estate speculation. In subsequent years, this logic would redirect the state's efforts to promote technological innovation—the stated goal of building all these science parks and high-tech experimental zones—toward land-based state capitalist accumulation.

42. Atsushi, "Industry-University Cooperation and University-Affiliated Enterprises in China."

43. Xuedong Ran, "Qinghua Kejiyuan 'Duoquan,' Ziguang 'Shaozhuangpai' Tongding Qinghuaxi" (The Power Struggle in Tsinghua Science Park: Unigroup's Young Clique Rules Over Tsinghua Enterprises), *The Economic Observer*, March 31, 2013, http://tech.sina.com.cn/it/m/2003-03-31/0834174561.shtml.

44. Jiangyu Wang and Tan Cheng-Han, "Mixed Ownership Reform and Corporate Governance in China's State-Owned Enterprises," n.d., 32; "Party-State Capitalism in China—Meg Rithmire," Mossavar-Rahmani Center for Business & Government, Harvard Kennedy School, https://www.hks.harvard.edu/centers/mrcbg/programs/growthpolicy/party-state-capitalism-china-meg-rithmire.

45. The parent company of TusHoldings, Tsinghua Holdings, is wholly owned by Tsinghua University and controls some of China's top university-affiliated high-tech enterprises.

46. Dan Liu, "Rushang de Diyun-Ji Qidi Konggu Gufen Youxian Gongsi Zongcai Wangjiwu" (A Confucian Businessman: On TusHoldings' CEO Wang Jiwu), *Shuimu Qinghua*, 2014, http://www.tsinghua.org.cn///upload//file//146035645 2191.pdf.

47. Liu, "Rushang de Diyun-Ji Qidi Konggu Gufen Youxian Gongsi Zongcai Wangjiwu."

48. Jing Huang, "Xiaoyou Wangjiwu Maxiaoming Fufu Juanzeng Xianli Xiaoyou Zonghui Chengli Baizhounian" (Alumni Couple Wang Jiwu and Ma Xiaoming Make Donation to the Alumni Association for Its 100th Anniversary), *Tsinghua News*, April 24, 2013, https://news.tsinghua.edu.cn/info/1012/60857.htm.

49. Tana Su, "Shandian Zhishang—Fang Qidi Konggu Youxian Gongsi Zongcai Wang Jiwu" (On the Mountaintop: An Interview with TusHoldings' CEO Wang Jiwu), *Tsinghua News*, September 5, 2014, https://news.tsinghua.edu.cn/info/1003/26850.htm.

50. One of TusHoldings' VC funds, THC Ventures, has managed the National SME Development Fund on behalf of the Ministry of Finance and other major state-owned banks and enterprises since 2006. Another fund, SinoKing Capital, works with the government of the Guangxi Zhuang Autonomous Region to manage its government-guided fund.

51. Jianyuan Shen, "Jiema Qidi Konggu—Yijia Keji Fuwu Jutou de 'Keji Xinyang' he 'Qianyi Buju' " (Decoding TusHoldings: A Tech Giant's "Tech Belief" and "Trillions Strategy"), *The Economic Observer*, April 30, 2018, http://www.tus holdings.com/h/qdmedia/show-63-703-1.html.

52. Zi Lin, "Tusholdings' CEO: Take Talent and Technologies to Xiong'an to 'Bite the Hard Bone,'" *Xinjingbao*, November 18, 2019, http://www.tusholdings.com /h/qdnews/show-60-1805-1.html.

53. Jiwu Wang, *Jiqunshi Chuangxin Lilun Yu Shijian* (Cluster Innovation Theory and Practice) (Beijing: Tsinghua University Press, 2016), 113.

54. Yining Zeng and Jing Xu, "Beida Qinghua Shuangxiong Hui? Xueyuanpai Chanye Dichan Qilu" (Peking University and Tsinghua University in Competition? The Misguided Path of University Enterprises in Real Estate), *China Real Estate Business*, September 6, 2012.

55. Orlik, *China*.

56. Yifan Chen and Xiuli Li, "Zhongguo Diyida Xiaoqi Bianju: Qinghua Konggu Dongshihui Tiaozheng Muhou" (The Transformation of China's No. University Enterprise Group: The Inside Story of Tsinghua Holdings' Board of Directors), *The Economic Observer*, August 4, 2018, http://finance.sina.com.cn/chanjing /gsnews/2018-08-04/doc-ihhhczfa1675278.shtml.

57. Jianfeng Zhong, "Qingli Guifan Gaoxiao Suoshu Qiye Congjin Gaoxiao Jinzhong Jingli Banxue" (Regulating University-Affiliated Enterprises and Encouraging Universities to Focus on Teaching and Research), *Zhongguo Jiaoyubao*, May 12, 2018, http://www.moe.gov.cn/s78/A27/s8544/201805/t20180514_335812.html.

58. Zhong, "Qingli Guifan Gaoxiao Suoshu Qiye Congjin Gaoxiao Jinzhong Jingli Banxue."

59. Chen and Li, "Zhongguo Diyida Xiaoqi Bianju: Qinghua Konggu Dongshihui Tiaozheng Muhou."

60. Lin, "Tusholdings' CEO."

61. Lin, "Tusholdings' CEO."

62. Di Su and Haizhen Wang, *Cheku Kafei: "Zhongguo Guigu" de Chuangyemeng* (The Garage Café: Entrepreneurial Dreams in "China's Silicon Valley") (Beijing: People's Press, 2013).

63. Su and Wang, *Cheku Kafei*.

64. Lindtner, Hertz, and Dourish, "Emerging Sites of HCI Innovation"; Wang, *The Other Digital China*.

65. Gong Zheng and Xue Hai, "'Cheku Kafei' Xianxiang Diaocha Yu Sikao" (An Investigation of and Thoughts on the "Garage Café" Phenomenon), *Zhongguancun Magazine*, February 2, 2018, https://www.zz-news.com/com/zhongguancun/news/itemid-968271.html.

66. Su and Wang, *Cheku Kafei*.

67. Su, "Cheku Kafei Chuangshiren Sudi."

68. Lin Yang, "Zongli Nihao: Wozai Zhongguancun Chuangye Dajie Xiu Jiapu" (Hello Prime Minister: I Am Compiling Family Genealogies on ZGC Inno-Way), *Boke Tianxia*, October 14, 2015, https://www.sohu.com/a/35616732_119666.

69. QQ is a popular instant messaging application operated by the Chinese internet company Tencent. The predecessor of WeChat, QQ was one of the first apps that many Chinese internet users learned to use.

70. This appropriation of "The Passion of the Christ" refers to his tortuous, sacrificial but ultimately symbolic experiences as a grassroots entrepreneur in China.

71. Lindtner, *Prototype Nation*, 23.

4. THE PLATFORMIZATION OF FAMILY PRODUCTION

1. See the 2021 Taobao Village Report issued by AliResearch, http://www.aliresearch.com/ch/information/informationdetails?articleCode=256317657652006912&type=新闻.

2. Hill Gates, *China's Motor: A Thousand Years of Petty Capitalism* (Ithaca, NY: Cornell University Press, 1997), 29. Gates differentiates petty capitalism from the Chinese state-centered tributary mode of production and Western industrial capitalism.

3. Tiejun Wen, Junna Zhang, and Jiansheng Qiu, *Ju Wei Si Wei: Guojia Anquan Yu Xiangcunzhili* (Be Prepared for Danger in Times of Danger: National Security and Rural Governance) (Beijing: Orient Press, 2016).

4. Philip C. C. Huang, "Rethinking 'the Third Sphere': The Dualistic Unity of State and Society in China, Past and Present," *Modern China* 45, no. 4 (July 1, 2019): 357, https://doi.org/10.1177/0097700419844962. According to Huang, much of the actual governance of rural society happens in the "third sphere," in between the formal system of the state and the informal system of society, where it is shaped by the interaction between the two systems and operates via mechanisms like the "community mediation system" or semiformal agents like the unsalaried quasi-officials known as *xiangbao* (乡保), who serve as a link between the county government and villages.

5. Li-An Zhou, "The Administrative Subcontract: Significance, Relevance and Implications for Intergovernmental Relations in China," *Chinese Journal of Sociology* 2, no. 1 (2016): 34–74.

6. Jonathan Unger, *The Transformation of Rural China* (New York: Routledge, 2016); Jacob Eyferth, *Eating Rice from Bamboo Roots: The Social History of a Community of Handicraft Papermakers in Rural Sichuan, 1920–2000* (Cambridge, MA: Harvard University Asia Center, 2009).

7. Huang, "Rethinking 'the Third Sphere,' " 365. According to Huang, the party-state set up formal township (commune) governments under the county level and replaced the Republican-era wards with the administrative village (brigade). Adopting a "mass line" ideology and campaign-style mobilization strategy, it embedded itself into the rural economy and society through village-based party branch committees.

8. Wen, Zhang, and Qiu, *Ju Wei Si Wei*.

9. Chun Lin, *The Transformation of Chinese Socialism* (Durham, NC: Duke University Press, 2006).

10. Yunxiang Yan, "The Chinese Path to Individualization," *The British Journal of Sociology* 61, no. 3 (2010): 489–512, https://doi.org/10.1111/j.1468-4446.2010 .01323.x.

11. Ho-fung Hung, *The China Boom: Why China Will Not Rule the World* (New York: Columbia University Press, 2017).

12. Yan, "The Chinese Path to Individualization."

13. Victor Nee, "Peasant Household Individualism," *International Journal of Sociology* 14, no. 4 (1984): 50–76. Nee describes the persistence of family-based economic logic in rural China as "peasant household individualism."

14. Alexander F. Day and Mindi Schneider, "The End of Alternatives? Capitalist Transformation, Rural Activism and the Politics of Possibility in China," *Journal of Peasant Studies* 45, no. 7 (November 10, 2018): 1221–46, https://doi.org /10.1080/03066150.2017.1386179.

15. Wen, Zhang, and Qiu, *Ju Wei Si Wei*.

16. Philip C. C. Huang, *The Peasant Economy and Social Change in North China* (Stanford, CA: Stanford University Press, 1988); Yasheng Huang, *Capitalism with Chinese Characteristics: Entrepreneurship and the State* (New York: Cambridge University Press, 2008).

17. Zhou, "The Administrative Subcontract."

18. Wen, Zhang, and Qiu, *Ju Wei Si Wei*.

19. Alexander F. Day, *The Peasant in Postsocialist China: History, Politics, and Capitalism* (Cambridge: Cambridge University Press, 2013); Huang, *Capitalism with Chinese Characteristics*.

20. Unger, *The Transformation of Rural China.*
21. Yan, "The Chinese Path to Individualization."
22. Yan, "The Chinese Path to Individualization."
23. Hairong Yan, Ku Hok Bun, and Xu Siyuan, "Rural Revitalization, Scholars, and the Dynamics of the Collective Future in China," *Journal of Peasant Studies* 48, no. 4 (January 20, 2020): 6, https://doi.org/10.1080/03066150.2019.1694911.
24. Wen, Zhang, and Qiu, *Ju Wei Si Wei.*
25. Nicholas R. Lardy, *The State Strikes Back: The End of Economic Reform in China?* (Washington, DC: Peterson Institute for International Economics, 2019).
26. Day and Schneider, "The End of Alternatives?" These voices eventually pushed the central state to announce more moderate and pro-rural policies between 2005 and 2008, promoting "in-place urbanization" (*chengzhenhua*, 城镇化), ecological civilization (*shengtai wenming*, 生态文明), and the construction of a resource-conserving and environmentally friendly society (*huanjingyouhaoxing, ziyuanjieyuexing shehui*, 环境友好型资源节约型社会).
27. Julia Chuang, *Beneath the China Boom: Labor, Citizenship, and the Making of a Rural Land Market* (Berkeley: University of California Press, 2020), 16–21.
28. Yan Hairong and Chen Yiyuan, "Agrarian Capitalization Without Capitalism? Capitalist Dynamics from Above and Below in China," *Journal of Agrarian Change* 15, no. 3 (2015): 366–91, https://doi.org/10.1111/joac.12121; "Inequality in China: Rural Poverty Persists as Urban Wealth Balloons," *BBC News*, June 29, 2011, https://www.bbc.com/news/business-13945072.
29. Wen, Zhang, and Qiu, *Ju Wei Si Wei.*
30. Thomas Orlik, *China: The Bubble That Never Pops* (New York: Oxford University Press, 2020), 119.
31. Orlik, *China*, 121.
32. Pun Ngai and Anita Koo, "A 'World-Class' (Labor) Camp/Us: Foxconn and China's New Generation of Labor Migrants," *Positions: Asia Critique* 23, no. 3 (August 1, 2015): 411–35, https://doi.org/10.1215/10679847-3125811.
33. Anthony H. F. Li, "E-commerce and Taobao Villages. A Promise for China's Rural Development?," *China Perspectives* 2017, no. 2017/3 (September 1, 2017): 57–62, https://doi.org/10.4000/chinaperspectives.7423.
34. W. Allyn Rickett, trans., *Guanzi: Political, Economic, and Philosophical Essays from Early China, Volume II* (Princeton, NJ: Princeton University Press, 1998). The earliest existing record of B County handicraft weaving can be traced to the *Guan Zi*, a seventh century BCE collection of political and philosophical texts attributed to the philosopher Guanzi (Guan Zhong), who also served as prime minister to Duke Huan of the Qi state. In the book, Guanzi advised the duke to protect the poor handicraft-weaving peasants living in the agriculturally poor

Northern Qi area, where modern-day W Village is located, by forbidding people living in other areas of Qi to enter the weaving trade.

35. Y. X. Shu, "Chenggong Zhilu-Ji Boxingxian Gongyi Meishu Erchang Changzhang Dangzhibu Shuji Sun Yingxi" (Road to Success; About Sun Yingxi, the Head of the Boxing No. 2 Handicraft Factory), in *Zouxiang Xinshiji* (Marching Toward the New Century) (Jinan: Huanyi Press, 1992), 510–23.

36. Jicheng Yao et al., *Huanghe Sanjiaozhou Minjian Yishu Shenmei Yanjiu* (On the Aesthetics of Handicraft Art in the Yellow River Delta Area) (Jinan: Qilu Press, 2011).

37. In a continuation of socialist danwei culture, for years some state-owned factories in China maintained protectionist or discriminatory recruitment policies that favored local residents with nonagricultural hukou, especially the children of employees. Migrant workers, especially those with agricultural hukou, were usually hired as temporary workers without full benefits. The Chinese state eliminated the agricultural vs. nonagricultural hukou category in 2016.

38. Tmall.com is an upgraded version of Taobao.com. It was introduced by Alibaba in 2010 as a way to differentiate brands or authorized distributors from Taobao's customer-to-customer merchants. For more information about Tmall, see chapter 5.

39. *Guanxi* is a Chinese term that refers to a system of social networks and influential relationships that can facilitate business and other dealings.

40. Weicheng Tang and Jin Zhu, "Informality and Rural Industry: Rethinking the Impacts of E-Commerce on Rural Development in China," *Journal of Rural Studies* 75 (2020): 20–29; Geng Lin, Xiaoru Xie, and Zuyi Lü, "Taobao Practices, Everyday Life and Emerging Hybrid Rurality in Contemporary China," *Journal of Rural Studies* 47 (October 2016): 514–23, https://doi.org/10.1016/j.jrurstud .2016.05.012; Linliang Qian, "Moral Diversification and Moral Agency: Contesting Business Ethics among Chinese e-Commerce Traders," *Journal of Chinese Sociology* 7, no. 1 (November 17, 2020): 21, https://doi.org/10.1186/s40711-020 -00137-4; Chiu-Wan Liu, "Return Migration, Online Entrepreneurship and Gender Performance in the Chinese 'Taobao Families,'" *Asia Pacific Viewpoint*, June 4, 2020, https://doi.org/10.1111/apv.12280.

41. Lin Zhang, "When Platform Capitalism Meets Petty Capitalism in China: Alibaba and an Integrated Approach to Platformization," *International Journal of Communication* 14 (January 1, 2020): 21.

42. Zhang, "When Platform Capitalism Meets Petty Capitalism in China."

43. David Barboza, "The Jack Ma Way," *New York Times*, September 6, 2014; Neil Gough and Alexandra Stevenson, "The Unlikely Ascent of Jack Ma, Alibaba's Founder," *New York Times*, May 7, 2014.

44. Yongle Chen, "Ma Yun: Wo Douneng Chenggong 80% de Nianqingren Yexing" (Jack Ma: If I Can Be Successful, So Can 80% of Young People), June 21, 2018, http://finance.sina.com.cn/roll/2018-06-21/doc-ihefphqk7758064.shtml.

45. Zhang, "When Platform Capitalism Meets Petty Capitalism in China," 123.

46. "China Auction Site Taobao Sees Sales Doubling in '09," *Reuters*, September 11, 2009, https://www.reuters.com/article/taobao-idUSSHA30977320090911.

47. Zhou, "The Administrative Subcontract."

48. Xiangdong Wang, "Shaji Moshi Jiqi Yiyi" (The Shaji Model and Its Significance), Sina Blog, December 15, 2010, https://tech.qq.com/a/20110221/000388.htm.

49. AliResearch, "Shaji Moshi Rang Nongmin Zhijie He Shichang Duijie" (The Shangji Model Directly Connects Peasants to the Market), December 22, 2010, http://pre.aliresearch.com/Blog/Article/detail/id/12607.html.

50. Xiangdong Wang, Qiping Jiang, and Xiumin Ye, *Hexie Shehui Yu Xinxihua Zhanlüe* (Harmonious Society and the Strategy of Informatization) (Beijing: The Commercial Press, 2014).

51. According to AliResearch's 2014 Research Report of Taobao Villages in China, a village has to meet the following three criteria to qualify as a Taobao village: (1) merchants are registered as residents of the village and conduct business there; (2) the annual ecommerce GMV should be no less than RMB 10 million; (3) the number of online merchants registered at the village should be no fewer than 50, or at least 10 per cent of the village households.

52. Li, "E-commerce and Taobao Villages. A Promise for China's Rural Development?"

53. Li, "E-commerce and Taobao Villages."

54. Wenxiao Zhang, "Rural E-Commerce Programs Can Work. So Why Do Some Fail?," *Sixth Tone*, February 8, 2021, http://www.sixthtone.com/news/1006806/rural-e-commerce-programs-can-work.-so-why-do-some-fail.

55. Xiangdong Wang and Hongbing Gao, *Dianshang Xiaopin* (Eradication of Poverty by E-commerce) (Beijing: The Commercial Press, 2016).

56. Leesa Shrader, "Microfinance, E-Commerce, Big Data and China: The Alibaba Story," *CGAP* (blog), October 11, 2013, https://www.cgap.org/blog/microfinance-e-commerce-big-data-and-china-alibaba-story.

57. Gough and Stevenson, "The Unlikely Ascent of Jack Ma, Alibaba's Founder."

58. Lingling Wei, "China Blocked Jack Ma's Ant IPO After Investigation Revealed Likely Beneficiaries," *Wall Street Journal*, February 16, 2021.

59. Lara Logan, "Jack Ma Brings Alibaba to the U.S.," *60 Minutes*, September 28, 2014, https://www.cbsnews.com/news/alibaba-chairman-jack-ma-brings-company-to-america/.

60. Leilei Ji, "Fanxiang Ruxiang Chuangye Chuangxin Renyuan Da 850 Wan" (The Number of Urban-to-Rural and Rural-based Entrepreneurs Reaches 8.5 Million),

Economics Daily, November 21, 2019, http://www.xinhuanet.com/fortune/2019
-11/21/c_1125255795.htm.

61. AliResearch, "2020 Chinese Taobao Villages Research Report," http://www.ali
research.com/ch/information/informationdetails?articleCode=1268604879
66199808.

5. MOVING BEYOND *SHANZHAI*?

1. Tao He, "Taobaocun Jishi: Yige Nongmin Bei Hulianwang Gaibian de Mingyun"
(Taobao Village Story: A Peasant's Life Changed by the Internet), *GQ*, October 8, 2015, https://www.gq.com.cn/topic/news_115g695f0deefff1.html.

2. Zhihong Liu, "Nituli Chanchu de Dianshang Wangguo" (An E-Commerce
Empire Sprouted from the Earth), *Xinhua Daily*, November 4, 2018, http://
jsnews.jschina.com.cn/shms/201811/t20181104_2017529.shtml.

3. Cara Wallis and Jack Linchuan Qiu, "Shanzhaiji and the Transformation of the
Local Mediascape in Shenzhen," in *Mapping Media in China* (New York: Routledge, 2012), 127–43; Lin Zhang and Anthony Fung, "The Myth of 'Shanzhai'
Culture and the Paradox of Digital Democracy in China," *Inter-Asia Cultural
Studies* 14, no. 3 (September 1, 2013): 401–16, https://doi.org/10.1080/14649373
.2013.801608; Josephine Ho, "Shanzhai: Economic/Cultural Production Through
the Cracks of Globalization," plenary speech in at the Crossroads Cultural Studies Conference, Hong Kong, 2010; Fan Yang, *Faked in China: Nation Branding,
Counterfeit Culture, and Globalization* (Bloomington: Indiana University Press,
2015); Silvia Lindtner, "Hacking with Chinese Characteristics: The Promises of
the Maker Movement Against China's Manufacturing Culture," *Science, Technology, & Human Values* 40, no. 5 (September 1, 2015): 854–79, https://doi.org
/10.1177/0162243915590861.

4. bunnie Huang, "Tech Trend: Shanzhai," *Bunnie's Blog* (blog), February 26, 2009,
https://www.bunniestudios.com/blog/?p=284; Silvia M. Lindtner, *Prototype
Nation: China and the Contested Promise of Innovation* (Princeton, NJ: Princeton
University Press, 2020); *Shenzhen: The Silicon Valley of Hardware (Part 1)*, *Future
Cities*, Wired video, 2016, https://www.youtube.com/watch?v=hp6F_ApUq-c.

5. Yinbin Hu, "'Shanzhai Dian' Beihou Shi Wangu de 'Shanzhai Siwei'" (Behind
"Shanzhai Shop" Lies Stubborn "Shanzhai Logic"), Xinhuanet, June 19, 2018,
http://www.xinhuanet.com/2018-06/19/c_1123000916.htm.

6. Lars Eckstein and Anja Schwarz, *Postcolonial Piracy: Media Distribution and
Cultural Production in the Global South* (New York: Bloomsbury, 2014), 7.

7. Wired, *Shenzhen*; Huang, "Tech Trend."

8. Township and village enterprises (TVE) were market-oriented public enterprises under the purview of local governments. These enterprises emerged in

the late 1970s and 1980s following China's economic reform. Many grew out of commune and brigade enterprises founded during the Great Leap Forward and the later years of the Cultural Revolution.

9. Michael Keane, *Created in China* (New York: Routledge, 2009); Jing Wang, "Culture as Leisure and Culture as Capital," *Positions: Asia Critique* 9, no. 1 (February 1, 2001): 69–104, https://doi.org/10.1215/10679847-9-1-69; Laikwan Pang, *Creativity and Its Discontents: China's Creative Industries and Intellectual Property Rights Offenses* (Durham NC: Duke University Press, 2012); Lily Chumley, *Creativity Class: Art School and Culture Work in Postsocialist China* (Princeton, NJ: Princeton University Press, 2016).

10. Connie Zheng, "Suzhi Development: Indigenous Approaches to Enhancing the Quality of Human Resources," *Journal of Chinese Human Resource Management* 5, no. 2 (January 1, 2014): 115–28, https://doi.org/10.1108/JCHRM-07-2014-0020.

11. Linliang Qian, "The 'Inferior' Talk Back: Suzhi (Human Quality), Social Mobility, and E-Commerce Economy in China," *Journal of Contemporary China* 27, no. 114 (November 2, 2018): 887–901, https://doi.org/10.1080/10670564.2018.1488104.

12. Anita Chan, *Networking Peripheries: Technological Futures and the Myth of Digital Universalism* (Cambridge, MA: MIT Press, 2013), 201. Chan observed parallel narratives emerging in rural Peruvian villages experiencing an export-oriented business boom. The first was a neoliberal discourse about entrepreneurially "flexible, mutual relations, [and] ever-present opportunities for self-advancement." The second was one of jealousy, deceit, exploitation, and the self-interested pursuit of success at all costs.

13. Michael Hardt and Antonio Negri, *Multitude: War and Democracy in the Age of Empire* (New York: Penguin Books, 2005), 108–9; Michael Hardt, "Affective Labor," *Boundary* 2 26, no. 2 (1999): 97, Hardt and Negri define immaterial labor as labor that "creates immaterial products, such as knowledge, information, communication, a relationship or an emotional response." According to them, this form of labor has gradually "achieved the dominant position of the highest value" in society since the late 1970s because, although the number of people engaged in immaterial labor remains relatively low in comparison to agriculture and industry, it nevertheless exerts hegemonic influence over "other forms of labor" and "society as a whole," forcing them to "informationalize, become intelligent, become communicative, become effective."

14. For more information about *baokuan*, see https://www.thatsmags.com/shanghai/post/22710/chinese-urban-dictionary-baokuan.

15. Lizhi Liu, "From Click to Boom: The Political Economy of E-Commerce in China," Stanford Institute for Innovation in Developing Economies, 2018.

16. Amanda Schiavo, "Alibaba's Jack Ma Seeks Harsh Sentences for Counterfeiters," *TheStreet*, March 7, 2017, https://www.thestreet.com/investing/stocks/alibaba-s-jack-ma-seeks-harsh-sentences-for-counterfeiters-14029609.

17. Liu, "From Click to Boom."

18. Lin Zhang, "When Platform Capitalism Meets Petty Capitalism in China: Alibaba and an Integrated Approach to Platformization," *International Journal of Communication* 14 (January 1, 2020): 127.

19. Henry Jenkins, Sam Ford, and Joshua Green, *Spreadable Media: Creating Value and Meaning in a Networked Culture* (New York: NYU Press, 2013); Yochai Benkler, *The Wealth of Networks: How Social Production Transforms Markets and Freedom* (New Haven, CT: Yale University Press, 2006); Peter Jaszi, "On the Author Effect: Contemporary Copyright and Collective Creativity," *Cardozo Arts & Entertainment Law Journal* 10 (1991): 293.

20. Xiaotong Fei, Gary G. Hamilton, and Wang Zheng, *From the Soil: The Foundations of Chinese Society* (Berkeley: University of California Press, 1992).

21. Pang, *Creativity and Its Discontents*, 227.

22. Alice E. Marwick, *Status Update: Celebrity, Publicity, and Branding in the Social Media Age* (New Haven, CT: Yale University Press, 2015), 166.

23. Sarah Banet-Weiser, *Authentic^TM: The Politics of Ambivalence in a Brand Culture* (New York: NYU Press, 2012).

24. Marwick, *Status Update*, 170. Marwick described how successful Silicon Valley self-branders sought to present their identities as "divorced from interpersonal and social ties." Instead, they existed "in a competitive, insecure business environment," and were acted out "primarily through social media." Chumley, *Creativity Class*, 125 Chumley, in a different context, described how art academy students in urban China learned to build personal brands "through practices of self-narration and self-expression."

25. Banet-Weiser, *Authentic^TM*; Lilly Irani, *Chasing Innovation: Making Entrepreneurial Citizens in Modern India* (Princeton, NJ: Princeton University Press, 2019).

26. Irani, *Chasing Innovation*, 199.

27. Irani, *Chasing Innovation*, 201.

28. Compared to Alibaba's Taobao platform, Tmall has a higher threshold of entry in terms of registration and maintenance fees.

29. Mitch Meisner, "Dazhai: The Mass Line in Practice," *Modern China*, August 15, 2016, https://doi.org/10.1177/009770047800400102; Norma Diamond, "Model Villages and Village Realities," *Modern China* 9, no. 2 (April 1, 1983): 163–81, https://doi.org/10.1177/009770048300900201.

30. Xiao was not able to travel to New York for the event because his visa application was denied.

31. Irani, *Chasing Innovation*.

32. Banet-Weiser, *Authentic^{TM}*, 10.

33. Angela McRobbie, *Be Creative: Making a Living in the New Culture Industries* (Cambridge: Polity Press, 2016), 90.

34. Under the one-child policy, rural residents were allowed to have a second child if their firstborn was a girl.

35. The street, consisting of a couple dozen small shops selling clothes, cosmetics, and snacks, had become popular in recent years among the area's growing population of young, middle-class women.

36. Yunxiang Yan, "Girl Power: Young Women and the Waning of Patriarchy in Rural North China," *Ethnology* 45, no. 2 (2006): 105–23.

37. Xiang Biao, "How Far Are the Left-behind Left behind? A Preliminary Study in Rural China," *Population, Space and Place* 13, no. 3 (May 2007): 179–91, https://doi.org/10.1002/psp.437.

38. Chiu-Wan Liu, "Return Migration, Online Entrepreneurship and Gender Performance in the Chinese *'Taobao* Families,'" *Asia Pacific Viewpoint*, June 4, 2020, https://doi.org/10.1111/apv.12280.

39. McRobbie, *Be Creative*, 90. Angela McRobbie observed in her study of gender in the British cultural industry that, for the daughters of working-class mothers, "normative femininity comes to be attached to the need to dis-identify with traditional female working-class values and lifestyles."

40. Amy Hanser, "The Gendered Rice Bowl: The Sexual Politics of Service Work in Urban China," *Gender & Society* 19, no. 5 (October 2005): 581–600, https://doi .org/10.1177/0891243205276794.

41. Haiqing Yu and Ling Cui, "China's E-Commerce: Empowering Rural Women?" *The China Quarterly* 238 (June 2019): 418–37, https://doi.org/10.1017/S0305 741018001819. According to Yu and Cui, women in rural e-commerce villages are "more confined by traditional patriarchal codes of self-sacrifice, domesticity and subordination" than their urban sisters.

42. Nick Srnicek, *Platform Capitalism* (Cambridge: Polity Press, 2016).

43. Tmall charges a fixed sum deposit that runs from 50,000 to 150,000 yuan, an annual service fee of 30,000 to 60,000 yuan, plus a commission fee in proportion to the shop's sales volume.

44. Srnicek, *Platform Capitalism*.

45. The village election is the only open election in contemporary China, although the party secretary of the village CCP branch is still an appointed position. For an analysis of China's village election system, see Kevin J. O'Brien and Lianjiang Li, "Accommodating 'Democracy' in a One-Party State: Introducing Village Elections in China," *The China Quarterly*, no. 162 (2000): 465–89.

46. Shuai Yang and Tiejun Wen, "Nongmin Zuzhihua de Kunjing yu Pojie" (The Predicament of and Solution to Farmers' Organization), *People's Forum* 29 (2011): 44–45.
47. Philip C. C. Huang, "Rethinking 'the Third Sphere': The Dualistic Unity of State and Society in China, Past and Present," *Modern China* 45, no. 4 (July 1, 2019): 355–91, https://doi.org/10.1177/0097700419844962.
48. Xiaozhou Su and Xing Ming, "Zhengfu Fuchi Nongcun Dianshang Ying Zouchu 'Saqian' Moshi" (Government Subsidies for Rural E-Commerce Should Avoid the "Throwing Money" Model), *Economic Information Daily*, December 15, 2016, http://politics.people.com.cn/n1/2016/1215/c1001-28951504.html.
49. Julia Chuang, *Beneath the China Boom: Labor, Citizenship, and the Making of a Rural Land Market* (Berkeley: University of California Press, 2020).
50. Tiejun Wen and Zhihui Tong, "Ziben He Bumen Xiaxiang Yu Xiaononghu Jingji de Zuzhihua Daolu-Jiandui Zhuanye Hezuoshe Daolu Tichu Zhiyi" (Capital and Government in the Countryside and the Road to Organizing the Small Peasant Economy: Doubts About the Co-op Path), *Open Times* 4 (2009): 5–26; Yan Hairong and Chen Yiyuan, "Debating the Rural Cooperative Movement in China, the Past and the Present," *Journal of Peasant Studies* 40, no. 6 (November 2013): 955–81, https://doi.org/10.1080/03066150.2013.866555.
51. Zhang, "When Platform Capitalism Meets Petty Capitalism in China"; Tarleton Gillespie, "The Politics of 'Platforms,'" *New Media & Society* 12, no. 3 (May 2010): 347–64, https://doi.org/10.1177/1461444809342738.

6. BETWEEN INDIVIDUALIZATION AND RETRADITIONALIZATION

1. Some examples of popular websites or apps used for reselling are Taobao.com, Ymatou, Sina Weibo, Tencent Weibo, WeChat, Instagram, and QQ.
2. CN FashionNetwork, "Zhongguo Jiang Daji Huise Shechipin Shichang: Daigou Daluanle Shechi Pinpai Gongying He Dingjia Jizhi" (China Will Launch a Strike Against Luxury Gray Market: Daigou Derails the Supply and Pricing Mechanisms of Luxury Brands), FashionNetwork.com, https://cn.fashionnetwork.com/news/zhong-guo-jiang-da-ji-hui-se-she-chi-pin-shi-chang—dai-gou-da-luan-le-she-chi-pin-pai-gong-ying-he-ding-jia-ji-zhi,677872.html.
3. That same year, a report released by the Chinese E-commerce Research Center revealed that the scale of the online reselling industry had reached US$4.35 billion in 2011, a year-over-year increase of 120 percent. Popular products include everything from baby formula to diamonds, but the most sought-after items are Western luxury brands such as Gucci, Prada, and Longchamp.

4. "What's 'Daigou' and What's It to Gucci and Beijing?" BloombergQuint, https://www.bloombergquint.com/quicktakes/what-s-daigou-and-what-s-it-to-gucci-and-beijing-quicktake.

5. Yuxue Zhang, "Kongjie Daigou'an Chongshen Pan Sannian" (Flight Attendant Sentence in Daigou Case Reduced to 3 Years), *BJNEWS*, December 18, 2013, http://www.bjnews.com.cn/inside/2013/12/18/297980.html.

6. Marcia Kaplan, "Chinese Consumers Are Eager to Buy Foreign Goods," *Practical Ecommerce* (blog), June 20, 2018. In 2017 alone, "Chinese consumers purchased $100.2 billion of goods from sellers in other countries, with an average spend per buyer of $882." Most of these "cross-border ecommerce shoppers" were affluent middle-class residents of large cities under the age of forty.

7. ZX, "Chinese Consumers' Rising Demand Drives Surge in E-Commerce Imports," *XinhuaNet*, June 29, 2016, http://www.xinhuanet.com/english/2019-06/29/c_138185220.htm.

8. Lisa Rofel, *Desiring China: Experiments in Neoliberalism, Sexuality, and Public Culture* (Durham, NC: Duke University Press, 2007).

9. Gail Hershatter, *Women and China's Revolutions* (London: Rowman & Littlefield, 2019), 1.

10. Arlie Hochschild and Anne Machung, *The Second Shift: Working Families and the Revolution at Home* (New York: Penguin Books, 1989); Andrew Ross, *No-Collar: The Hidden Cost of the Humane Workplace* (New York: Basic Books, 2002); C. Wright Mills, "The New Middle Class, I," in *The New Middle Classes* (New York: Springer, 1951), 189–202; Gina Neff, *Venture Labor: Work and the Burden of Risk in Innovative Industries* (Cambridge, MA: MIT Press, 2012); Alice E. Marwick, *Status Update: Celebrity, Publicity, and Branding in the Social Media Age* (New Haven, CT: Yale University Press, 2015).

11. Kathi Weeks, "Life Within and Against Work: Affective Labor, Feminist Critique, and Post-Fordist Politics," *Ephemera: Theory and Politics in Organization* 7, no. 1 (2007): 233–49; Angela McRobbie, "Reflections on Feminism, Immaterial Labour and the Post-Fordist Regime," *New Formations* 70, no. 70 (2011): 60–76; Kylie Jarrett, *Feminism, Labour and Digital Media: The Digital Housewife* (New York: Routledge, 2016), 33; Christine L. Williams and Catherine Connell, " 'Looking Good and Sounding Right': Aesthetic Labor and Social Inequality in the Retail Industry," *Work and Occupations* 37, no. 3 (2010): 349–77.

12. Jarrett, *Feminism, Labour and Digital Media*, 102–3. Centering on the concept of the "digital housewife," Kylie Jarrett has sought to demystify the romanticized figure of the inalienable, autonomous, and self-determining individual. According to her, this constructed authenticity was neither achievable nor necessarily appealing to those who fell outside the bounds of the "white, European, heterosexual, able-bodied cis-male" subject. Instead, Jarrett focuses on

"relational identities and other-oriented caring practices from which women have historically drawn their agency and meaning and which are often found in cultures that do not draw on Western European paradigms of individuality." Kathi Weeks, "Life Within and Against Work," 428. Kathi Weeks has warned against the recurring Marxist tendency to couch cultural critiques in a constructed authentic space, instead putting forth a different vision, in which the antagonistic relationship between productive work in the public sphere and reproductive work in the private sphere—a distinction more suited to the Fordist imaginary of life and labor than the current moment—is reconceptualized as the mutually transformative realms of "work and life," and women's experiences of affective, socialized, and communicative labor deployed to reimagine a different "quality of life." Michele White, *Producing Women: The Internet, Traditional Femininity, Queerness, and Creativity* (New York: Routledge, 2015), 56. Turning to entrepreneurial mothers with shops on platforms like eBay and Etsy, Michele White observed the disconnect between the demands of "intensive motherhood" and e-commerce's promises of liberation, empowerment, and a more community-oriented and ethical career path than traditional wage work. However, she also notes that mother-entrepreneurs have revised "the more limiting conceptions of stay-at-home mothers and femininity" by profiting from "their maternal position."

13. Bingchun Meng and Yanning Huang, "Patriarchal Capitalism with Chinese Characteristics: Gendered Discourse of 'Double Eleven' Shopping Festival," *Cultural Studies* 31, no. 5 (September 3, 2017): 10, https://doi.org/10.1080/09502386.2017.1328517.

14. Nancy Fraser, "Contradictions of Capital and Care," *New Left Review* 100, no. 99 (2016): 117.

15. Patricia Ebrey, *Women and the Family in Chinese History* (New York: Routledge, 2002); Sherry J. Mou, *Gentlemen's Prescriptions for Women's Lives: A Thousand Years of Biographies of Chinese Women* (New York: Routledge, 2015).

16. Dorothy Ko, *Teachers of the Inner Chambers: Women and Culture in Seventeenth-Century China* (Stanford, CA: Stanford University Press, 1994); Mou, *Gentlemen's Prescriptions for Women's Lives*.

17. Mou, *Gentlemen's Prescriptions for Women's Lives*.

18. Shaopeng Song, "Geming Lishi de Heli Yichan—Weirao Zhongguo Funü Yanjiu de Taolun" (The Legacy of Revolutionary History: A Discussion on the Study of Chinese Women's History), *Wenhua Zongheng*, July 20, 2018, http://www.21bcr.com/gemingshiguandeheliyichanweiraozhongguofunvshiyanjiudetaolun/; Gail Hershatter, Lisa Rofel, and Tyrene White, *Engendering China: Women, Culture, and the State* (Cambridge, MA: Harvard University Press, 1994); Ko, *Teachers of the Inner Chambers*; Gail Hershatter and Wang Zheng, "Chinese

History: A Useful Category of Gender Analysis," *The American Historical Review* 113, no. 5 (December 2008): 1404–21, https://doi.org/10.1086/ahr.113.5.1404.

19. Ko, *Teachers of the Inner Chambers*, 10. Calling for "a concept of power that focuses not on static structures or institutions but on the dynamic processes through which power is exercised," Dorothy Ko observed that "even in imperial China . . . there was much fluidity and possibilities for individuals to constitute themselves in everyday practice."

20. Tani Barlow, *The Question of Women in Chinese Feminism* (Durham, NC: Duke University Press, 2004); Joan Judge, "Talent, Virtue, and the Nation: Chinese Nationalisms and Female Subjectivities in the Early Twentieth Century," *The American Historical Review* 106, no. 3 (2001): 765–803.

21. Lydia H. Liu, Rebecca E. Karl, and Dorothy Ko, eds., *The Birth of Chinese Feminism: Essential Texts in Transnational Theory* (New York: Columbia University Press, 2013); Joan Judge, "Talent, Virtue, and the Nation," 40. Despite the preponderance of male voices in early Chinese feminism, educated women, especially those from well-off families who could afford to send their daughters overseas for an education, were able to articulate their own positioning in the public sphere through writing and engaging in public campaigns, usually by appropriating radical nationalist agendas or proposing anarchist feminist alternatives.

22. Shaopeng Song, *Xiyangjinglide Zhongguo Yu Funv* (*China and Chinese Women Through a Western Lens.*) (Beijing, Social Sciences Academic Press, 2016).

23. Song; Liu, Karl, and Ko, *The Birth of Chinese Feminism*.

24. Judge, "Talent, Virtue, and the Nation."

25. Chun Lin, *The Transformation of Chinese Socialism* (Durham, NC: Duke University Press, 2006).

26. Meng and Huang, "Patriarchal Capitalism with Chinese Characteristics."

27. Zheng Wang, *Finding Women in the State: A Socialist Feminist Revolution in the People's Republic of China, 1949–1964* (Berkeley: University of California Press, 2016); Gail Hershatter, "Women and China's Socialist Construction, 1949–78," in *Women and China's Revolutions* (Lanham, MD: Rowman & Littlefield, 2019), 23. According to Hershatter, slogans such as "women hold up half the sky" and propaganda images of gender-neutral "iron girls" (*tieguniang*, 铁姑娘, or *nüqiangren*, 女强人), who were every bit as strong as their male model worker counterparts "shaped the self-perceptions and sense of possibility" of a generation of women during the socialist years.

28. Shaopeng Song, "The State Discourse on Housewives and Housework in the 1950s in China," in *Rethinking China in the 1950s*, ed. Mechthild Leutner (New Brunswick, NJ: Transaction Publishers, 2007), 49–63.

29. Hershatter, "Women and China's Socialist Construction, 1949–78."
30. Zheng Wang, "Gender, Employment and Women's Resistance," in *Chinese Society*, ed. Elizabeth J. Perry and Mark Selden (New York: Routledge, 2003), 176–204.
31. Chingkwan Lee, *Against the Law* (Berkeley: University of California Press, 2007); Lin, *The Transformation of Chinese Socialism*; Wang, *Finding Women in the State*.
32. Meng and Huang, "Patriarchal Capitalism with Chinese Characteristics."
33. Lisa Rofel, *Desiring China: Experiments in Neoliberalism, Sexuality, and Public Culture* (Durham, NC: Duke University Press, 2007); Zhen Zhang, "Mediating Time: The 'Rice Bowl of Youth' in Fin de Siècle Urban China," *Public Culture* 12, no. 1 (January 1, 2000): 93–113.
34. Fang Lee Cooke, "Women's Managerial Careers in China in a Period of Reform," *Asia Pacific Business Review* 11, no. 2 (June 1, 2005): 149–62, https://doi.org/10.1080/1360238042000291216.
35. Qi Wang, Dongchao Min, and Ærenlund Sørensen Bo, *Revisiting Gender Inequality: Perspectives from the People's Republic of China* (New York: Palgrave Macmillan, 2016).
36. Wang, Min, and Bo, *Revisiting Gender Inequality*, 71.
37. Jie Yang, "Nennu and Shunu: Gender, Body Politics, and the Beauty Economy in China," *Signs: Journal of Women in Culture and Society* 36, no. 2 (January 1, 2011): 333–57, https://doi.org/10.1086/655913.
38. Maryam Cheraghi, "Innovation by Entrepreneurs in China: The Increasing Prominence of Women," *Journal of Knowledge-Based Innovation in China* 5, no. 3 (January 1, 2013): 172–87, https://doi.org/10.1108/JKIC-08-2013-0016.
39. Tonia Warnecke, Lucas Hernandez, and Nicholas Nunn, "Female Entrepreneurship in China: Opportunity or Necessity-Based?," *Student-Faculty Collaborative Research*. Paper 23, 2012.
40. Tao Qin, "Zhaoge Meinü Zuo Laoban" (Find a Beautiful Woman to Be the Boss), *Internet Weekly*, January 8, 2001.
41. "Zhang Shuxin: Tech Martyr," China Pictorial, July 2, 2014, http://www.chinapictorial.com.cn/en/features/txt/2014-07/02/content_627343.htm. Some of the most prominent Chinese female IT entrepreneurs, such as Zhang and first generation ZGC entrepreneur Jin Yanjing, would be ousted in political and commercial power struggles and turned into martyrs of the new economy.
42. Hernandez, Nunn, and Warnecke, "Female Entrepreneurship in China," 412; Hershatter, *Women and China's Revolutions*, 265. When the country's SOEs were reformed in the 1990s, a large number of women were laid off from state-owned factories by male-dominated middle management. This came despite the sacrifices women had made during the socialist years and left many with no

choice but to seek alternative self-employment opportunities in the urban informal sector, often as street vendors or convenience store owners. Tamara Jacka, "Working from Within: Women and the State in the Development of the Courtyard Economy in Rural China," in *Women and the State: International Perspectives*, ed. Shirin M. Rai and Geraldine Lievesley (Bristol, PA: Taylor & Francis, 1996), 143–62. According to Jacka, the state promoted women's involvement in the courtyard economy as a flexible and cheap source of labor. By 1986, 35 percent to 55 percent of all "specialized households" (*zhuanye hu,* 专业户)— household businesses engaged in a particular agricultural or sideline business for economic benefit—were run by women.

43. Susan Greenhalgh, *Cultivating Global Citizens: Population in the Rise of China* (Cambridge, MA: Harvard University Press, 2010).

44. Fengshu Liu, *Urban Youth in China: Modernity, the Internet and the Self* (London: Routledge, 2013).

45. Binli Chen and Hailan He, "Falling Behind the Rest? China and the Gender Gap Index," *Social Inclusion* 8, no. 2 (April 28, 2020): 10–22, https://doi.org/10.17645/si.v8i2.2810.

46. Angela Xiao Wu and Yige Dong, "What Is Made-in-China Feminism(s)? Gender Discontent and Class Friction in Post-Socialist China," *Critical Asian Studies* 51, no. 4 (October 2, 2019): 12, https://doi.org/10.1080/14672715.2019.1656538.

47. Bingchun Meng, "When Anxious Mothers Meet Social Media: Wechat, Motherhood and the Imaginary of the Good Life," *Javnost—The Public* 27, no. 2 (April 2, 2020): 171–85, https://doi.org/10.1080/13183222.2020.1727276; Greenhalgh, *Cultivating Global Citizens.*

48. Wu and Dong, "What Is Made-in-China Feminism(s)?" 12. In June 2021, China's leaders announced they had approved the implementation of a three-child policy.

49. Wang, Dongchao, and Sørensen, *Revisiting Gender Inequality.*

50. Wang, *Finding Women in the State*; Wang, Dongchao, and Sørensen, *Revisiting Gender Inequality.*

51. Wang, *Finding Women in the State,* 260.

52. Wang, Dongchao, and Sørensen, *Revisiting Gender Inequality,* 61.

53. Wang, Dongchao, and Sørensen, *Revisiting Gender Inequality,* 62.

54. Wang, Dongchao, and Sørensen, *Revisiting Gender Inequality,* 67.

55. John Osburg, *Anxious Wealth:Money and Morality Among China's New Rich* (Stanford, CA: Stanford University Press, 2013).

56. Hershatter, *Women and China's Revolutions.*

57. Ying Fang and Alan Walker, " 'Full-Time Wife' and the Change of Gender Order in the Chinese City," *Journal of Chinese Sociology* 2, no. 1 (December 2015): 8, https://doi.org/10.1186/s40711-015-0006-x.

58. Yalan Huang, "'Re-Feminization' of Dependent Women Migrants: Negotiating Gender Roles in the Chinese Digital Diaspora," *Asian Journal of Women's Studies* 26, no. 2 (April 2, 2020): 159–83, https://doi.org/10.1080/12259276.2020 .1747249.
59. For more information, see http://www.199it.com/archives/539618.html.
60. Xiujuan Gao et al., "2019 Alibaba Quanqiu Nüxing Chuangye Jiuye Yanjiu Baogao" (2019 Alibaba Global Female Entrepreneurship and Employment Research Report) AliResearch and China Women's University, 2019, https://www.startupgrouphk.com/wp-content/uploads/2019/11/2019全球女性創業就業研究報告.pdf.
61. Xingmin Geng, "Tuijin Chuangxinchuangye Jinguo Xingdong" (Advance Women's Innovation and Entrepreneurship and Create an Upgraded Version of the Mass Innovation and Entrepreneurship Campaign), cnwomen.com.cn, August 30, 2019, http://www.cnwomen.com.cn/2019/08/30/99170695.html.
62. Meng and Huang, "Patriarchal Capitalism with Chinese Characteristics," 8–9.
63. "Yiou Gongsi 2019 Zhongguo Nüxing Chuangyezhe 30 Ren Baogao" (EqualOcean's 30 Chinese Women Entrepreneurs 2019), EqualOcean, December 7, 2019, https://www.iyiou.com/p/119718.html.
64. Sarah Banet-Weiser, *Authentic^{TM}: The Politics of Ambivalence in a Brand Culture* (New York: NYU Press, 2012); Ann Gray, "Enterprising Femininity: New Modes of Work and Subjectivity," *European Journal of Cultural Studies*, July 24, 2016, https://doi.org/10.1177/13675494030064003.
65. The "West" in this context also includes more developed Asian nations and regions such as Hong Kong, Macau, Korea, and Japan.
66. "UNWTO: Chinese Outbound Tourism Spending Grew 8% in 2018—Blue Swan Daily," Corporate Travel Community, June 7, 2019, https://blueswandaily.com /unwto-chinese-outbound-tourism-spending-grew-8-in-2018/.
67. Rofel, *Desiring China*, 2007, 128.
68. Hershatter, *Women and China's Revolutions*, 20.
69. Rofel, *Desiring China*, 2007.
70. Huang, "'Re-Feminization' of Dependent Women Migrants," 159.
71. Huang, "'Re-Feminization' of Dependent Women Migrants," 159.
72. "2019 Niandu Zhongguo Jiating Yuyu Fangshi Baipishu" (2019 Chinese Family Reproduction and Child-Rearing White Paper), *Baobao Shu*, January 9, 2020, http://zhiku.hsw.cn/system/2020/0109/2835.shtml.
73. Candace West and Don H Zimmerman, "Doing Gender," no. 2 (1987): 124-151,
74. Banet-Weiser, *Authentic^{TM}*, 8.
75. Rofel, *Desiring China*, 223.
76. Sharon Hays, *The Cultural Contradictions of Motherhood* (New Haven, CT: Yale University Press, 1998); Jarrett, *Feminism, Labour and Digital Media*.

77. Marwick, *Status Update.*
78. Marwick, *Status Update.*
79. "Dianshangfa Jijiang Shishi Daji Daigou, Shechipin de Hao Rizi Yao Jieshu Le?" (The E-commerce Law Is Going to be Implemented, Are the Best Days of Luxury Brands Over?), FashionNetwork.com, https://cn.fashionnetwork.com/news/—dian-shang-fa—ji-jiang-shi-shi-da-ji-dai-gou—she-chi-pin-pai-de-hao-ri-zi-yao-jie-shu-le—,1030007.html.
80. Meng, "When Anxious Mothers Meet Social Media."
81. Greenhalgh, *Cultivating Global Citizens.*
82. Diane Negra, *What A Girl Wants?* (New York: Routledge, 2008).
83. Meng, "When Anxious Mothers Meet Social Media;" Meng and Huang, "Patriarchal Capitalism with Chinese Characteristics."
84. Elizabeth Wissinger, "Modeling Consumption: Fashion Modeling Work in Contemporary Society," *Journal of Consumer Culture* 9 (July 2009): 281, https://doi.org/10.1177/1469540509104377.
85. Minh-Ha T. Pham, *Asians Wear Clothes on the Internet: Race, Gender, and the Work of Personal Style Blogging* (Durham, NC: Duke University Press, 2015).
86. Jie Zhang, "From Self Isolator to Business Owner: Social Standing and Economic Mobility Among Chinese Housewives in Japan," *Journal of Asia-Pacific Studies* 36 (July 2019): 14; Fran Martin, "Rethinking Network Capital: Hospitality Work and Parallel Trading Among Chinese Students in Melbourne," *Mobilities* 12, no. 6 (November 2, 2017): 890–907, https://doi.org/10.1080/17450101.2016.1268460; Huang, "'Re-Feminization' of Dependent Women Migrants."
87. Wang, *Finding Women in the State*, 252.
88. Ding Hei and Shuang Ling, "Qian Kongjie de Haiwai Daigou Men" (The Overseas Daigou Scandal of a Former Flight Attendant), *Prosecutor Review*, 2012.
89. Sun Yun, "Haiwai Daigou Fengxian Da: Liuxuesheng Xiaoxin Chufan Mei Falü" (Overseas Daigou Is Risky: International Students Shouldn't Break the Law in the United States), www.epochtimes.com, June 13, 2013, https://www.epochtimes.com/gb/13/6/13/n3892730.htm.
90. Sun, "Haiwai Daigou Fengxian Da."
91. Ling, *China's New Revolution.*
92. Ko, *Teachers of the Inner Chambers*, 1–2.
93. Wu and Dong, "What Is Made-in-China Feminism(s)?" 16.
94. In 2010, the General Administration of Customs issued a new regulation that made any personally mailed item into China taxable if its value exceeded 50 yuan. General Administration of Customs P.R. China, "Guanyu Tiaozheng Churujing Geren Youdi Wupin Guanli Cuoshi Youguan Shiyi" (Regulations Regarding Inbound and Outbound Personal Postal Items), July 2, 2010,

http://www.customs.gov.cn/customs/302249/302266/302267/357036/index.html.

95. "Dianshangfa Jijiang Shishi Daji Daigou, Shechipin de Hao Rizi Yao Jieshu Le?"; Keith Bradsher, "How China Lost $1 Trillion," *New York Times*, February 7, 2017.

96. Jacky Wong, "China's Campaign Against Online Reselling Will Be Ugly for Cosmetics," *Wall Street Journal*, July 3, 2019. Methods used include limiting overseas credit card spending, cash withdrawals, and the amount of Renminbi international travelers were allowed to carry.

97. Xie Yu, "Duty-Free Boom Fuels Surge in Chinese Tourism Stocks," *Wall Street Journal*, August 11, 2020; "Beijing Raises Duty-Free Quotas for Cross-Border e-Commerce," *South China Morning Post*, November 23, 2018. Methods used include increasing the annual quota on cross-border e-commerce purchases for individual buyers (from 20,000 to 26,000 yuan), the tax-free limit on single transactions (to 5,000 yuan), and tripling the annual limit on duty-free purchases in the country's first "domestic free trade zone" of Hainan Province (to 100,000 yuan)

98. Pham, *Asians Wear Clothes on the Internet*; Tu Lan, "Politics of Visibility in the Chinese Community in Prato, Italy," in *Transcending Borders: Selected Papers in East Asian Studies*, ed. Ikuko Sagiyama and Valentina Pedone (Newcastle, UK: Cambridge Scholars Publishing, 2016), 27–46; David N. Pellow and Lisa Sun-Hee Park, *The Silicon Valley of Dreams: Environmental Injustice, Immigrant Workers, and the High-Tech Global Economy* (New York: NYU Press, 2002).

99. Kaiser Kuo, "White Privilege, American Hegemony, and the Rise of China," *SupChina*, August 21, 2020, https://supchina.com/2020/08/21/white-privilege-american-hegemony-and-the-rise-of-china/.

100. McKinsey & Company, "China Luxury Report 2019: How Young Chinese Consumers Are Reshaping Global Luxury," April 2019, 29. https://www.mckinsey.com/~/media/mckinsey/featured%20insights/china/how%20young%20chinese%20consumers%20are%20reshaping%20global%20luxury/mckinsey-china-luxury-report-2019-how-young-chinese-consumers-are-reshaping-global-luxury.ashx

101. Mike Cherney, "To Reach Chinese Consumers, Brands Market in Australia," *Wall Street Journal*, October 3, 2018.

102. Xinyu Zhang, "Chuan Zhongguo Daji Daigou, LV Jifanxi Mu Gongsi: Haoxiaoxi" (It Is Said That China Is Going to Strike Hard on Resellers: The Parent Companies of Louis Vuitton and Givenchy Say That's Good News), Huxiu.com, October 12, 2018, https://www.huxiu.com/article/266534.html; Taosheng Yang, "Shou Zhongguo Haiguan Daji Daigou Yingxiang, Riben Huazhuangpin He Lingshouye Gujia Pubian Xiadie" (Impacted by Chinese Customs' Strike Hard Campaign Against Resellers, Japanese Cosmetics and Retail Industry Stock

Prices Fall Across the Board), LUXE.CO, October 5, 2018, https://luxe.co/post/89795.

103. Minh-Ha T. Pham, "Couture's Chinese Culture Shock," *The American Prospect*, January 27, 2012. Minh-ha Pham documented Western fashion gatekeepers' snarky comments about Chinese luxury consumers, such as, "You can't pretend to have lots of taste if you're simply buying all that shit and spending tons of money." In the process, she observed how critiques of taste served as a "surrogate for definitions of race and class" and that "the tacky Chinese luxury consumer stereotype is a form of coded racial discourse that links fakeness to race" to reaffirm "the whiteness of the ideal fashion subject."

104. Carol Ryan, "Luxury-Goods Industry Has a China Problem," *Wall Street Journal*, January 1, 2019.

105. Zhuoxiao Xie, "Im/Materializing Cross-Border Mobility: A Study of Mainland China–Hong Kong Daigou (Cross-Border Shopping Services on Global Consumer Goods)," *International Journal of Communication* 12 (September 25, 2018): 14.

106. Tu Lan, "Politics of Visibility in the Chinese Community in Prato, Italy" *In Transcending Borders: Selected Papers in East Asian Studies, edited by Ikuko Sagiyama and Valentina Pedone, 27–46.* (Florence: Firenze University Press, 2016).; Pun Ngai, *Made in China:Women Factory Workers in a Global Workplace* (Durham, NC: Duke University Press, 2005).

107. Pham, *Asians Wear Clothes on the Internet.*

EPILOGUE

1. Evelyn Cheng, "China's Premier Talks up Education in the Country's Bid to Boost Innovation," CNBC, March 11, 2021, https://www.cnbc.com/2021/03/11/chinas-premier-talks-up-education-in-a-bid-to-boost-innovation.html.

2. Lao Dong, "Beiguan yu Xingdong de 2020: Shida Gongren Weiquan Xingdong Pandian" (Pessimism and Action Coexist in 2020: An Overview of the Top Ten Labor Movements), *Service Worker Notes* (blog), January 1, 2021, https://serviceworkercn.com/workers-year-of-2020/.

3. Lin Qiqing and Raymond Zhong, "'996' Is China's Version of Hustle Culture. Tech Workers Are Sick of It," *New York Times*, April 29, 2019.

4. Arif Dirlik, "The Idea of a 'Chinese Model': A Critical Discussion," *China Information* 26, no. 3 (2012): 208.

5. Silvia M. Lindtner, *Prototype Nation: China and the Contested Promise of Innovation* (Princeton, NJ: Princeton University Press, 2020), 36.

6. Arif Dirlik and Maurice J. Meisner, *Marxism and the Chinese Experience: Issues in Contemporary Chinese Socialism* (Armonk, NY: M. E. Sharpe, 1989), 22.

7. Dirlik and Meisner, *Marxism and the Chinese Experience*, 26.
8. Ha-Joon Chang, *Kicking Away the Ladder: Development Strategy in Historical Perspective* (London: Anthem Press, 2002); Steven K. Vogel, "Neoliberal Ideology and the Myth of the Self-Made Entrepreneur," Social Science Research Network (SSRN) Scholarly Paper, August 13, 2020, https://doi.org/10.2139/ssrn.3698179.
9. Joseph E. Stiglitz and Lin Justin Yifu, eds., *The Industrial Policy Revolution I: The Role of Government Beyond Ideology* (New York: Palgrave Macmillan, 2013).
10. Peter L. Berger, *In Search of an East Asian Development Model* (New Brunswick, NJ: Routledge, 1988); Theodoros Papadopoulos and Antonios Roumpakis, "Family as a Socio-Economic Actor in the Political Economies of East and South East Asian Welfare Capitalisms," *Social Policy & Administration* 51, no. 6 (2017): 857–75, https://doi.org/10.1111/spol.12336; Theodoros Papadopoulos and Antonios Roumpakis, "Familistic Welfare Capitalism in Crisis: Social Reproduction and Anti-Social Policy in Greece," *Journal of International and Comparative Social Policy* 29, no. 3 (October 1, 2013): 204–24, https://doi.org/10.1080/21699763.2013.863736.
11. Papadopoulos and Roumpakis, "Familistic Welfare Capitalism in Crisis," 206.
12. Tiejun Wen et al., *Quanqiuhua yu Guojia Jingzheng: Xinxing Qiguo Bijiao Yanjiu* (Globalization and National Competition: A Comparison of Seven Emerging Countries) (Beijing: Dongfang Chubanshe, 2021).
13. Fred L. Block and Matthew R. Keller, *State of Innovation: The U.S. Government's Role in Technology Development* (New York: Routledge, 2015); Stiglitz and Yifu, *The Industrial Policy Revolution I*; Ji Yingchun, "A Mosaic Temporality: New Dynamics of the Gender and Marriage System in Contemporary Urban China," *Temporalités: Revue de Sciences Sociales et Humaines* 26 (December 1, 2017), https://doi.org/10.4000/temporalites.3773; Papadopoulos and Roumpakis, "Familistic Welfare Capitalism in Crisis."
14. Tang Frank, "What Is China's Dual Circulation Economic Strategy and Why Is It Important?," *South China Morning Post*, November 19, 2020.
15. See Kaiser Kuo and Jeremy Goldkorn's discussion of China's Red New Deal of September 16, 2021, at https://supchina.com/2021/09/16/red-new-deal-or-raw-new-deal-unraveling-chinas-astonishing-barrage-of-regulatory-action/.
16. For more information about the "Build Back Better Framework," see https://www.whitehouse.gov/build-back-better/.
17. Deirdre Walsh and Caitlyn Kim, "The House Passed a Bill Aimed at Boosting U.S. Competitiveness with China," NPR, February 4, 2022.
18. Eric Schewe, "Semiconductor Shortages End an Era of Globalization," *JSTOR Daily*, April 8, 2021, https://daily.jstor.org/semiconductor-shortages-end-an-era-of-globalization/.

Index

business incubators: innovation incubators, 73; local government subsidies, 73–74; privately owned incubators, 70–71, 72–73; state-owned incubators, 68–70; state subsidies, 73–74, 82, 88–89, 91–92, 99–100; Torch Plan, 67; Wuhan Donghu Pioneers Center, 66–67. *See also* Garage Café; InnoWay; Tsinghua Science Park Business Incubator (TusStar)

business incubators (U.S.), 67–68

ByteDance, 25, 40

campaign-style entrepreneurship promotion, 41–43, 51, 91

capital, access to: international sanctions, 9; start-ups, 39, 93–94

capitalist accumulation, 106–7, 108, 142, 148, 160, 196

celebrity entrepreneurs, 10, 34. *See also* Ma, Jack

centralized minimalist governance, xv, 13, 20, 29, 113, 157–58, 230, 235; family-driven individualization, 106, 107–11, 134–35

"chain of contempt," 47. *See also* hierarchies of entrepreneurship

"China model," xiv–xv, 230, 233; legitimacy of, 11

"China paradigm," xv, 230–36; spatiotemporally- and culturally-specific nature of, 233–34

"China threat," xiv–xv, 219, 232

Chinese Communist Party (CCP): corporate governance, 77; entrepreneurial reinvention, 7, 8–9, 41–42, 46–47, 49, 64–65, 77, 82–83, 90; GDP-driven developmentalism, 11; Long March, 202; management

autonomy, 83; mass mobilization strategy, 108; new core socialist values, 195; private/public fusion, 49; state-managed marketization, 8–9; supply-side reforms, 82–83; technocratic elite, rise of, 30–31; threats to legitimacy, 11, 30–31, 33; township and village enterprises, 9; TusStar, 64–65

Chinese exceptionalism, xiv, 11, 230, 233

class inequalities, xii–xiii, 217; emergence of technocratic-commercial elite, 31–32; researcher-founding firms, 75; rural areas, 167–68; urban work regime, 7–8

class inequalities (U.S.), xii–xiii; 99 percenters, 4

coliving spaces, 71

competition: digital platforms, 171–72; e-commerce entrepreneurs, 138–42, 146, 147–49; family businesses, 138–42, 146; foreign competition, 33–34, 35; tariffs, 33, 202, 216, 218, 222

Confucian entrepreneurialism, 3, 48, 78, 107

Confucian ideals: family values, 8, 168, 186, 187–88, 189, 195, 229–30; gender norms, 187–88, 189, 195–96, 209, 223

consumerism, 189, 202, 223; *daigou* entrpreneurship, 187; purchasing power, 194, 219; women, 191, 192–96, 197–99

"copy-to-China" business model, 35

copyright infringement, 138–39; criminalization, 143, 145–46. *See also* counterfeiting; intellectual property rights

coronavirus, xi–xii, 46, 235

corporate governance: Chinese Communist Part involvement, 77–78

economic bust. *See* boom-bust cycles

economic expansion, ix, 41–43; O2O platforms, 60. *See also* boom-bust cycles

elite entrepreneurs: emergence of technocratic-commercial elite, 31–32; grassroots entrepreneurs compared (case studies), xii, 46–61

empowerment: digital empowerment, 105, 119, 127, 193; e-commerce, 160–61, 162, 168, 170, 173, 178–79; feminist empowerment, 185–86, 188–90, 206; grassroots entrepreneurs, x, 3–5, 12, 159–61, 173; industrial policy, 41–42, 81, 87–88, 141; social equity, 141; women, 160–61, 162, 168–70, 185, 189–90, 193–94, 197–99, 200–206, 211, 214

entrepreneurialism as an ideology, 3–4, 230

entrepreneurial reinvention (Barbados): reputational flexibility, 2

entrepreneurial reinvention (China), vii–xi, 1; CCP policy, 7; critics, 32; family production, 231; hybridization, xi–xii, 6–7, 61–62; IT-related entrepreneurialism, 5–6, 31–34; kinship networks, 7; limits of entrepreneurialism, 6; Maoist China, 7–8, 30–31; People's Republic of China, 7; petty capitalism, 7, 107; post–Cold War, 2, 4; post-financial crisis, 27–30, 37–39, 232–33, 234–35; post-Mao China, 2–3, 31–34, 234; tributary mode of production, 7, 107

entrepreneurial reinvention (India): entrepreneurial citizenship, 1–2

entrepreneurial reinvention (UK): entrepreneurialization of arts and culture, 1

entrepreneurial reinvention (U.S.): individualized cultural entrepreneurialization, 1, 4–5; IT-related entrepreneurialism, 5–6; limits of entrepreneurialism, 6; Silicon Valley, 4–5

entrepreneurship defined: Cantillon, 2; culturalism, 3; laissez-faire capitalism, 2–3; neoclassical economics, 2; neoinstitutionalism, 2–3; neoliberalism, xv–xvi, 1–3; post–Cold War, 2, 4; post-Mao China, 2–3

entrepreneurship mobilization, 41–44

Ezubao, 44

family-driven individualization, 106, 107–11, 141–42, 147–48

family handicraft production, 14–15; case study, 113–27; collectivization of, 108; commune enterprises, 115; e-commerce businesses, 120–21, 126–27; factory production, 115–16; financial crisis, 116–17; migrant returnees, 117–23; opening-up policy, 116; People's Republic of China, 108; post-financial crisis, 117–19; post-Mao, 116; privatization, 116; reinvention of, 231; small family/peasant businesses, 114–15, 117–19

family values: centralized minimalist state, 107–11; Confucian norms, 8, 168, 186, 187–88, 189, 195, 229–30; family businesses, 14–15; family-driven individualization, 107–11; ideological tensions, 194–96

female *daigou* entrepreneurs, 16–17, 184–87; class, 192–93; empowerment, 160–61, 162, 168–70, 185, 189–90,

193–94, 197–99, 200–206, 211, 214;
family-based gendered division of
labor, reinvention of, 205–6;
full-time and part-time work
compared (case studies), 199–201,
222; immigrant wives, 204–5;
generational differences, 192–94,
202–4; ideological tensions, 194–96;
personal relationships, 213–14;
purchasing power, 194; redressing
gendered structural inequalities,
198–99, 206, 208, 214–24;
refeminization, 205; self-branding,
206–14
feminist empowerment, 185–86,
188–90, 206. *See also* women
feminization of labor, 185–86, 189–92;
feminized sectors, 197, 216–17;
impact on women, 197–98,
216–17; post-financial crisis, 223;
transnational middle-class *daigou*
entrepreneurs, 17, 184, 219. *See also*
female *daigou* entrepreneurs
financial crisis of 2008, vii–viii, xi,
11–12, 112; entrepreneurial
reinvention, 4–5, 27–30, 37–39,
232–33, 234–35; family handicraft
production, 116–19; feminization of
labor, 223; ideological tensions
post-financial crisis, 27–30, 38–39;
investor state model, 29–30, 111–12;
Mass Entrepreneurship and
Innovation Spaces, 71–74;
platformized family production,
111–13
financialized approach to governance,
12, 27–28, 39–41. *See also* investor
state model
financialized approach to innovation,
xi, 4, 41–42, 46, 230

foreign competition, 33–34, 35
foreign direct investment (FDI), viii, ix,
10, 109–10, 111–12
foreign monopolies, ix

Garage Café, 27, 38, 40–41, 65–66, 72,
83–84; benefits of coworking spaces,
87–88; decline, 92–94; grassroots
entrepreneurship, 90; mass
entrepreneurship and innovation,
88–94; model incubator space, as,
90–91; origins, 84–87; subsidies,
88–89, 91–92. *See also* coworking
spaces
GDP-driven development, 10–11,
45–46, 83, 109–10, 111, 178; tensions,
13, 35–36
gendered consumerism, 169–71
gender inequalities: Confucian China,
188–89; devalorization of handicraft
labor, 161–71; #MeToo, 4; modern
China, 191–92; post-Mao China,
189–90; socialist China, 189; urban
work regime, 7–8. *See also* division
of labor; women
generational inequalities, 189–90;
family businesses, 121; gendered
handicraft labor, 161–71; migrant
workers, 121–22, 123–27; rural-
urban divide, 121–22, 123–27
geographical disparities, xv–xvi, 9,
109–10, 189, 231–33. *See also*
rural-urban divide
global capitalism, xi–xii, xv, 2–6, 229,
232–33; Chinese integration, 8–9, 10,
20, 28–31, 140–41, 218–19, 234–35
global recession. *See* financial crisis of
2008
government-controlled data, access to,
48–49, 51, 60

JD.com, 25, 113, 134, 184, 218, 228

Keynesian economics, 2, 12
kinship networks, xi, 6–7, 107, 108–10

labor migration. *See* migrant workers
laissez-faire capitalism, 2–3, 34–35,
    109, 127
Lenovo, 25, 34, 51–52, 54, 72, 91
liberal capitalist universalism, xiii, 7,
    34, 46, 230, 234
Li Keqiang, 12, 42–43, 91, 98, 132,
    133–34, 197, 227
limits of entrepreneurialism, 6, 66,
    99–100; awareness of, x, 20; female
    daigou entrepreneurs, experiences
    of, 183–87, 214–24; redressing
    structural inequalities, 173–79;
    transnational gendered
    entrepreneurial citizenship,
    214–24
local government subsidies: business
    incubators, 73–74

Ma, Jack, 10, 117–18, 128–29, 135, 149,
    157, 158, 228
Made in China 2025 initiative, 27, 41,
    42–43, 73
"maker culture," 28, 46–47
makerspaces, 43, 45, 56, 63–64, 71–72,
    85. *See also* coworking spaces
management autonomy, 83
Mao Zedong, 202; death, 30–31;
    legitimacy of CCP, 30; technocratic
    elites, 30
market liberalism, 2–3, 34
market reforms, viii–ix, 77, 91,
    130–31
Marxism, xiv, 78

mass entrepreneurship and innovation,
    promotion of, xi–xii, 5–6, 12, 17–18,
    20, 25, 42–43, 227
Mass Entrepreneurship and Innovation
    Spaces, 63–64; local government
    subsidies, 73–74; post-financial
    crisis, 71–74; state subsidies, 73–74,
    82, 88–89, 91–92, 99–100. *See also*
    Garage Café; InnoWay; Tsinghua
    Science Park Business Incubator
    (TusStar)
mass mobilization strategy, 28, 30,
    38–39, 42, 46, 90, 108, 157–58
media management: Alibaba and
    Taobao villages, 131–36;
    e-commerce entrepreneurs, 131
Meituan, 40, 44
#MeToo, 4
middle class labor subjects:
    transnational *daigou* entrepreneurs,
    xvi, 17–18, 184, 219; women, 17–18,
    169–70, 184, 191–92, 219
migrant returnees, 105; family
    handicraft production, 117–23;
    generational inequalities, 121–22,
    123–27
migrant workers: eviction from cities,
    18–19; grassroots entrepreneurs, 43,
    93–94; individualization of peasant
    migrant workers, 110–11, 141–42;
    peasant workers, 10–11, 104;
    reinvention of, 225–36; rural-urban
    migration, 10–11, 108, 110, 116, 156;
    urban-rural migration, 10–11, 104,
    112–13, 116–17, 123–27, 129, 138
minimalist governance. *See* centralized
    minimalist governance
mixed economy model, 5–6, 11–12, 41,
    115, 186–87

mixed-ownership reform (MOR), 5, 42, 47–49, 73, 77–78; TusHoldings, 78–83

multiculturalism, 2, 229–30

Nail House. *See* InnoWay

nationalism, 61, 186, 187–88, 223, 229; technonationalism, xii, 12–13, 28, 38, 41, 46–47, 56, 66, 72, 228–29, 231

neoclassical economics, xiii, 2–3, 230, 233

neoinstitutionalism, 2–3

neoliberalism, xv–xvi, 1–2; bureaucratic capitalists, 9; laissez-faire capitalism, 2–3; post–Cold War, 2, 4; post-Mao China, 2–3, 8–9, 234; state-managed marketization, 8–9

new core socialist values, 195

"new socialist countryside," 11, 108, 111

99 percenters (U.S.), 4

office space and equipment, access to, 7. *See also* coworking spaces

"one thousand counties" campaigns, 134

online-to-offline (O2O) platforms, 40, 51, 60, 79; economic bust, 44–45, 59

outsourcing: family businesses, 14–15; immigrant workers, 8

overseas returnees, 19, 30, 35, 40, 43, 47; case study, 51–56

peasant workers, 10–11, 104; family handicraft production, 114–15, 117–19; individualization of peasant migrant workers, 110–11; migrant workers, 110–11, 141–42. *See also* migrant workers

peer-to-peer (P2P) platforms, 40, 51, 61; economic bust, 44–45

people-centric management, 26

People's Republic of China, 7, 11, 75; collectivized agriculture, 108; collectivized family-based industries, 108; family handicraft production, 108, 115; feminism, 188–89; women, 188–89

petty capitalism, 7, 15, 107, 109

Pinduoduo, 40, 113, 149

piracy, 143, 145–46

platformized family production, 104–5, 230; origins, 116–17; post-financial crisis, 111–13; *Shanzai* logic of production, 147–52; social and economic context, 111–13; state-capital-village relations, 127–37; W Village case study, 106–7, 113–27. *See also* family handicraft production

Polanyian capitalism, xv

political networks, access to, 32

Pompeo, Mike (U.S. Secretary of State), xiv

post–Cold War: entrepreneurial reinvention, 2, 4, 234

post-financial crisis: entrepreneurial reinvention, 27–30, 37–39; family handicraft production, 117–19; ideological tensions, 27–30, 38–39; investor state model, 29–30, 111–12; Mass Entrepreneurship and Innovation Spaces, 71–74; platformized family production, 111–13

post-Mao China: entrepreneurial reinvention, 2–3, 8–9, 31–34, 234; family handicraft production, 116; gender inequalities, 189–90; ideological tensions, 28–29, 31–34; neoliberalism, 2–3, 8–9, 234; women, 189–90

middle-class women, xvi, 17–18, 169–70. *See also* female *daigou* entrepreneurs
tributary mode of production, 7, 107
Tsinghua Science Park (TusPark), 63, 76, 79, 81
Tsinghua Science Park Business Incubator (TusStar), 73, 79–81, 83; intellectual property protection, 76
Tsinghua University, 25, 38, 74; university-affiliated enterprises, 75–77
TusHoldings, 45, 64, 73, 76–77, 78–83

Uber, 4–5, 44, 59–60, 229
unemployment rates, 12, 20, 38–39, 110–11, 190–91; financial crisis, 29–30, 112, 129; investor state policy, 61; mass entrepreneurship and innovation campaign, 42–44; urban unemployment, 108, 129
United States: Biden administration, 236; business incubators, 67–68; "China threat," xiv–xv, 6; discontentment, intersectionality of, 4; individualized cultural entrepreneurialization, 1, 4–5; influence of, 11–12, 52, 67–68, 143, 232–33; Silicon Valley, 4–5; Trump administration, 235–36; U.S.–China trade agreement 1999, 10; U.S.–China trade relations, xi–xii, xiv, 6, 10, 15, 20, 26–27, 38, 46, 235–36
university-affiliated enterprises, 63–65, 74; mixed-ownership reform, 78–79; origins, 75–76; public-private hybrids, as, 75–77; Tsinghua, 75–77, 78–79; TusHoldings, 78–79
"Up to the Mountain, Down to the Countryside" campaign, 44, 108–9

urban workers: inequalities, 7–8; rural-urban divide, 8, 10–11, 44; rural-urban migration, 10–11, 108, 110, 116, 156; socialist social contract, 7–8; urban reform, 9, 10; urban-rural migration, 10–11, 104, 112–13, 116–17, 123–27, 129, 138
U.S.–China trade relations, 10; Biden administration, 236; collaborative optimism, 38; trade war, xi–xii, xiv, 6, 15, 20, 26–27, 46; Trump administration, 235–36

valorization of labor: digital entrepreneurship as labor, 15, 105, 141, 148, 154–55, 162; gendered handicraft labor, 161–71; individualization of workers, 15, 231; physical labor, 161; women, 161–71, 185–86, 195–96, 206–7
value-added innovation, 38–39
venture capital markets, 25, 43, 227–28; coworking spaces, 71–72; privately owned incubators, 70–71, 72; state-guided venture capital funds, 5; state-owned venture capital firms, 26–27
"village rationale," 107–8

W Village: Bulrush and Wicker Handicraft Industry Association, 175–79; platformized family production (case study), 106–7, 113–27; *shanzhai* production, 143–47. *See also* Taobao village phenomenon
Washington consensus, 230, 234
Wen Jiabao, 38
Western gaze, xiii–xiv, 2–3, 143–44, 218–19, 231–32

WeWork, 4, 63, 71
Willow Leaf Industry Society, 115
women, xii; Confucian China, 187–88;
  daigou entrepreneurs, 184–87;
  digital entrepreneurship, 187, 197,
  202–3, 205; discrimination in the
  workplace, 188–89, 191–92, 194, 205,
  223–24; e-commerce, 196–99;
  employment rates, 190–91;
  empowerment, 160–61, 162, 168–70,
  185, 189–90, 193–94, 197–99,
  200–206, 211, 214; gendered division
  of labor, 188–92; individualization
  of workers, 17, 169–70, 187, 189–90,
  192–93, 214; informal economy, 16,
  184–87; modern China, 191–92;
  People's Republic of China, 188–89;
  post-Mao China, 189–90; self-
  branding, 206–14; service-oriented
  social media, 206–14; socialist
  feminist project, 189; valorization,
  161–71, 185–86, 195–96, 206–7;
  weavers, 116, 161–71. See also female
  daigou entrepreneurs
work-life balance, 195–96, 198, 203, 213
World Trade Organization: China's
  admission, ix, 10, 70, 146, 193
Wuhan Donghu Pioneers Center,
  66–67; subsidies, 67

Xi Jinping, 27, 82–83; Confucian family
  values, 195; Made in China 2025

initiative, 27, 41; supply-side
  reforms, 44–45
Xi-Li administration, 5; investor state
  model, 28, 41–42; Made in China
  2025 initiative, 27, 41

Yiren Digital, 40

Zhang, Charles, 10, 34, 96
Zhidong Wang, 34
Zhitongche, 149–50
Zhongguancun Development Group
  (ZGC Group), 39–40
Zhongguancun (ZGC) neighbourhood,
  vii, 227–28; coworking spaces, xii,
  18–19, 20, 27, 58, 60–61, 65–66,
  83–94, 100; dot-com entrepreneurs,
  34–35; economic boom, 41–43;
  economic bust, 43–46; electronics
  vendors, 35–37; expansion, 35–36;
  Garage Café, 18–19, 27, 38, 65–66,
  83–94, 197; High-Tech Experimental
  Zone, 69; intellectual property
  protection, 39; IT start-ups, ix–x,
  18–20; Maoist China, 30–31;
  National Indigenous Innovation
  Demonstration Zone, 39; national-
  level science park, 34–35; post-Mao
  state-led entrepreneurial
  reinvention, 28–29, 31–34; state-
  owned incubators, 68–70
Zhu Rongji, 34, 69

Printed and bound by CPI Group (UK) Ltd, Croydon, CR0 4YY

16/02/2023

03192472-0003